THE
IRON
PEN

Portrait of Frances Burney by her cousin Edward Francesco Burney. Reproduced from *The Musical Times,* August 1, 1904. Courtesy Henry W. and Albert A. Berg Collection, The New York Public Library, Astor, Lenox and Tilden Foundations.

THE
IRON
PEN

Frances Burney and
the Politics
of Women's Writing

Julia Epstein

Published by Bristol Classical Press

First published in Great Britain by
Bristol Classical Press, 226 North Street, Bedminster,
Bristol BS3 1JD.

British Library Cataloguing in Publication Data

Epstein, Julia
The iron pen: Frances Burney and the
politics of women's writing
1. Fiction in English. Burney, Fanny 1752–1840
I. Title.
823'.6

ISBN 1-85399-078-7
ISBN 1-85399-079-5 Pbk

For Betsy

Oh that my words were now written!
oh that they were printed in a book!
     That they were graven with an iron
pen and lead in the rock for ever!
                                    Job 19:23-24

She saw the immense volumes of Eternity,
and her own hand involuntarily grasped a
pen of iron . . .
                    Frances Burney, *Camilla*

Contents

Acknowledgments

I have incurred many debts to friends and colleagues in the course of writing this book. I owe special thanks to Mary Poovey and Ellen Cronan Rose, who generously and thoughtfully read early drafts of the entire manuscript and made valuable suggestions, and to Ellen Pollak for spirited conversation about eighteenth-century literature. Several others also read portions of the manuscript, and their advice has improved this book: Paula Marantz Cohen, Irene Raab Epstein, Madelyn Gutwirth, Elaine Tuttle Hansen, Alvin B. Kernan, Judith Newton, George Ovitt, Jr., Douglas L. Patey, M. Elizabeth Sandel, M.D., Kathleen Henderson Staudt, John Wright, and the members of Constantia. Beth Kowaleski-Wallace and the anonymous reader for the University of Wisconsin Press reviewed my manuscript insightfully and constructively. Margaret Anne Doody and Kristina Straub were kind enough to share their books on Burney, which appeared as this one was going to press, in manuscript, and I have profited greatly from conversations with them.

Financial support came from a William Andrews Clark Memorial Library Fellowship, a Drexel University Research Scholar Award, and a National Endowment for the Humanities Summer Seminar Fellowship. Thomas L. Canavan, Dean of the College of Humanities and Social Sciences at Drexel University, provided several awards of released time from teaching to support this work. Haverford College provided a grant for the final preparation of the manuscript, for which I am grateful to then Provost and Acting President Harry C. Payne and to Acting Provost Sidney Waldman. Cheryl Mills, Edmund Myers, Lucy Barber, and the competent staff of the Academic Computing Center at Haverford offered their technical expertise. Meredith Levin, Emily Rose, and Michael Wilson helped with proofreading, and Sharon Nangle and Adeline Taraborelli provided excellent typing. My editors at the University of Wisconsin Press—Barbara Hanrahan, Jack

Kirshbaum, Carol Olsen, and Rama Ramaswami — have been kind, smart, and thorough. I am also grateful to Violet Brown, whose meticulous efficiency and secretarial skills are exceeded only by her patience.

A shorter version of chapter 1 appeared as "Fanny Burney's Epistolary Voices" in *The Eighteenth Century: Theory and Interpretation* 27 (1986): 162–79. A small piece of my "Jane Austen's Juvenilia and the Female Epistolary Tradition," *Papers on Language and Literature* 21 (1985): 399–416, also appears in chapter 1. A different version of chapter 2 appeared in *Representations* 16 (1986): 131–66, with the title "Writing the Unspeakable: Fanny Burney's Mastectomy and the Fictive Body." A brief version of chapter 3 titled "Evelina's Deceptions: The Spirit and the Letter" was published in *Fanny Burney's "Evelina"*, ed. Harold Bloom, Modern Critical Interpretations Series (New Haven: Chelsea House Publishers, 1988), 111–29. I thank all four publications for permission to reprint this material here. Permission to reproduce illustrations from archival materials was kindly granted by Lola Szladits, Curator of the Henry W. and Albert A. Berg Collection of the New York Public Library.

Some friends helped more than they realized by putting up with my mania for the eighteenth century and providing generous hospitality, good food, lots of humor, and above all the gift of their friendship. I would especially like to thank Carolyn Anderson, Marta Dabezies, Seth Frohman, Sima Godfrey and Paul Krause, Nelly Furman, Raphael Hoch, Georgeann Iacono, Anne Koedt, Ellen Levine, Melvin and Rita Reier, Patricia Rose, and George and Kathryn Sandel.

My family has offered continuous and generous support in more forms than I could list here. My parents, Aubrey Epstein and Irene Raab Epstein, taught me about the powers of the printed word (to mention only one of their many gifts), and my brother Paul's critical intelligence has been an inspiration. My daughter Anna tried valiantly to reach the Delete button at the corner of my keyboard, no doubt because she sees little point to books without pictures. Her disdain for academicism has had its salutary effects, as has her ability to make me laugh. And finally, I could not have completed this book without the intellectual example, the astute criticism, the wit, and the encouragement of M. Elizabeth Sandel, to whom it is dedicated.

THE
IRON
PEN

Introduction

Instability and displacement characterize names and naming conventions for Frances Burney's heroines: their names are always unsettled and unsettling. A name bestows a public identity, and female protagonists in Burney's novels seek their place in the social sphere in part by locating and securing legitimate names for themselves. Naming is never a simple process in these novels, tied as it is to the empowering social institutions of class, family, marriage, lineage, and inheritance. It is especially ironic, then, that Burney's own name contains problems for scholars. She was commonly known as Fanny Burney but frequently catalogued in libraries as Madame d'Arblay, and her literary reputation has in some ways been tied to her name. Many reviewers of her later works remark that her style "went to seed" when "Fanny Burney" the sprightly wit became the ponderous and moralizing "Madame d'Arblay." In addition, "Fanny," a common and popular eighteenth-century woman's name, is a particularly diminutive, super-feminized, and private name.[1] Indeed, Burney has suffered from some critics who patronize and infantilize her, and who thereby diminish or ignore her achievement. Following the practice of the Oxford World's Classics editions of Burney's novels and of Margaret Anne Doody's major new literary biography, I have used "Frances Burney" in the title of this book. It is time to restore Burney's given name.

The project of this book might be said to be to convert Burney from the status of a "minor" writer to that of a "major" writer. But those terms — major and minor — lean on issues of canonization and the politics of literature course reading lists, and to use them begs the question that this study engages. This is not a project of "rehabilitation"; Burney no longer needs to be rehabilitated. Rather, I have tried to approach Burney's prose writings as a vantage point from which to ask certain questions about the representation of women in late eighteenth-century fiction and about the interpretations one woman's writings have received. Burney has been read as a clever observer of manners and character and as an acute social satirist, and she was both. She has also been read as a comic artist who saved her *bons mots* for her journals because she was too diffident to utter them in public. There is a gaping chasm between the portrait that derives from this alleged diffidence and depicts Burney as a timid, prudish snob, and what I believe I have uncovered in her writings: the masked simmering rage of a conflicted but self-conscious social reformer. Critical attention has been lavished on the accommodations of Burney's life, an attention that has then been extrapolated for use as a strategy in interpreting her art. Much less attention has been paid to the far richer problem, in my account, of Burney's obsessive hostilities. Recently, scholars have begun to recognize that she was not the sheepish simperer she has been portrayed as being: such a character could not have written the acutely critical work she produced. To analyze the complex reasons Burney wore a public veil while skewering her social milieu in writing, however, would require the sort of psychological study that this book cannot pretend to supply. I start here with a different question: Why has the gulf between social self/proper lady and private self/angry writer been dismissed or glossed over for two centuries? Why has Burney's aggressive violence not been read?

While I will discuss how and why critics have trivialized the Fanny Burney/Madame d'Arblay of the 1790s and after, and how and why her value in the literary marketplace has ebbed and flowed in the particular pattern that it has, it is important here to state that Burney has been taken seriously, in the last ten years especially, as a writer and cultural figure. Her first novel, in particular, has received decisive new critical attention. Readings of *Evelina* by Susan Staves, Judith Newton, Mary Poovey, Catherine Parke, Mona Scheuermann, and Kristina Straub have illuminated that novel's dissection of woman's place in the eighteenth-century gender economy as it is filtered through the refracting lenses of contemporary conduct manuals and of the social and legal conditions that dominated women's lives in the late eighteenth century.[2] Patricia Meyer Spacks, Katharine Rogers, and Judy Simons have taken a broader look at Burney's relation to authorial production and verbal art.[3] Margaret Anne Doody has written a monumental literary biography of Burney, and Kristina Straub has contributed an intelligent reassessment of Burney's artistic and feminist accomplishment.[4] Indeed, readings of Burney's work as "feminist" have taken such hold that there has even appeared a critique of such readings.[5] Other critics — most notably Rose Marie Cutting and Terry Castle — have offered readings of portions of Burney's *oeuvre*.[6] Finally, Edward A. Bloom, Lillian D. Bloom, and Joyce Hemlow have done invaluable textual studies of Burney without which critical revaluations would be impossible because the materials themselves would be unavailable.[7] While I take issue with some of these readings and build on others, I have learned from them all. I have chosen here to focus on a particular aspect of Burney's work that I believe shades all of her writings, provides one possible key to an understanding of her literary power, and has not been adequately taken into account: her obsession with violence and hostility. This obsession emerges in scenes of assault and moments of disguised anger throughout Burney's writings, and focusing on it allows me to open up her texts in ways they have not been opened before. While this represents only one facet of Burney's achievement, and an insistence upon it that leaves no space for other interrogations of Burney's work would defeat itself, in my view its dark cast informs and even pervades all of her work.

It is true that Burney outwardly appeared as a "proper lady" throughout her life, submitting to the exigencies of social and family expectation. It is also true that her writings trace the invisible costs of this propriety. Surface propriety was purchased at the price of internal rage; that the cauldron was covered only made it boil with greater heat. It is these reservoirs of rage in Burney's prose — fictional, epistolary, and journalistic — that I wish to mark: it was the intensity with which I found myself submerged in these reservoirs of Burneyan anger and frustrated desire that led me to write this book. I have tried to uncover this indirect but endlessly erupting anger in a body of work that has received attention for very different kinds of literary accomplishment from those that interest me here. It is my contention that the chaos, ferocity, and violence of Burney's prose allow us to unravel the constrained cultural situation not just of her own but of women's writing in general during a period crucial for the entrance of women into the mainstream literary marketplace, the turn of the nineteenth century.

In what kind of marketplace did Burney ply her trade? Many historians have seen the decade of the 1770s as representing a dearth of fiction writing, claiming that Tobias Smollett's death after *The Expedition of Humphry Clinker* in 1771 sent the novel into a tailspin from which it did not begin to emerge until Jane Austen published *Sense and Sensibility* in 1811. Certainly, women as writers of fiction had not yet fully established themselves, despite the interesting and important early efforts of novelists such as Jane Barker, Eliza Haywood, Charlotte Lennox, Sarah Scott, Frances Sheridan, Frances Brooke, and Sarah Fielding, and I too agree that after *Humphry Clinker, Evelina* is the only landmark novel from the 1770s. However, *Evelina* is also more than merely a small, bright beacon in an otherwise dim decade. It both built on the several novelistic traditions Burney inherited — the itinerant orphaned *pícara* inserts herself into the sentimental romance — and it made a historically significant new departure into social and domestic critique. The presence of an apparently innocent but actually calculating heroine marks this departure.

Burney has been called a snob in *Evelina* (and she is one there, though the charge must be mitigated in her later novels). But *Evelina* also provides a crucial and critical delineation of the social fragmentation beginning to be effected by what E. J. Hobsbawm calls "the rising new business classes" in England.[8] The aristocracy does not escape Burney's satiric pen in her first novel, and it falls prey to this satire precisely because Burney recognized the outmoded and decaying nature of aristocratic values and public behaviors. It is no accident that she uses public events such as assemblies and ridottos and public watering places such as Vauxhall and Ranelagh as platforms from which to launch attacks against social regulations that constrained female conduct and thereby endangered the very women they were allegedly established to protect. Such a critique does not emerge in any systematic fashion in novels that predate *Evelina*.

Burney's second novel, *Cecilia*, foretold the entrance of labyrinthine politics and of Gothic "terror" into the novel of the 1790s. Though Burney's later work is usually compared to the Richardsonian model into which *Evelina* has been critically assimilated, it can be argued that it makes more sense to read it beside the work of contemporary writers from the later part of the century such as Charlotte Smith, Ann Radcliffe, Elizabeth Inchbald, Robert Bage, Thomas Holcroft, Mary Wollstonecraft, William Godwin, Mary Hays, and Jane West. Burney's work should especially be read in relation to the writings of other women. After Burney, women were recognized not only as the established primary audience for fiction, but as the novel's central core of writers as well. As the American and French revolutions influenced the overt politics of fiction in the later eighteenth century, it was women writers who were able not only to thematize political upheaval but also to internalize it with subtle psychological analysis, that is, to write about the political importance of the internal, the private, and the domestic. While writers such as Bage, Holcroft, and Godwin used their fictions didactically to promote their political theories, women novelists invented an inverted Gothicism that permitted them to displace their repressed and politically significant desires into complex psychological and social narratives. Burney practiced an especially sophisticated version of this Gothicism in her social fictions, if we accept a definition of the "Gothic" as a literature of entrapment and engulfment, a literature that inscribes closure as at once stifling, inevitable, and necessary and that thematizes and textualizes the twin creations of domesticity and subjectivity as deriving from female intensity.[9]

The political strategies of Burney's narratives can be correlated to a changing economic situation for women. Burney's entrance into the literary marketplace—and her need to draw a financial return from her productions—coincided with major shifts in the economic position of women as well. While women remained the property of their fathers and husbands and without useful legal status, and continued to serve as pawns in an increasingly competitive marriage market with complex rules of property settlement and entail still supporting the powers of the patriarchal family, their status in the home had altered for the worse by the end of the eighteenth century. The increasing availability of leisure time for women has been commended as a boon to freedom, but the shift away from cottage industry in the home and toward domestic specialization and enforced idleness made it difficult for women to achieve any measure of independence, despite the power they exercised within the home itself.[10] At the same time, women were beginning to arrive on the Victorian pedestal eventually epitomized by Coventry Patmore's term "Angel in the House," an evolution traced by Mary Poovey in her analysis of the concept of the "proper lady."[11] Nancy Armstrong reads this new figure of female subjectivity more positively, and sees in it a reconstruction of cultural semiology.[12] Ellen Pollak calls this "women's rise to economic superfluity" and marshals it to counter Lawrence Stone's now controversial argument about the rise of "affective individualism."[13] As numerous feminist critics have noted, this contradictory situation left creative middle-class women in a limbo between conduct-book prescriptions for modesty, deference, and quiet virtue on the one hand, and their individual drive for self-expression, for acknowledgment of their importance as mothers and as participants in family enterprise, or simply for an autonomous sense of self, on the other.[14] The history of *Evelina*'s secretive and anonymous publication is the best-known example of Burney's ambivalent participation in this double bind, but the struggle to synthesize propriety with public achievement stalked her all her life, as it stalked women writers from Aphra Behn to Virginia Woolf. If feminist criticism has made any point with absolute clarity and persuasion, this is it.

Indeed, by opening up the political functions of literature that have been elided in traditional reading strategies, feminist criticism has enabled us to look not only at the ways women felt confined by cultural codes but also at the ways novels by women have reshaped our conceptions of domesticity, of individual development in relation to social norms, and of the constitution of subjectivity itself in the way the public world was imagined. Nancy Armstrong has argued convincingly that domestic novels recodified what constituted the feminine and indeed what constituted desire. She suggests that "a modern form of gendered subjectivity developed first as a feminine discourse in certain literature for women" and novels "performed the operations of division and self-containment that turned political information into the discourse of sexuality." Enlightenment fiction, Armstrong asserts, used the Rousseauian model of the social contract to "[create] a language for social relationships that was immensely useful for purposes of an emergent capitalism."[15] We could go even further. The woman in the private sphere of the home and the work of art proffered in the public marketplace of culture both depend upon the creation and sustenance of desire in others for their livelihood. In the very historical moment that middle-class novels invented, codified, and challenged domestic relations and sanctioned the philosophy of individualism, they were also entering the sphere of commerce and threatening to blur not only gender but also class boundaries and categories.[16] Domestication, feminization, and commodification went hand in hand. The book that enclosed the heroine, the book whose very status as a physical object could cover and house female interiority in all its privacy, also went forth in public wearing only a price tag.

My argument about Burney's narrative strategies, and their participation in a politics and economics of late eighteenth-century women's writing, proceeds initially from an effort in the first part of this book to understand the development and deployment of Burney's private voices in her letters and journals. I have tried in Chapter 1 to suggest the contours of Burney's writing life through an analysis of particular moments in her private papers in which the question of her feminine identity foundered on the rocks of internal rage and the aggressively faced hardships of a difficult life. I look, therefore, at passages that describe her alleged childhood "dyslexia," the internal violence done her during her years at court, an adventure that left her stranded in a coastal cave flooded by the rising tide, and her endurance of the last illness and death of her husband. In traumatic "crisis" passages such as these, I believe, Burney reveals and comes to terms with the place of writing in her life. Writing, I argue, obsessed Burney; she was a compulsive writer, and wrote in order to permit herself to live. Chapter 2 continues this analysis by focusing on the 1811 mastectomy Burney underwent in Paris and the extraordinary document she left to commemorate that event. In that document, Burney transforms her body into a sign system, into a hieroglyph whose decoding leads her to an analysis of gender oppression. The mastectomy letter can also be read, I argue, as a series of paradigmatic strategies for the integration of feminist social theory into the "domestic" novel — the narrative of social ideology — that Burney invented.

In the second and third parts of this book, I offer readings of Burney's four novels. I have ordered these discussions not chronologically, but in accordance with the two major strains of analysis I believe Burney displayed in them. *Evelina* and *Camilla,* it seems to me, concern themselves primarily with female modes of communication and with the dangerous silences into which contradictory eighteenth-century social ideologies enclosed women who aspired to be judged appropriately decorous and feminine. Both heroines eventually manufacture and manipulate an indirect feminine language that can liberate them from this enclosure, though while Evelina manages this with witty craftiness, Camilla pays the steep price of temporary madness (and the steeper price still, some might want to argue, of marriage to a judgmental prig). But Evelina and Camilla both retain access, albeit problematic access, to "protection," whereas Cecilia and *The Wanderer*'s Juliet are cut off from traditional social and familial structures and enter the world wholly alone. *Cecilia* and *The Wanderer,* while also concerned to inscribe enforced female silence into the social history of women, take on, thereby, more political and economic themes. Cecilia and Juliet are both heroines defined not so much by their status as "proper" women, though that status haunts them as well, as by their unprecedentedly independent relationship to money and to the means to earn it. Language is subordinated to more complicated powers of action in *Cecilia* and *The Wanderer,* in large measure because Evelina and Camilla still circulate in the orbit of the bourgeois family as Cecilia and Juliet do not.

Finally, the last section of this book looks at the ways Burney has been read, beginning with the reviews her work received during her lifetime, reviews that moved her from lionized best-seller celebrity status in 1778 and again, though a bit less so, in 1782, to waning and ultimately pitiably depleted storyteller, accused of slavishly imitating a borrowed Johnsonian style unsuited to her, in 1796 and 1814. By 1832, when she published a memoir of her famous father, the musicologist Charles Burney, she was treated with unconcealed contempt. Then a different "Fanny Burney," an official gossip and historian of the hectic times, emerged with the first publication of her journals in 1842, and a new set of reviews appeared. This revised view of Burney, as public wallflower and closet satirist, held sway through the nineteenth century until *Evelina* began to insinuate itself again, eventually landing in the mid-twentieth century on many university reading lists, at least for specialized courses in the eighteenth-century English novel. At this point, Burney became a "major minor" writer, but with the standard critical caveat that she began brilliantly and then got worse and worse. Chapters 3 through 6 of this book propose, instead, that she got better and better both as a narrative stylist and as a social theorist.

The editorial project headed by Joyce Hemlow, inaugurated with Hemlow's comprehensive biography of Burney in 1958 and continued by the publication of Burney's later journals and letters begun in 1972 and completed in 1984, has made Burney's familiar writings widely available for the first time. All this newly accessible material has led scholars to reconstruct a new Burney who challenges the received view of the writer as witty but withdrawn, socially insightful yet politically listless. Her works have begun to reappear in print, with *Camilla,* a reprinting of *Cecilia* as well as a new annotated edition, and the play *A Busy Day* all seeing print in the 1980s, and an annotated edition of *The Wanderer,* its first reissue since 1814, in progress. New interpretations of Burney's life have come to light in reviews of her journals and letters as well as in Margaret Anne Doody's book, and several new readings of *Evelina* have appeared in scholarly journals and recent books on women's fiction.

This latest rebirth into a critical afterlife is characterized predominantly by feminist interpretation and by an effort to read Burney within the context of a marketplace that accepted women producers of literature in large numbers for the first time. This is not the same thing as arguing that Burney herself was a feminist — to use the term anachronistically — though it does not preclude such an argument. Rather, I mean by "feminist criticism" to designate an empowering discourse that permits critics to uncover the ways Burney's work was embedded in the eighteenth century's gender constructions and to read her narrative strategies of indirection, understatement, and irony as peculiarly female strategies.[17] My own project clearly fits into the latest wave of Burney criticism. But while tracing this critical trajectory, I argue that each manifestation of engagement with Burney has reflected a particular generation's need to mine certain kinds of ore from literature: literature as it is portrayed in critical readings serves the hegemonic interests represented by the classism and elitism of the profession of *belles lettres.*

The answer to the question of why critics have not been able to read Burney's aggression resides, I believe, within the ideological boundaries of literary critical practice, and the project of this book is an ideological one. I want to locate and interpret the narrative strategies of a writer who embodied both social and self-contradictions as she struggled to define herself and her art within a coercive structure of social, political, economic, and cultural relations. Burney cannot be read outside the context of the material conditions that produced her writings; her work makes sense only within the structure of social relations that framed the increasingly class-specific world of England and France at the end of the eighteenth and the beginning of the nineteenth centuries. Ideological constructions control the production of both literature and criticism, a phenomenon that engenders the hermeneutic circularity of critical reading: the cultural and political circumstances that define the production of literary criticism in a given moment (say, 1988) encroach on our reading of the cultural and political circumstances of Burney's writing. This is what I mean when I call my argument ideological; it reflects an understanding of ideologies as those systems of social relations and values and representations that dominate in a particular period, place, and situation by being taken for granted as inalterable givens, and thereby masking social contradictions by apparently fostering a univocal world view.[18]

I try in the last chapter of this book to question the relationship between Burney's work, produced as it was during a period characterized by upheaval in its positioning of women and of class distinctions, and the ideological critical readings it has elicited. If certain ideologies have typified each generation of Burney critics, we are not doing anything different to try now to "recuperate" Burney for a feminist (or Marxist, or psychoanalytic, or deconstructive, or new historicist) political project. This project allows me to read deliberately as a woman (how else might I read?) a set of woman-generated texts, and to make a political case for both parties in that reading. I am, among other things, doing just that. If I situate my interpretation in this way, however, I also fall into the apparent trap of undercutting and even dismissing my own critical enterprise by subjecting it to the same accusations of self-interest that, I contend, underlie all critical readings. But I also want to argue that the acts of writing literature and of writing literary criticism participate in a matrix of power relations in which the question always turns on the constitution of authority in a text. Finally, in order to write literary criticism, it is necessary to take a political stand, to argue that some kinds of reading are better than others. "Criticism," Terry Eagleton has reminded us, "is not an innocent discipline, and never has been." Indeed, Eagleton asserts, it "has become a locus of political contention rather than a terrain of cultural consensus."[19] And Jim Merod has argued that "literary critics need to ask how they are positioned within the culture and how they are used, how their work is used, and how they lend themselves to those uses." In criticizing Wayne Booth's embrace of feminist criticism as critical freedom, Merod characterizes Foucault's (and, he adds, Nietzsche's) notion that "writers who succumb to codes and disciplines are in a distinctly unfree or operationally limited, institutionally mandated situation that does not leave them free to commit any particular inventive act except within rigorous conceptual, procedural, and even political boundaries."[20] I argue in chapter 7 that this book both participates in an ideological project and offers a valid interpretation of Burney's literary achievement.

One

Private Voices

Frances Burney d'Arblay's life story reads almost like the stories of her fictional heroines, except that Burney did not find romantic love until she was nearly forty, and even then, she did not live happily ever after despite what appears to have been a nearly ideal marriage. Burney belonged to a large and complicated family that occupied the edges of polite society. When she married the French émigré General Alexandre-Jean-Baptiste Piochard d'Arblay in 1793, her position became politically as well as socially precarious. The fourth daughter of the first marriage of Charles Burney, author of *The History of Music* (1776–89), Burney competed with eight siblings (three of her brothers died, however, in infancy), two half siblings, and three stepsiblings. Her mother, Esther Sleepe, died in 1762 when Burney was ten years old, and to say that none of Charles Burney's older children was particularly delighted when he married Elizabeth Allen in 1767 understates their antipathy. Burney was especially distressed by this second marriage. Much has been written about her close relationship with her family, especially with her father; many have tried, indeed, to argue that a family pathology of no small dimensions was at work in this motley household.[1] Certainly Burney was close to her father and avidly sought his approval, and she maintained affectionate relations with her siblings, particularly eldest sister Esther (Hetty), younger sister Susanna (who died tragically on 6 January 1800, a date Burney commemorated ever after and on which, ironically, she herself died in 1840), and, in her later years, youngest sister Charlotte. It is hard to determine the motivations and explanations that would illuminate a life removed from us by two centuries, and I leave it to others to apply the insights of modern psychology and psychobiography to Burney's childhood and filial commitments. But I will argue in my readings of her work that appearances and reality almost never mesh in the way Burney imaginatively depicts the world. We can speculate, therefore, that this may have been the case in her life as well as in her fiction. She seemed demure and self-deprecating, whereas there is ample evidence that she was driven, proud, and enormously ambitious. She seemed to defer to the views and rules of others, whereas her written social critiques demonstrate that she had a rigorously willful mind of her own.

As a child and throughout her life, Burney was a voracious reader and a compulsive and prolific writer. In her youth, she studied French and Italian; she read all the standard histories (Charles Rollin on the ancient world, Nathaniel Hooke on Rome, David Hume on England, William Robertson on Scotland), the periodicals (the *Spectator* of Richard Steele and Joseph Addison, Steele's *Guardian,* Eliza Haywood's *Female Spectator,* and Samuel Johnson's *Rambler, Adventurer,* and *Idler*), the poetry of John Milton, Alexander Pope, Edward Young, and James Thomson, Pope's translations of Homer and versions of Horace along with the works of Epictetus, Cicero, and Pliny, collections of sermons (including those by Laurence Sterne and James Fordyce), and the array of advice books and conduct manuals available for moral instruction in the mid-eighteenth century. She was familiar with the works of Shakespeare, Corneille, La Bruyère, and Voltaire. Because of her father's prominence as a music master and music historian and critic, Burney met cultural figures such as Edmund Burke, Johnson, Hester Thrale, Richard Brinsley Sheridan, David Garrick, Sir Joshua Reynolds, Elizabeth Montagu, and Mary Granville Delany. These connections earned her the dubious honor of preferment to a position at court, a preferment that was to lead to the bleakest five years of her life following the publication of her second novel. She observed and recorded the trial of Warren Hastings and the aftermath of the Battle of Waterloo. She lived for ten years in France in exile with her husband, bore her first child when she was forty-two, and endured a mastectomy without anesthesia when she was fifty-nine. Later, after her return to England, her own fame gained her audiences with Sir Walter Scott and Charles Lamb. Hers was a rich and busy life, not the life of the attentive but sidelined bystander some literary commentators have portrayed.

Burney's life spanned nearly a century—from 1752 to 1840—and while she wrote no fiction after *The Wanderer* appeared in 1814, and nothing at all for public consumption after the execrably reviewed *Memoirs of Doctor Burney* in 1832, Burney's writings, in particular her journals and letters, provide a unique social history of an unstable period in transition from a patronage and patrimony system to a full embrace of bourgeois capitalism. Her novels are preoccupied with this instability in relation to the uneasy emergence and mingling of distinct social and economic classes, and her works taken collectively offer a powerful critique of the superficial codes of behavior that condemned the working classes to social inferiority and promoted the landed gentry to a supercilious sense of its own moral aristocracy. Much has been written about Burney's incisive and meticulous record of social experience in the late eighteenth century, a record that stands alongside that of Samuel Pepys from a century earlier for the brilliance of its distillation of a particular time, place, and class in England.

In these first two chapters, I examine darker material that has largely been excluded from discussions of Burney's journals and letters. While all of her writing betrays her particular vision of a social world that at once fascinated and repelled her, I focus here on a series of narratives that involve traumatic events in Burney's life. I do not wish to claim anything like normative status for these passages within Burney's canon, nor do I wish even to argue that they are "typical" of Burney's private writings. I have selected these narratives for two reasons. First, in narrating moments of tension, danger, or violence Burney reveals most clearly the place of the act of writing for her narrative creation of a particularly female subjectivity. Second, Burney's responses to social impediments in the construction of this subjectivity may be most nakedly witnessed when the conflicting pressures of traumatic events build to such a pitch that Burney's ordinarily checked and controlled rage loses its covert status and appears unmistakably on the page. Burney's lifelong attempts to construct a "self" were all conducted in and through writing, and I have selected her accounts of several disturbing episodes—her physical torture at court, a near drowning, and her husband's death in chapter 1, and her mastectomy in chapter 2—as spectacular outcroppings of the issues at stake in this project of self-construction.

1

Compulsive Writing

In her third novel, *Camilla; or, A Picture of Youth* (1796),[1] Burney systematically isolates and alienates her heroine in scenes of increasing frustration and loss: her father is in debtor's prison because of her; her uncle's house is boarded up and echoing; her sister is incarcerated by an evil husband; her mother remains silent in response to Camilla's letter asking forgiveness. Finally, an encounter with the corpse of her villainous brother-in-law sets up a climactic delirium that leads to the novel's key vision: Camilla has a nightmare in which the gaunt, aggressive figure of Death challenges her to enter her merits and claims in the Records of Eternity. She at first resists writing in these imposing volumes, answering the challenge with a "voice from within, over which she had no control, though it seemed issuing from her vitals, low, hoarse, and tremulous" (874–75). "Let me not sign my own miserable insufficiency!" she pleads. Nevertheless, under an inner compulsion, "her own hand involuntarily grasped a pen of iron" and began to write "with a velocity uncontroulable." The words Camilla composes—a blinding self-condemnation—become "guilty characters . . . illuminated with burning sulphur" (875). But

when she takes up the iron pen a second time—"again, unlicensed
by her will"—and dashes it across the page, the paper remains blank,
the pen makes no mark upon it.[2] And, as the page explodes and the
bound volume "burst[s] open," Camilla is assailed by "voices then, by
hundreds, by thousands, by millions, from side to side, above, below,
around, called out, echoed and re-echoed" (876). She is imprisoned,
as was her creator, by a disembodied primal language, a language
both unwritable and ineradicably embedded in her imagination, clam-
oring for attention and shattering silence. Camilla's vision fictively
enacted—and finally exploded—a tension that had been building
throughout Burney's writing career, and that controlled her literary
and autobiographical voices and silences.

This tension in Burney's writing between two poles of authorial self-
definition, defiance and submission, is dramatized most tellingly in
the harrowing climax of *Camilla*, an exemplary scene that embodies
literally Burney's defensive attitude toward the writing process. Camilla's hostile writing implement usurps its user's power to express
herself and bars her access to language. The iron writing tool, the
graven letters, and the gaping blank page in *Camilla* figure Burney's
understanding that her writing represented an inexorable public unveiling. The iron pen, both tool and weapon, is clearly an awkward
implement for her, and objectifies the relation Burney understood between silence and exposure, and ultimately, between narrative and
its interpretations; it represents an industrial rather than a domestic
image, a masculine rather than a feminine means of communication:
it is a sign of profound discomfort.[3]

Compare *Camilla*'s writing metaphor—the "iron pen"—to another
contemporary metaphor of writing, the "rural pen" in William Blake's
poetic "Introduction" to his 1789 *Songs of Innocence*.[4] After a child asks
the poet first to "pipe" and then to "sing" a "song about a Lamb," he
issues a third invitation:

> Piper sit thee down and write
> In a book that all may read—
> So he vanish'd from my sight.
> And I pluck'd a hollow reed.
>
> And I made a rural pen,
> And I stain'd the water clear,
> And I wrote my happy songs
> Every child may joy to hear

(7)

Blake's complex relation to his writing and printing implements was not always this unconflicted, of course, but here writing for Blake occurs within a social institution embodied by this public request from one child who speaks for "every child." When the poet pipes and sings, he entertains an individual child who constitutes a private, intimate audience for an oral/aural performance. The child "hears" his song. But after asking him to write "a book that all may read," this singular auditor vanishes, and the poet's voice attenuates into writing, now distanced, formal, and public. But Blake's poet has manufacturing control over his pen and the materials of its production. And the "hollow reed" become "rural pen" makes a permanent mark in the world: it "stain'd the water clear." Blake's "stain" endures for "every child"; Camilla's scorched sulfuric letters, in contrast, fade into a blank page.

Blake too associated the instruments of his creative trade with burning letters. In the first "Memorable Fancy" from *The Marriage of Heaven and Hell,* the poet describes a walk through the fires of hell and on his return home

> I saw a mighty Devil folded in black
> clouds, hovering on the sides of the
> rock, with corroding fires he wrote the
> following sentence now percieved by the
> minds of men, & read by them on earth.
>> How do you know but ev'ry Bird that
>> cuts the airy way,
>> Is an immense world of delight,
>> clos'd by your senses five?
>
> (35)

Depicted in plate 7, Blake's image of the Devil's corrosive writing suggests, as does the writing in Camilla's dream, an *imposition* of letters. In plate 14 of *The Marriage of Heaven and Hell,* the poet returns to his imagery of fiery consumption and argues that he will "expunge"

> the notion that man has a body distinct
> from his soul . . . by printing in the
> infernal method, by corrosives, which in
> Hell are salutary and medicinal, melting
> apparent surfaces away, and displaying
> the infinite which was hid.
>
> (39)

Blake does not here dismiss the murderous quality threatened by
Burney's similar image of the iron pen, but converts the threat into
a cleansing illumination and opening out of the "narrow chinks of
[man's] cavern." In plate 15, Blake describes "a Printing house in Hell"
whose method involves melting metals into "living fluids" by "flaming
fire," casting the metals into the infinite expanse of the cave to be "re-
ciev'd by Men" who "took the forms of books & were arranged in libraries" (40). While Blake too, then, employs an imagery that marries
writing and burning, letters and fire, and that gives to creative production the simultaneously destructive and generative power of cor-
rosion, the poet's emphasis finally "stains" and endures in its infernal
as well as its rural modes, while Burney's iron pen with its sulfuric
ink burns *through* and disappears.

Yet permanence also resides in the iron pen's authoritative inscrip-
tions. Camilla's dream recalls Job's anxious desire that "my words were
now written! . . . That they were graven with an iron pen and lead
in the rock for ever!" (Job 19:23–24). In addition the letters "illuminated with burning sulphur" recall the biblical tablets of the law burned
into both sides of the stone by the finger of God as well as the pen
of iron in Jeremiah.[5] Iron in the Bible is an impure metal, unlike silver, gold, or even brass. God asks Moses not to use his iron tool to
build the stone altar, because iron symbolizes destruction, severance,
and estrangement.[6] A kind of hieroglyphic primal scene of writing
for Burney, a Rosetta stone embedded in her *oeuvre,* the dream of the
iron pen and its etchings in the Records of Eternity is Burney's feminist revision of Moses' reception of the stone commandments and a
fruition of Job's desire for a permanent written record. Camilla as
writer is a figure of female divinity and autonomy, an inscriber of
herself into the Book of Life. However, Burney always struggles against
the primordial permanence of the record writing leaves, the permanence Blake celebrates, even as she desires it. For her, writing constitutes an irrepressible expression of inner self. As such, writing
represents vulnerability, exposure, indelicacy. We shall see that as a
consequence Burney never achieves either the distanced impersonal-
ity of public gesture that Blake accomplishes in the short excerpt from
his "Songs of Innocence" or the consuming power of creativity inscribed in *The Marriage of Heaven and Hell.*

Burney's charged relation to her writing culminates in *Camilla*'s ex-
plosive climax, but it had been with her throughout her career. When
she wrote the *Memoirs of Doctor Burney* in homage to her deceased father, Burney produced an autobiographical and retrospective history
of herself as well, a history that illuminates her relation to language,

rhetoric, and writing as a kind of exorcistic therapy.[7] In that work, she confessed the visual-perceptual deficits she may have suffered from as a child. This condition has been diagnosed as severe childhood dyslexia—a learning disability with neurological implications.[8] But Burney's voracious reading, her copious citations of other writers in her journals and letters, the ambitious reading lists she set herself, and the evidence of her own manuscripts and handwriting call into question whether her lack of reading ability at age eight may correctly be labeled as "dyslexia," or even as odd for a young girl in the eighteenth century: it seems more likely that her status as a middle child and her mother's illness and death took family attention away from her instruction. She was seventy-four when she wrote this third-person account of not being able to read: "At eight years of age she was ignorant of the letters of the alphabet; though at ten, she began scribbling, almost incessantly, little works of invention; but always in private; and in scrawling characters, illegible, save to herself" (*Memoirs* 2:123). Despite, or perhaps in consequence of, her early inability to read, she developed the facility to memorize poetry recited aloud to her along with an early obsession with writing, which she refers to as "this writing mania." While her brother James mocked her by holding books upside down to pretend to teach her to read, a ruse she was unable to discern, "these scrambling pot-hooks had begun their operation of converting into Elegies, Odes, Plays, Songs, Stories, Farces, — nay, Tragedies and Epic Poems, every scrap of white paper that could be seized upon without question or notice." And the secret nature of her writing obsession derived from these public humiliations: "She grew up, probably through the vanity-annihilating circumstances of this conscious intellectual disgrace, with so affrighted a persuasion that what she scribbled, if seen, would but expose her to ridicule, that her pen, though her greatest, was only her clandestine delight" (*Memoirs* 2:123). Only in old age could she recount the history of her early reading disability, which she understood as an "intellectual disgrace."[9] But by this confession of retroactive amused embarrassment, Burney repossesses an arena of language. It is not by accident that this distanced third-person narrative of childhood humiliation is interpolated in Burney's final published work, because to write the history of her own language dysfunction is by definition to overcome it, to prove it cured. And I shall argue that she had similarly conquered other obstacles—among them, breast cancer, imprisonment in a flooded cave, and the death of her husband—by writing about them.

On the one hand, Burney's desire to write was always radically irrepressible—she was a compulsive writer, as unable to stop writing as a compulsive gambler is unable to stop gambling. Her image of "scrambling pot-hooks" reflects that. On the other hand, writing for Burney represented a challenge to received notions of feminine behavior that included modesty, artlessness, submissiveness, passivity, and silence on the list of feminine virtues, and Burney wanted to minimize her own defiance in issuing that challenge. Later, her financial predicament and the necessity to support a politically renegade husband and a sickly child would provide Burney with a practical rationalization for writing. But that situation did not occur until after the appearance of *Evelina,* whose ambivalently anonymous publication has been well-documented, and *Cecilia,* works whose popular success had made Burney the reigning novelist in England. By the time she published *Camilla,* the first fragmentary jottings for which were made during her disastrous five years (1786 to 1791) as an oppressed second keeper of the robes to Queen Charlotte at the dreary, insular court of George III, Burney's view of herself as a writer had been nearly strangled by contradictions.[10] To be an author was to flout social prescriptions for feminine conduct; to stifle her authorial voice was to stifle her very selfhood. The tensions created by this problem emerged in the tentative but resentful personae who inhabit Burney's letters and novels, and in her conscious manipulation of both dialogic silences and written white space. Identifying that tension allows us to locate repositories of anger, defiance, and self-conscious authorship in Burney's writings.

The self-willed "pen of iron" in Camilla's nightmare vision pictured the most troubled and insistent relationship between writing and writer that Burney ever presented when she characterized her composing process. In January of 1778, when she was twenty-five, her first completed manuscript, *Evelina; or, a Young Lady's Entrance into the World,* appeared in print anonymously. "There seems something very formidable in the idea of appearing as an authoress," wrote Burney in her diary later that year, "I ever dreaded it."[11] At first, Burney had feared, or at least pretended to fear, being "found out" as an author and censured by her father. But when both her family and the literary coterie surrounding the Thrales and Samuel Johnson fêted and approved her, she became apprehensive about expectations for future production:

> I am now at the summit of a high hill; my prospects on one side are bright, glowing, and invitingly beautiful; but when I turn around, I perceive, on the other side, sundry caverns, gulfs, pits, and precipices, that, to look at, make my head giddy and my heart sick. I see about

me, indeed, many hills of far greater height and sublimity; but I have
not the strength to attempt climbing them; if I move, it must be downwards. (*DL* 1:11)

Already, with the awkwardly short-lived anonymity of her first published work, Burney was unsettled by the public relations of writing.

Camilla's dream effectively raises and consolidates the central problem that haunted Burney's writing career, the problem of authorship
and authority.[12] Burney was plagued all her life by the political contradictions encoded in the ambivalent social status of a woman writer.
In 1769, the year her *Essay on Shakespeare* appeared, Elizabeth Montagu
defined this ambivalence in a letter to her father-in-law:

> When I was young, I should not like to have been classed among
> authors, but at my age [nearly fifty], it is less unbecoming. If an old
> woman does not bewitch her neighbor's cows, nor make any girl in
> the parish spit crooked pins, the world has no reason to take offence
> at her amusing herself with reading books or even writing them.[13]

Burney had articulated a version of this view, minus Montagu's cheerful irony, in the voice of the elder Mr. Delvile speaking to Cecilia in
Burney's second novel, *Cecilia; or, Memoirs of an Heiress* (1782).[14] "Let
me counsel you to remember that a lady," he tells his charge, "whether
so called from birth or only from fortune, should never degrade herself by being put on a level with writers, and such sort of people" (2:26).
And Burney herself, distressed that her name "had got into print . . .
I had always dreaded as a real evil my name's getting into print" in
a satirical pamphlet, tells family friend Samuel ("Daddy") Crisp that
"I would a thousand times rather forfeit my character as a writer, than
risk ridicule or censure as a female." "I have never set my heart on
fame," she continues, "and therefore would not, if I could, purchase
it at the expense of all my own ideas of propriety" (*DL* 1:101-2).

Addressing her father in the dedication of her last novel, *The Wanderer; or, Female Difficulties* (1814),[15] Burney reported her struggles against
the impulse to write imaginative literature:

> So early was I impressed myself with ideas that fastened degradation
> to this class of composition [the novel], that at the age of adolescence,
> I struggled against the propensity which, even in childhood, even from
> the moment I could hold a pen, had impelled me into its toils; and
> on my fifteenth birth-day, I made so resolute a conquest over an in-
> clination at which I blushed, and that I had always kept secret, that
> I committed to the flames whatever, up to that moment, I had com-

mitted to paper. And so enormous was the pile, that I thought it prudent to consume it in the garden.

You, dear Sir, knew nothing of its extinction, for you had never known
of its existence. . . .

The passion, however, though resisted, was not annihilated: my
bureau was cleared; but my head was not emptied; and, in defiance
of every self-effort, Evelina struggled herself into life. (1:xx–xxi)

This passage's incendiary language reveals the Faustian intensity of
Burney's internal fight. Writing novels was a "degradation," something
"at which I blushed, and that I had always kept secret." She speaks
of writing fiction as a "propensity" that "impelled" her, an "inclination" that it was necessary to conquer, a "passion" to resist: in other
words, writing became, in Burney's childhood and youth, a shameful
vice. All her life Burney was conscious that attempts to tamp down
her desire to write would be futile, "in defiance of every self-effort."

Critics who write about Burney tend to be both intrigued and
put off by the split narrative persona, at once self-effacing and self-
congratulatory, she portrays in her journals and letters. Burney's apparent prudishness masks a strong will along with an obsessive, almost uncontrollable authorial energy, and many eighteenth-century
scholars have seen her effort to struggle against the creative impulse
she understood to be "unbecoming" as a mousy fearfulness. Patricia
Meyer Spacks, for example, while arguing that Burney "may write
better fiction than other women of her era partly because she has come
to terms more fully than they with the realities of the female condition," also castigates her for requiring "permission to rebel" from her
father when she married.[16] Lillian D. Bloom and Edward A. Bloom
call her "the prototype of her pseudonymous Miss Nobody" and assert
that "she was undeveloped emotionally."[17] Peter Glassman sees Burney as self-repressed, a woman whose life was "marked . . . by her
willful, by her no doubt actually diseased, submission to imposed and
invented criteria of behavior" and calls her "this fixed and fixated
woman" who "refused to enter her appropriate arc."[18] Irma S. Lustig
describes Burney as a "prude of contained heart . . . excessively prim
and righteous."[19]

Burney worked at understating the ways in which she knew writing
represented a challenge to feminine decorum and complacency, and
to judge from this critical view of her, she succeeded. In fact, however,
Burney manipulated her narrative voices in order to direct her ideas
about sexual politics, and about the tyranny of propriety and its rules,
into an analysis of how powerlessness can be turned around to protect

women. Burney critics have tended to equate the writer's diaries and journals, letters, novels, and plays as all equivalent transcripts of actual life. This tendency—a tendency that has plagued male writers as well, but more often in the form of the intentional fallacy—has obscured the distinctions in every writer's work both between literature and life in general, and between the differing ways Burney's sensibility rendered experience in nonfictional prose and in imaginative literature. While it makes no sense to read intimate private writings as necessarily "authentic" in contrast to the fictions that are always "contrived," it also makes no sense to yoke the two kinds of writing and to read them in consequence merely as glosses on each other, as does, for example, Peter Glassman when he reads Burney's letters as appendices to her novels. The critical assessments cited above fail to investigate Burney's ironic manipulations of narrative voice, and reflect only the conventional surface of her literary production. That surface is cracked by a split between defiance and compulsion in Burney's approach to the act of writing.

Burney's biography illustrates the chronology of her sense of writing as public self-interpretation, and explains her consistent attachment to letter writing. The dramatic manuscript bonfire she staged when she was fifteen and mentioned in *The Wanderer*'s preface (burning, among other juvenilia, a preliminary version of *Evelina* titled *The History of Caroline Evelyn*), her flirtatious mixture of pride and blushing apprehension at the reception of *Evelina,* and the continuing conflicts with her father and with Samuel Crisp, especially over her desire to write for the stage, all point to the problems of authorship for Burney. As an adolescent she was warned by her stepmother that keeping a journal held dangers for young girls, so she devoted herself to needlework in the mornings, "by which means my reading and writing in the afternoon is a pleasure I cannot be blamed for by my mother, as it does not take up the time I ought to spend otherwise."[20] The same Burney who in 1778 referred to herself, wryly but with legitimate pride, as "the ingenious, learned, and most profound Fanny Burney" (*DL* 1:1) also remarked in 1778 that she "instantly put away my book, because I dreaded being thought studious and affected" (*DL* 1:22) during a visit to the Thrales at Streatham.

Burney's desire to appear to bow to conventions of femininity may have fueled her commitment to letter writing, a kind of composition recognized as a decorous female mode of discourse by the eighteenth century. The privacy of epistolary form offered Burney a protected textual space in which to experiment with her narrative voices.[21] The letter form, more than any other kind of literature, forbids anonymity: a letter must be signed, because an unsigned letter becomes radically contextless (a ransom note; extortion or blackmail), a floating sea of words disconnected from the meaning-imparting gesture of the signature, a gesture that seals relationship into the text. "Let me not sign my own miserable insufficiency," Camilla begs. The signature, of course, is also a claim to authorship and to an authoritative voice. In her journals and letters Burney forthrightly embraces this claim, while her novels each contain different codes for it. She had already amply displayed a knowledge of the manipulative rhetorical possibilities intrinsic to the letter form, for example, in the epistolary *Evelina*. Evelina signs her letters to her guardian Villars with the anagrammatic name "Evelina Anville," but in the period between learning her legitimate surname and giving it up for that of her husband, her signature options blur. The novel's plot hinges on Evelina's struggle to legitimate herself with the name "Belmont," to be "owned" by her biological father. To "own" the name here means both to possess it through social and legal sanction, and to admit to it, to claim it by signing it.

Burney's second heroine, Cecilia Beverley, also grapples with issues of authority and selfhood, and again these issues are centrally connected with the status of her name, and her ability and willingness to sign it. *Cecilia* encodes the signature and authorial claim directly in the sound — "seal" — embedded in its title and in its protagonist's name, and enacted throughout in the heroine's obstacle-strewn efforts to maintain both her wealth and her name. An heiress enjoined to marry only if her prospective husband agrees to take her surname and to relinquish his own, Cecilia Beverley struggles to integrate ownership of self with ownership of property. She seeks to put her "seal" (her name — her confirmation and authentication) on her lover, Mortimer Delvile, on her secret marriage (a "seal" is also a vow of secrecy), and on the material possessions her name bestows. So Cecilia "owns" her signature in as problematic a fashion as Evelina "owns" hers, though Cecilia's struggle is to keep and impose her name, while Evelina seeks legitimacy in order to exchange her birth name for another. Juliet Granville, the "wanderer" of Burney's last novel, possesses no name at all and spends most of the narrative worrying that her given name will expose her. Camilla's signature stamp, more graphic than either Evelina's or Cecilia's but as materially threatening to her identity, is also spiritually threatening in ways that go beyond the metaphoric and literal "seals" of the heroines who preceded her: the burning, sulfuric letters she etches in her nightmare mark the page as a signet and

demand, finally, that she take responsibility for herself as a writer.
If she does not, the page, supreme threat, will remain empty, unsigned,
and a blank page frightened Burney almost as powerfully as a page
whose irrepressible writing put her in mind of adolescent bonfires.

The letter form that prompted Burney to "sign" herself most readily and to embrace authorship least suspiciously also permitted her
to dramatize her deepest angers. Burney's virtually continuous dread
of public exposure and explosion and her compulsion to document
it derived from her experience at court, that most code-bound and
therefore most dangerous of social milieus. Her writings from the court
of George III in the years 1786 to 1791 demonstrate her preoccupation
with the metonymic power of uncanny forms of violation and violence, and her efforts to dramatize her hostilities in controlled compositions. She disclosed her opening impressions of court etiquette
to her sister Esther in a famous letter dated 17 December 1785. Burney
was thirty-three and unmarried when she wrote this letter; her father
had arranged for her to be considered for a place at court, and she
was presented to the royal family as part of an interview for this position. Burney's deep resentment of her powerlessness to resist this pet
plan of her father's social vanity erupts in the letter she wrote after
that interview in which is incorporated her "Directions for coughing,
sneezing, or moving, before the King and Queen," a passage that bristles with ironic detachment. This extraordinary letter deserves full
citation:

My dearest Hetty
    I am sorry I could not more immediately write; but I really have
not had a moment since your last.
    Now I know what you next want is, to hear accounts of kings, queens,
and such royal personages. O ho! Do you so? Well.
    Shall I tell you a few matters of fact?— or, had you rather a few mat-
ters of etiquette? Oh, matters of etiquette, you cry! for matters of fact
are short and stupid, and anybody can tell, and everybody is tired
with them.
    Very well, take your own choice.
    To begin, then, with the beginning.
    You know I told you, in my last, my various difficulties, what sort
of preferment to turn my thoughts to, and concluded with just starting
a young budding notion of decision, by suggesting that a handsome
pension for nothing at all would be as well as working night and day
for a salary.
    This blossom of an idea, the more I dwelt upon, the more I liked.
Thinking served it for a hot-house and it came out into full blow as

I ruminated upon my pillow. Delighted that thus all my contradictory
and wayward fancies were overcome, and my mind was peaceably settled
what to wish and to demand, I gave over all further meditation upon
choice of elevation, and had nothing more to do but to make my elec-
tion known.

My next business, therefore, was to be presented. This could be
no difficulty; my coming hither had been their own desire, and they
had earnestly pressed its execution. I had only to prepare myself for
the rencounter.

You would never believe — you, who, distant from courts and court-
iers, know nothing of their ways — the many things to be studied, for
appearing with a proper propriety before crowned heads. Heads without crowns are quite other sort of rotundas.

Now, then, to the etiquette. I inquired into every particular, that
no error might be committed. And as there is no saying what may
happen in this mortal life, I shall give you those instructions I have
received myself, that, should you find yourself in the royal presence,
you may know how to comport yourself.

Directions for coughing, sneezing, or moving,
before the King and Queen.

In the first place, you must not cough. If you find a cough tickling
in your throat, you must arrest it from making any sound; if you find
yourself choking with the forbearance, you must choke — but not cough.

In the second place, you must not sneeze. If you have a vehement
cold, you must take no notice of it; if your nose membranes feel a great
irritation, you must hold your breath; if a sneeze still insists upon making its way, you must oppose it, by keeping your teeth grinding together; if the violence of the repulse breaks some blood-vessel, you must
break the blood-vessel — but not sneeze.

In the third place, you must not, upon any account, stir either hand
or foot. If, by chance, a black pin runs into your head, you must not
take it out. If the pain is very great, you must be sure to bear it without wincing; if it brings the tears into your eyes, you must not wipe
them off; if they give you a tingling by running down your cheeks, you
must look as if nothing was the matter. If the blood should gush from
your head by means of the black pin, you must let it gush; if you are
uneasy to think of making such a blurred appearance, you must be
uneasy, but you must say nothing about it. If, however, the agony is
very great, you may, privately, bite the inside of your cheek, or of your
lips, for a little relief; taking care, meanwhile, to do it so cautiously
as to make no apparent dent outwardly. And, with that precaution,
if you even gnaw a piece out, it will not be minded, only be sure either
to swallow it, or commit it to a corner of the inside of your mouth till
they are gone — for you must not spit.

I have many other directions, but no more paper; I will endeavour, however, to have them ready for you in time. Perhaps, meanwhile, you will be glad to know if I have myself had opportunity to put in practice these receipts?

How can I answer in this little space? My love to Mr. B. and the little ones, and remember me kindly to cousin Edward, and believe me, my dearest Esther,

Most affectionately yours,
F. B.
(*DL* 2:53–55)

The opening and closing of this epistle suggest a bantering irony and contrast sharply with the brutal tone of the stylized middle section. Far from being apprehensive that she might not gain a court preferment, she actually dreads being offered the position. The court passage sardonically and savagely parodies the then popular conduct manuals with their self-righteous rhetoric. Lord Chesterfield's injunction to his son condemning laughter—that "disagreeable noise" that occasions a "shocking distortion of the face"[22]—does not even seem harsh in comparison with Burney's bitter narrative of the need to control private and natural physical acts. Each succeeding paragraph of the court passage grows longer and more horrifically detailed; each sentence expands internally as the dread it contains threatens increasingly to reveal itself. Coughing becomes choking; sneezing yields to broken blood-vessels. The final discourse on motionlessness—a state of absolute imprisonment in the body—explodes into a literal bloodbath, a portrait of controlled agony ending, astonishingly, in self-cannibalism. The self-inflicted but other-imposed violence escalates exponentially as the tone shifts from irony to blackest comedy in a cynical narrative of monumental enforced frustration in which Burney parallels control over bodily response with control over her elaborate prose: all those balanced sentences beginning with "If." Everything about this text is self-conscious, including the way its author set it off as a free-standing essay from the letter's coy, affectionate conventional opening. Its rhetorical deliberateness and careful pacing argue that Burney approached this letter not simply as an amusing family communication, but as a literary production. This composition reveals a writer whose skill at manipulating language is impressive indeed, and who channels her intense and volatile emotions into narrative control.

The next year Burney's diary contained a report on "the true court retrograde motion," the requirement that royal attendants walk backwards before the king and queen. Burney practiced this unnatural motion for hours in order to learn the skill "without tripping up my own heels, feeling my head giddy, or treading my train out of the plaits," and she was especially impressed by one stoic attendant, faced with a retreat of twenty yards: "She therefore faced the King, and began a march backwards, — her ankle already sprained, and to walk forward, and even leaning upon an arm, was painful to her; nevertheless, back she went, perfectly upright, without one stumble, without even looking once behind" (*DL* 2:146–47). Burney's resentment of the oppressive life at court grew from her own multifaceted lack of choice in the face of her father's insistence that she accept the position as second keeper of the robes. In her court diaries of 1788, three years after her savage etiquette parody, Burney described her situation as acute indeed: "banished from every friend, confined almost to a state of captivity, harrowed to the very soul with surrounding afflictions, and without a glimpse of light as to when or how all might terminate" (*DL* 3:91). The five years she served Queen Charlotte were the grimmest of her life, and her only outlet to express the violation of self she endured at court was in her writing: along with letters and journal entries, the court years yielded materials for several plays as well as the outlines of *Camilla,* a novel whose heroine's relation to language as both compulsive disability and brutal exorcism reflects Burney's own.

The powerful court letter is paradigmatic of a certain authorial stance that Burney adopts in order to narrate crucial moments of stress, conflict, and trauma both in her own life and in the lives of her fictional female protagonists. Her ambition to write and to act independently was frustrated by social and cultural impediments; her heroines' independent impulses are equally impeded. Often through the kind of stylistic hyberbole exemplified in the court letter, Burney turns social and physical trauma into knowledge and uses language to distance herself from and to control, at least retrospectively, experiences of pain. The traumatic incidents I discuss in these first two chapters are not, however, all of the same type, though I would like to argue that Burney deploys similar techniques for their narration. The court letter details institutions of self-inflicted pain: the explicit rules she suffered at court (signs for the implicit rules suffered everywhere else) were oppressive, but the actual assault described here comes from within (*she* bites her own cheek). While a certain amount of externally imposed physical violence occurs here (the injunctions, for example, to remain standing and to refrain from eating), the most important site of violence is not the external events, but the writing itself. Burney does not merely report or mirror institutions of oppression; she posits and dramatizes violence as an effect — the inevitable effect — of oppression.

The most notable narration of violence in Burney's *oeuvre* is a text I analyze at length in the next chapter, the account of Burney's surgical ordeal when she underwent a mastectomy for what was diagnosed as breast cancer in 1811. She struggled *not* to struggle against her physicians during that ordeal very much as she had struggled not to write as a young woman. In the mastectomy letter, Burney encodes a series of contradictions into her writing: self-control and violence; acceptance and protest; passivity and rebellion. I leave the detailed discussion of the mastectomy narrative itself until the next chapter, but those contradictions also appear in two of the longer and heavily edited "journal-letters," the report of her adventures in a cave at Ilfracombe and the depiction of Burney's husband's protracted dying from the ravages of cancer.[23] These incidents, a near-drowning and the suffering of someone she loved, do not narrate violence so explicitly as do the court and mastectomy writings, where physical assault — externally imposed but self-inflicted at court; voluntarily submitted to but enacted by others on the operating table — is literally invasive for the writer. In the cave, Burney believes she may die. In her account of her husband's final illness, she narrates her emotional trauma far more effectively than she narrates his physical ordeal.

We need to differentiate between assaults upon Burney's autonomy from the outside world, as at court and under the knife, and Burney's responses to and dramatizations of those assaults. In other words, we need to differentiate between external violence and internal response, and between overt bodily pain and social violation of self. The peculiar quality of these narratives — and we may add to them the various assaults of psyche, of social space, and of body discussed in parts 2 and 3 with respect to the novels — comes from Burney's insistence on physicality. Burney and her heroines experience social oppression with and through their bodies. The intense outcroppings in Burney's private writings of concern with aggression and with violent experience, a concern matched in her novels, supply illustrative keys to the relationship she forged between lived events and the memory of them she recorded. In each case, Burney's narrative recapitulation of incidents fueled by anger, fear, courage, and defiance constitutes a reclamation project. By writing about experiences that rendered her radically vulnerable, she turns her very vulnerability and emotional and physical precariousness into a position of creative power that allows Burney to purify and recreate herself.

In 1823 Burney composed "Adventures at Ilfracombe," an account

of an incident that had occurred six years earlier at a seaside resort
in Devonshire where she had accompanied her son, Alexander. This
long journal-letter reads like a scene from one of Burney's novels, and
bears close scrutiny. She had set off down the beach with her dog, Diane,
and a large bag for collecting rocks (Burney's husband was an ama-
teur mineralogist, and she sought specimens for his collection). Thinking that the tide was ebbing, Burney became preoccupied with her
collecting, and wandered toward the entrance of Wildersmouth, a series
of recessed caves formed by the rocks along the beach and accessible
only at low tide. Burney ventured into the chamber of the last cave:

> The top was a portly Mountain, rough, steep, & barren; the left side
> was equally Mountainous, but consisting of layers of a sort of slate,
> intermixed with moss; the right side was the elevated Capston, which
> here was perpendicular, & at the bottom were the Sands by which I
> entered it, terminated by the Ocean. The whole was alltogether strik-
> ingly picturesque, wild, & original. There was not one trace of Art,
> or even of any previous entrance into it of Man. Almost, I could imag-
> ine myself its first Human Inmate. (*JL* 10:693)

Enchanted by a glittering stone at the top of the cave, Burney climbed
and continued with her collecting. Diane disappeared, then returned
and began to whine, but her mistress thought the dog was only anxious about her week-old puppies. When the dog started to tug at her
piteously, she finally discovered that the entrance to the cave had filled
with water:

> I now rushed down to the Sea, determining to risk a [w]et Jerkin,
> by wading through a Wave or two, to secure myself from being shut
> up in this unfrequented place: — but the time was past! —The Weather
> suddenly changed, the Lake was gone, — & billows mounted one after
> the other, as if with enraged pursuit of what they could seize & swallow.
> I eagerly ran up & down, from side to side, & examined every nook
> & corner, every projection & hollow, to find any sort of openning
> through which I could any way pass. But there was none. (*JL* 10:694)

As an editorial note in the journals reports, the Bristol channel coasts
have the greatest tide range in Great Britain, and a high tide with
a following wind could easily imprison an unwary tourist. Burney probably did not realize this. What she did realize was that her frenzied
panic at the discovery of her entrapment was not new to her. The language that conveys this panic in the Ilfracombe journal resonates with
the memory of the nearly identical language Burney had employed

to write about other trapped women: Evelina in the pleasure gardens; Cecilia at the masquerade and in the carriage; Camilla on the platform with Dubster and in her dream; Juliet on stage and in the summer house. Entrapment and the rising panic it produces might even be termed the quintessential Burney anxiety, in life as in fiction, and dramatizing it was her specialty.

Diane, as intrepid and indefatigable as Mortimer Delvile's dog Fidele in *Cecilia,* found a small opening through the rocks and escaped, howling for her mistress to follow, but the hole was far too tiny to admit the passage of an adult woman. The slates crumbled at Burney's grasp, her hands slid off the moss, and she could locate no secure foothold to prevent her from falling onto the jagged rocks "that must almost inevitably have dashed out my brains" (*JL* 10:695). A storm arose, making the chamber smaller every moment:

> The roughness of the Rock tore my cloaths; its sharp points cut now my feet, & now my Fingers, & the uncooth distances from each other of the holes by which I could gain any footing for my ascent painfully writhed my whole person. . . . the pressing danger gave me both means & fortitude to accomplish it [climbing], — but with so much hardship that I have ever since marvelled at my success. My Hands were wounded, my Knees were bruised, & my feet were cut; for I could only scramble up by clinging to the Rock on *all fours.* (*JL* 10:696–97)

In the process, Burney lost a shoe, and used her parasol to snare it and replace it on her bleeding foot. She hung on to a rock and tried to retain her balance while the tide continued to rise. Burney was sixty-five years old in 1817, had had a breast surgically removed, and would not, given prevailing fashion, have been suitably dressed for such exertion. She turned her attention to the prospect of being swallowed up in a watery grave as the waves foamed around her. "I did not breathe — I felt faint, — I felt even sea-sick.— . . . Giddy I now felt.— in my fear of losing my strength, or self-command, & falling" (*JL* 10:701):

> What a situation for a Female Alone — without power to make known her danger — without any resource for escaping its tremendous menace, but by painfully, laboriously, & perillously standing upright, & immoveably on the same spot, till it should be passed — without any human being knowing where to find her, or suspecting where she might be — a Female, & past 60 years of age! (*JL* 10:701–2)

A "Male Alone," particularly one her age, might not have fared much better, of course.

Burney consoled her shivering dog and recited lines from *Paradise Lost* about thunder that bellows "through the vast and boundless deep," a poem she and her son, Alexander, read in its entirety while at Ilfracombe.[24] At length, the storm abated and the tide, Burney was overjoyed to notice, gave signs of receding, but it had begun to rain and grow dark, and the water's ebbing was as frustratingly slow as its rising had been terrifyingly precipitous. She was cold, hungry, and worried about her son's anxiety at her disappearance: "Thus passed this, to me, most memorable Day" (*JL* 10:707). Eventually, a rescue party headed by John Lefevre arrived, and afterward "many asked how I had escaped Fainting away. Others wondered I had not screamed the whole time" (*JL* 10:713). Burney later learned that she had been caught in a semiannual changing of the tides: two days hence, and she could not have been saved.

In September 1824, Burney referred to the Ilfracombe event in a letter to her sister Esther, who, having heard of the "truly extraordinary, & so nearly fatal adventure," had expressed surprise that Burney "had not been my own Historian." Afraid that her husband would be frightened at the rumor (he was in Paris at the time) as she had been afraid her father would find out about her breast surgery six years earlier, "I did not dare risk its relation, well knowing I ought to tell it myself to make it heard with serenity! yet never a moment was it out of my thoughts even for Weeks" (*JL* 11:551). To Esther, she refers to "the awful *10 Hours* of Danger & Affright, & for so narrow an escape of abruptly ending my career unknown & unheard of, in becoming food to Whales or Sharks" (*JL* 11:552). In her account of her husband's last months, written in 1819 and 1820, she also reports that he had "charged me to write the account.—I made memorandums immediately & it is NOW, even NOW [after his death], a comfort to me that I have a wish of his I can fulfill" (*JL* 10:846). These requests offer partial answers to the question of why, six years later in 1823, Burney finally took pen in hand to relate this adventure in such detail. Here is her own explanation:

> All Ilfracomb, I was told, went afterwards to visit this place. And the impression made by the frantic agony of Alexander is still alive, this 6th year after the adventure; for it is now 1823. & Lady Keith & her Daughter, Miss Elphinstone, the other day demanded of me the truth of the reports of his dreadful distress, & my alarming disappearance, for a lady then resident at Ilfracomb, had related so strange & frightful a history, that Georgina had thought of it continually, & they had both determined upon examining into its authenticity. (*JL* 10:714)

To write about the adventure is to offer proof of its credibility: the calamity happens again in the writing, but this time because she wields the pen, she has control over character, plot, and outcome.

A letter dated 1912 from her rescuer's son, George John Lefevre, suggests that Burney's narrative memory might be open to question in another kind of challenge to her authenticity:

> The lady's account of her adventure was greatly exaggerated—She was in no real danger—The sea had not come up to her. She was not clinging to the rocks—She was seated on the sand—The incident of the little dog Fidele [*sic*] was an invention as far as my father recollected—He could not be said to have saved her life but his happy suggestion that she might have been caught by the tide saved her from enough inconvenience. (*JL* 10:714, note)

Of course, Lefevre's son was not born until 1831, so his "memory" is inherited and secondhand, and in Burney's account, the rescue occurred in darkness. But whether this incident in truth occurred as Burney recounts it or not, her narrative produces a characteristic Burneyan ambivalence. A proper, decorous heroine in ribboned shoes and parasol, complete with lapdog—in other words, the quintessential "Female Alone" of her novels—grapples with brute physical strength in the muck and mire of crisis, and barefoot at that. On the one hand, she takes pride in her endurance and ingenuity; on the other hand, she wants to do the correct "feminine" thing, to swoon and scream.

The writing itself represents a site of struggle between these personae. In many ways it is as though the writing is Burney's effort not to assert her valor or gain sympathy for her sufferings, but rather to reclaim her parasol, her shoes, and her decorous demeanor. There is potential violence here in the threat of drowning, and actual minor violence in the scrapes and bumps and discomforts of climbing and waiting to be rescued, but what is striking about this narrative written so many years later is its rhetorical insistence on the physicality of the experience. The waves are in "enraged pursuit" and "seize & swallow"; the graphically described rough and sharp rocks provide only enough footing to tear clothes, cut feet, and "painfully writhe [. . .] my whole person"; reduced to "all fours," Burney is "wounded," "bruised," "cut." Given the danger, whether it had been actual or not, Burney came away with only very minor injuries. Her privileging of the physical over the psychological or social content of this ordeal (she must have feared to die; she was publicly found in a state of some undress;

she was frightened and alone for ten hours) is therefore particularly striking. Burney asserts through this account that women experience oppression, fear, and danger with their bodies: the body both encases and represents. By highlighting the bodily aspects of this ordeal, Burney marks the boundaries of an arena in which her own subjectivity holds primacy.

In the Ilfracombe journal, Burney refers to 1817 as "the last year of my happiness!" (*JL* 10:691); her husband, General Alexandre d'Arblay, died on 3 May 1818. As she has done retrospectively for the misadventure in the cave, as she did after her surgical trauma in 1811, and as she did for her wartime travels in the journals of Dunkirk and Waterloo, as she did indeed after each key event or emotion of her life, Burney sat down months after d'Arblay's death to compose an account of his dying. Written later and heavily edited, this account survives in a fair copy bound in a red leather notebook marked with a black ribbon and titled "Narrative of the Last Illness and Death of General d'Arblay." The notebook numbers 147 pages. These long and carefully revised sections of Burney's journal constitute a kind of "semiprivate" voice: not quite familiar letters or diaries, they beg to be read as self-conscious literary texts even though they are not presented as such. Meant to be seen by a plural but deliberately selected audience, these letters-cum-journal entries represent arranged family documents. That Burney chose her most traumatic, most intimate, rawest experiences as subjects for these documents suggests that she composed them as a kind of psychotherapy. Certainly the converting into theater of d'Arblay's illness and death and his wife's grief displaces the writer from her subject and turns her into its object. Reliving these experiences as a writer, Burney also reorganizes them for her memory.

The "Narrative of the Last Illness and Death of General d'Arblay" was begun on 17 November 1819 with this apology:

> My soul visits ever more my Departed Angel — & I can devize no means
> to soothe my lonely woe so likely of success, as devoting my Evening
> solitude to recollections of his excellencies, & of every occurrence of
> his latter days — . . . . I think it will be like passing with Him — with
> Him Himself — a few poor fleeting — but dearly cherished moments. . . .
> With my Pen I shall seem still to address Him! at least, to call his loved
> Image & Idea before me! — . . . . I will call back the history of his last
> Illness — ever present as it is to me, it will be a relief to set it down:
> & its lecture may both solace & aid me in supporting my own final
> seizure. (*JL* 10:843–44)

D'Arblay's dying was ugly and insistent, and Burney's choice to write about it finds its clearest motive in her reference to "relief." D'Arblay first felt ill in the fall of 1817, though his disease — probably rectal cancer — had no doubt silently invaded earlier. In June, he left London for Paris hoping to improve his health: a bout with jaundice had afflicted him in February. It was in September 1817, with d'Arblay out of the country, that Burney and her son visited Ilfracombe. They returned to Bath in October to meet the elder d'Arblay. Burney found him thin, weak, and easily fatigued; his efforts to garden in the crescent fields only made matters worse. D'Arblay's final appearance in public turned out to be a duty visit to the queen in the Pump Room shortly before Christmas 1817. The d'Arblays returned home abruptly when the general, regaled for the last time in his military honors, fainted from pain. Burney never saw the queen again — she died in November 1818 — and Burney's brother Charles suffered a fatal stroke shortly after Christmas. It was a bleak holiday season for the d'Arblays.

Both her husband and her friends tried to talk to Burney of the severity of d'Arblay's illness, but she evaded the subject:

> Again, therefore, I became the Dupe — the willing Dupe! of solacing expectation. My sister Burney [Esther] & Miss Maltby sought to find means & opportunity to warn me of my errour — but I flattered myself the errour was theirs, & evaded, therefore, by assuming spirits that embarrassed them, to hear their warning voices. I felt that I could not sustain a sound of condemnation. I flew, therefore, all discussion, & parried their dreadful hints by appearing not to understand them, & shewing an even inexorable repugnance to every attempt at explanation. (*JL* 10:855)

No wonder she needs to write about it afterward, having postponed and evaded her own grief. George Edmund Hay, a Bath apothecary, attended the patient and reassured Burney in January that there was "no reason . . . for Anxiety" (*JL* 10:856). Meanwhile, d'Arblay quietly arranged his papers and affairs in anticipation of his death. William Tudor, the surgeon who had attended the queen at Bath, was called in when d'Arblay told Hay "that he felt an internal growing ossification that menaced his life" (*JL* 10:858). In the meantime, Burney entertained her husband by reading aloud to him. One of her texts consisted of "my juvenile Journals, which were commenced when I was fifteen, & continued till my marriage" (*JL* 10:860). Intertextuality reigns in this narrative; large chunks of it comprise Burney's transcriptions of her husband's final diary entries (these stopped in April with the words "Patienza! Patienza!" [*JL* 10:868]).

D'Arblay spoke only of his coming death and plans for his wife and son, while Burney resolutely refused to recognize that he was dying even when he talked to her about wearing mourning (*JL* 10:881). This narrative, despite its title, remains more a narrative of Burney's emotional denial than of d'Arblay's physical suffering, as the account of her interview with the physicians illustrates:

> When I was alone with Mr. Tudor, I parried the subject with so much agitation, that I believe I frightened him from enforcing the dread sentence I saw menacing; & Mr. Hay returned while yet nothing unusual had been pronounced. I saw them both disturbed & embarrassed: I would have taken the opportunity to escape: but they then began both together to point out the encrease of weakness — the thinness — the unabating pains — — — I felt to what this led, & could endure no more; breaking in upon them with a tremulous eagerness that startled them to silence, "Well, Gentlemen," I cried, "the greater the difficulty, the more honour will redound to your skill; — —"
> Mr. Hay hung his head, in undisguised depression, & Mr. Tudor tried to articulate some words of Cases incurable: but I interrupted him with "there are NONE, sir! — No mortal man ought to pronounce such words!" (*JL* 10:882)

Tudor and Hay began to resent this stubbornness, but they subsided nonetheless.

Burney unveils in this narrative a favorite technique of her heroines — and one that gets them chin-deep in trouble — in relating one of her final conversations with her ailing husband. In response to his urgent "Qu'a [*sic*] tu, donc? . . . Dis le moi, donc!" Burney reports, "It was vain to try to elude, & I could not deceive him. Oh never, — from the time I was his, never did I deceive him! *Where I could not be silent, or evasive,* on subjects I had any reason to wish to avoid, I was ever, ever faithfully sincere" (my italics) (*JL* 10:889). Silence and evasion on many subjects pervade Burney's copious, and copiously "prepared," diaries and letters, as silence and evasion dominate the speech of her heroines. Just before his death, d'Arblay withdrew into reflection, and asked for silence: "He told me not to utter one word to him; even of reply, beyond the most laconic necessity; & never, upon any consideration, to speak uncalled" (*JL* 10:894).

When words cease to flow for Burney, she ceases to exist, a condition clear from her agonizingly drawn-out account of d'Arblay's final days. Just before she recorded his last moments, she writes:

My Pen lingers now! — reluctant — nay laborious it becomes to finish
the brief little that remains — & that deprives me, thence forward, of
the precious, though heart-piercing, occupation of inscribing these too
dear recollections! Yet, the brief little that remains is wholly sweet &
consolatory — & recurs ever as the best & most sacred of balms to my
poor, wounded, festered heart. (*JL* 10:906)

General Alexandre d'Arblay died peacefully in his sleep, with his wife
and son at his beside, 66 printed pages and 147 handwritten ones after
his health began to deteriorate. At the end, after Tudor pronounced
him dead, Burney claimed the madness that overtakes Cecilia and
Camilla in similar emotional emergencies, but the very details of the
narrative she composed make her claim seem specious:

> I had certainly a partial derangement — for I cannot to this moment
> recollect any thing that now succeeded with Truth or Consistency; my
> Memory paints things that were necessarily real, joined to others that
> could not possibly have happenned, yet amalgamates the whole so to-
> gether, as to render it impossible for me to separate Truth from in-
> definable, unaccountable Fiction. (*JL* 10:908)

The narrative serves its purpose nevertheless. Burney emerges from
it the consummately devoted wife and helpmeet, loyal to the end, sto-
ically nursing her suffering husband and mindless with grief when
he breathes his last. Whether this account bears relation to the truth
we have no way of knowing — no letter such as Lefevre's has surfaced
to question it — but we do learn from it a great deal about Burney's
ideal and idealized image of herself.

The journal of General d'Arblay's illness and death, even more than
the Ilfracombe journal, raises questions of the relation of truth to fiction in Burney's writings or, more to the point, the relation of experience to its imaginative representation. Perhaps not accurate renderings of things as they were, these narratives nevertheless capture what
we might call Burney's retrospective memorialization of herself at
moments of trauma. She denies, she suffers, and ultimately she endures. If these narratives must finally be read as hybrids between fiction
and factual truth, then Burney appropriately chooses a hybrid structure in which to house them. The familiar letter form provided her
with a narrative vehicle defined by its slippery configuration of private and public selves, a configuration that is metaphorically punc-
tured in the court letter on coughing and sneezing, literally violated
in the mastectomy letter by the invasive act of surgery, challenged by

the ocean at Ilfracombe, but oddly celebrated by death in Burney's
tale of d'Arblay's final illness.

The slipperiness of privacy in opposition to publication exists as a
rhetorical strategy within epistolary form itself, a strategy Burney uses
to brilliant effect in *Evelina*. But the distinctions also extrude from the
form in these accounts of trauma and allow Burney to recreate herself
in memory by narrating material that violates and thus escapes the
conventions of the familiar letter. Writing about moments of helplessness represents a doubly recuperative process. Burney reclaims in her
letters the self she had surrendered in court, on the operating table, in
the cave, and at her husband's bedside. Her letters reveal an uncommon genius at depicting and analyzing the intimate experience of violence, violation, and fear, the transformation of pain into knowledge.

The language of real and metaphorical violence also appears less
explicitly in many of Burney's other narrative letters. She often framed
her narratives of illness and catastrophe with reflections on letter
writing. She had referred to the mastectomy account as "this doleful
ditty" (*JL* 6:612); she wrote "a second melancholy ditty" (*JL* 7:15) to
Esther early in 1815 to relate the d'Arblays' unfortunate crossing to France
in that year. Again here, as she had done in the breast operation letter
and the Ilfracombe journal, Burney composes the narrative in such
a way that it could serve as a scene in one of her fictions. The crossing
is stormy, and Burney suffers badly from "the deadly sea malady" (*JL*
8:12), so weak from nausea and vertigo upon arrival at Calais that she
must be carried to an inn. As d'Arblay seeks succor and medicine for
his wife, a cart strikes him and throws him to the ground. Each of
them "insensible" by turns, with Burney fainting and d'Arblay bleeding, this scene provides all the melodrama of the madness sequence
in *Cecilia* mingled with some of the same overwrought comedy Jane
Austen used in her juvenile "sensibility" send-up, *Love and Freindship*.
Burney brackets her "tragical" (*JL* 8:14) tale with a lengthy apology
to Esther for her epistolary neglect: "What pain — suffering — & alarm
have fallen to my lot since our separation!" (*JL* 8:12) she begins. Then,
comparing this missive to the surgery account, she predicts that Esther "will never like the sight of a long letter from me again!" (*JL*
8:15). That Burney characterizes the letter as an emissary of self is
common enough practice in eighteenth-century epistolary literature
and belongs to the conventions of representation in familiar letters,
but here the reflexive references to a symbolic letter-text so accumu-
late that the very paper on which she writes comes alive.

Burney repeatedly characterized letters and letter writing as metaphorical enterprises. To her brother James, she wrote in 1815:

> If Letters are to be considered in their best light, i.e. as marks of Friend-
> ship, — how many have you not written me — of late — without holding
> a Pen? I would not exchange, for Value, your hospitality & kindness
> to my Alexander, for the best collection of Epistles left by Cicero, Pliny,
> or even Madame de Sévigné. (*JL* 8:316)

Letter writing for Burney is a mental gesture, an act of love, intellect,
and will. This characterization makes the complex classification of
Burney's own private papers particularly interesting. She always kept
a diary, at first addressed to the famous "Nobody" but frequently containing direct addresses to members of her family, and especially to
her sisters Susanna and Esther. She also composed extended narratives
for her family in the form of long letters that seem to belong to their
own genre and that, Burney admits, she revised and recopied. The
Waterloo journal, for example, narrates events that took place between February and July 1815, covering the period from the time Burney
learned that Bonaparte had returned from Elba to his surrender to
the English (a period of fear for Burney during which she searched
for her missing husband), but not written until 1823. This account,
unsentimental and filled with political commentary, was not written
until long after the events it narrates, and again its voice is causally
and crucially connected to pain and to the possibility that pain can
be exorcised through writing. As she explained to Alex: "And how I
arrived — through what dangers, what impediments, & what difficulties, I must reserve to relate in my future Letters. — I can bear to write
now — & you can desire to read, exclusively of our beloved sufferer,
again thus cruelly the victim of baleful accident" (*JL* 8:465).

But while pain and violence often charge Burney's voice in her letters, she also repeatedly emphasizes her pleasure in writing, a pleasure that overflowed from her literary manuscripts to augment the
length of her private writings. To her husband, she admonished, "Could
you seriously believe that I had neglected to Write? O no! — on the
contrary, I have *un si doux plaisir* in this reciprocated communication,
that I have the *retenue* to write little enough, & have always a sheet
in hand over & above what I can send" (*JL* 10:569). And a week later,
she tells him, "how must I have been changed, to have read SUCH
Letters, & not have answered them! The truth is, I have written *too
much*, not *too little*, for, by always going on with my Journal, I have
always had by me a sheet or two more than I could end, so that I
have often seemed in arrears, not to cost you both of information &
on postage, by ending up to the Date of the day that my Letter went
to the post" (*JL* 10:576).

That habit of carrying her journal about with her had begun at least fifty years earlier, in 1768, the first year from which the Burney diaries are extant. In July of that year, she had written, "You must know I always have the last sheet of my Journal in my pocket, and when I have wrote it half full I join it to the rest, and take another sheet—and so on" (*ED* 1:17). Burney kept both journal and letters constantly in an "in-progress" state so that the process of their composition becomes part of their content. Her private words, therefore, come to read very much like the epistolary continuations of a Pamela or an Evelina, the same entry incorporating mood shifts and tonal variation. Thus for Burney the familiar letter and journal forms intermingle and fuse into a generic hybrid characterized by the very compulsion that inspires her to cover sheet after sheet with adventures and observations.

Discussions of Burney's compulsion to write, and the impulse to still her pen that accompanied it, recur so frequently in her journals and letters that in their revelations of internalized violation these discussions serve as a leitmotif that parallels the obsessive recurrences of violence. Two episodes deserve particular mention. First, the earliest diaries and letters document Burney's "embarrassment" (in Johnson's dictionary sense of "entanglement") at both the concealment and the unveiling of her authorship of *Evelina*. She pretends to be unable to tolerate hearing herself praised, an affected stance that earns her a deserved lecture from Hester Thrale (*DL* 1:52), yet she signs a July 1778 letter to her father "Francesca Scriblerus" (*DL* 1:9). Does she really desire anonymity? Clearly not. In fact, the diaries and letters of 1778 expose a woman who longs for recognition, though not necessarily for approval. But she wants to pay only a discreet price for that recognition, and it is when she appears as *Evelina*'s author in a pamphlet titled "Warley: A Satire" that she claims to Crisp, "I had always dreaded as a real evil my name's getting into print" (*DL* 1:101). It must be remembered, however, that Crisp is no more a correspondent with whom Burney can be candid than is her guardian, the Reverend Mr. Villars, an unproblematic interlocutor for Evelina. And even a cursory perusal of these early papers reveals a woman who would not offend the male elders—Crisp and Charles Burney—to whom she owes emotional and economic allegiance, yet who basks in the admiration of the Thrales, Johnson, and Reynolds, and will not relinquish her supposed public discomfort without a struggle.

The second episode that highlights Burney's conflicted sense of herself as compulsive writer concerns the composition history of *The*

Witlings, her first play as well as her initial effort after the success of *Evelina.* Urged to turn her pen to dramatic comedy by Sheridan and assorted persuasive others, Burney met with loud disapproval from her father and from Crisp, with their explicit accusation that writing for the stage is "unfeminine"; indeed, Burney's "daddies" were to be a plague on her thwarted career as a playwright throughout her writing life. Yet her acquiescence to their complaints rings false. "When my Daddy Crisp says, 'that it would be the best policy, but for pecuniary advantages, for me to write no more,' is exactly what I have always thought since 'Evelina' was published," she tells Crisp in a 1779 letter. "But I will not now talk of putting it in practice, — for the best way I can take of showing that I have a true and just sense of the spirit of your condemnation, is not to sink sulky and dejected under it, but to exert myself to the utmost of my power in endeavours to produce something less reprehensible" (*DL* 1:170).

Put down her pen? Unthinkable, says Burney, in her most deferential and ladylike prose. While six years later Burney pleasantly reported Queen Charlotte's public comment that "her character . . . is too delicate to suit with writing for the stage" (*DL* 2:19) and Mary Delany's remark that she "would as soon die!" (*DL* 2:21) as read aloud from her own works, Burney never had any intention of giving up writing, either for the stage or for reading audiences (there are seven finished plays and one dramatic fragment extant, though only one was performed during Burney's lifetime, and only two can be found in print today: the meddling daddies were largely successful in publicly stifling Burney's theatrical voice). That she dissembled to her father and father-surrogate is not an argument that she dissembled to herself. Burney needed, and knew that she thrived on, the written renderings of her narrative imagination. She could not have stopped structuring her life as a series of fictive narratives, nor could she have surrendered her pen.

Burney's experience in composing *Camilla* illuminates her approach to the act of writing. *Camilla* was rigorously criticized for its allegedly excessive five-volume length; Burney worked on a second edition with a sharp pruning pen, and continued to labor over a third version until only a few years before she died.[25] This book represented her legacy to her son, Alexander, as she intended its royalties for his inheritance, so *Camilla* took on significance for her beyond its literary merit. Critics have underestimated both Burney's artistic commitment to this work (it was not written merely as a money-maker) and its literary worth, seeing *Camilla* as the first downswing in Burney's powers as a novel-

ist.[26] But the extraordinary period — 1786 to 1836 — that the work ab-
sorbed her, and the intensity of that absorption, suggest that she saw
Camilla as her most troubling work, as the potential star in her literary crown.

Burney's reflections on composing her novels illuminate this compulsive approach to the private act of writing in letters and journals.
Burney speaks of her writing, as she had reported in the preface to
The Wanderer, as a force against which she is powerless to struggle: "Our
Gardening Hobby-Horse has given way, of late, to a literary Courser —
how long that will run I know not; — but if the Race will continue thus
alternately mental & corporal, I can have no wish, and no fear, each
rectifying whatever in either may be excessive" (*JL* 3:6). In July of
1796, shortly after *Camilla* appeared, Burney reported in a letter to her
father a conversation she had had with King George III when she
travelled to Windsor to present sets of *Camilla* to the royal family. The
king asked her how much of her time she had devoted to writing. "'*All
my time, sir*'," she replied, "'— from the period I planned publishing it,
I devoted myself to it wholly; — I had no Episode — but a little baby! —
My subject grew upon me, and increased my materials to a bulk —
that, I am afraid, will be still more laborious to wade through for the
Readers, than the Writer!'" (*JL* 3:176). She had written to her husband,
"I am very careful of myself, I assure you, except in the one article
of writing late — but — it is so delicious to stride on, when *en verf* !" (*JL*
3:157). And the new novel took its place next to the infant Alexander:
"The mother of Camilla left her daughter asleep in order to nurse
for a short time her brisk and lively boy" (*JL* 3:169). That reference
corresponds to the dismissive "I had no Episode — but a little baby!";
Burney's literary productions *were* her children and, like an infant,
this one insisted on long periods of her mother's undivided attention.

The same energy of imagination and composition that Burney had
to rein in while writing *Camilla* resurfaced in her journals and private letters. In those writings, unmindful of eventual reviews and the
harsh judgments of outsiders, Burney could indulge her writing passion unchecked. It is perhaps not so ironic, then, that the letters read
like fiction. During Burney's courtship with d'Arblay — a picturesque
courtship in the eighteenth-century sentimental tradition as Burney
presents it, and fittingly carried out almost entirely through quasi-
illicit correspondence — she wrote in 1793 to her brother Charles for
advice:

> Were I with you, I should relieve myself from the extreme embar-
> rassment of opening my own Cause by employing you in various con-

jectures, & keeping your imagination in play, till, by skill or chance,
you came near to my subject: — but at this distance, I am forced to
mount my Pegasus without any Esquire —

My Pegasus? — No! — I have nothing to do with Poetics — nothing with
fiction — all is plain though perhaps you may not hold it to be plain —
or common sense. —

In brief — & to give you — at once — some little scope for conjecture —
Do you remember seeing, at a Concert in Titchfield Street, a Gentleman — whose Face, you said, looked *anything* but French? —

Now your Eye brows begin to arch — (*JL* 2:175)

The unstoppable flow of teasing narrative mingles here, as in most
of Burney's letters, with her compulsion to arrange and orchestrate
her tale, to tell a suspenseful, witty story, to manipulate language and
rhetorical structure so that they both forge a bond between writer and
addressee and at the same time distance them.

The composition history of Burney's journal-letters and the way
she handled her private papers in her bequest to her niece Charlotte
Barrett, their first editor — editing, cataloging, and elaborately mark-
ing these writings with codes — suggest that Burney took the same
care with this work as she did with her novels.[27] She demonstrates
a lively, purposeful sense of audience in her epistolary writings, and
she viewed these manuscripts as an important part of her literary
oeuvre. The rhetorical and narrative sophistication of her long, com-
plexly structured journal-letters shows that Burney practiced the art
of letter writing as a literary form akin both to the essay and to the
novel. While she did not think of her letters as a public literary act,
despite the editorial evidence she prepared for Charlotte Barrett, her
obsessive embrace of violation and pain as engenderers of her epistolary voice connects Burney's letters to her more self-consciously "literary" productions.

Eighteenth-century letter writers such as Burney inherited the familiar epistolary form they used from its protean appearances in
eighteenth-century conduct manuals, periodicals, travel narratives, and
didactic essays. Letters appeared in such periodicals as Richard Steele's
Tatler (1709–11) and Eliza Haywood's *Female Spectator* (1744–46), framed
a wide variety of philosophical and political polemics, and insinuated
their paratactic, pseudo-oral form into the general merger of prose gen-
res in the eighteenth century.[28] Eighteenth-century writers changed
conceptions of correct style in letters by shifting away from the formal
conventions and neoclassical ideals of Renaissance and Restoration
epistolary dogma and moving toward a looser, more emotive and ex-
pressive style.[29] The rhetoric of gallantry yielded to the language of

sentimentality, and in the process the letter moved from the arena of official public discourse (the classical and medieval *ars dictaminis* tradition) to a world of privacy and intimacy, of advice and seduction.

This movement from public to private, from oracular to conversational, and from labored discourse to spontaneous flow of thought and emotion brought the letter to the special attention of an array of women writers who had been trained in the art of letter writing as in the arts of needlework, singing, and drawing, and who knew what Virginia Woolf expressed in a discussion of Dorothy Osborne, that "letters did not count" as literature.[30] For eighteenth-century women, letters represented an especially tricky mode of writing, a form circumscribed and intellectually suspect by its classification as a feminine "accomplishment." If a woman wrote in order to support herself or to assert her intellect, she defied propriety in the eighteenth-century's gender economy; on the other hand, if she wrote for private expression, using a genre by definition (but not in fact) destined for private audiences only, she did not transgress against the virtues of modesty, obedience, decorum, and silence.

The letter's peripheral or paraliterary status made it available to writers who otherwise might not have entered the literary marketplace so aggressively and who have become known, some primarily, as *épistolières:* with Burney are Osborne, Margaret Cavendish, Madame de Sévigné, Mary Astell, Lady Mary Wortley Montagu, Madame de Graffigny, and even Jane Austen, whose earliest writings were predominantly composed in epistolary form. This female epistolary tradition continues, of course, into the twentieth century with writers like Virginia Woolf and texts such as the *Three Marias* and Alice Walker's *The Color Purple.* Many of these letter writers in the eighteenth century also wrote poetry, essays, plays, or novels, but they were most "at home," in a quite literal sense, in private writings intended for particular and contained audiences. It is in their letters that we may locate a "natural" voice, a voice unconstrained by expectation or apology or, often, conventional femininity. Letters and diaries had been validated as permissible for respectable women, and had become, thereby, connected with female narrative; indeed, by the end of the seventeenth century letters had become inextricably tied to female modes of self-expression and to a social world over which women presided. Burney felt defensive about her novel writing—not so about letters. The letter, an alleged repository for the female voice in an unguarded mode, was also therefore potentially subversive.

Burney was especially adept at calculatedly overturning the eighteenth-century familiar letter's claim to be an imitatively oral form, a claim that connects the feminine virtue of artlessness with a para-literary mode of discourse apt to camouflage a sophisticated rhetoric of disguise. That connection explains the letters of epistolary heroines such as those of Richardson and Burney, and it provides a clue for reading the letters of women who prized their private correspondence and openly labored over it, while remaining nervous and ambivalent about more official forays into print.[31] "I have now attained the true art of letter-writing," Jane Austen wrote to her sister Cassandra, "which we are always told, is to express on paper exactly what one would say to the same person by word of mouth; I have been talking to you almost as fast as I could the whole of this letter."[32] But that claim—as Samuel Johnson pointed out when he asserted that "no transaction . . . offers stronger temptations to fallacy and sophistication than epistolary intercourse . . . [and] a friendly Letter is a calm and deliberate performance in the cool of leisure"[33]—masks a polite fiction.

"It is truly a communication with spectres," Kafka wrote of the letter in his *Briefe an Milena,* "not only with the spectre of the addressee but also with one's own phantom, which evolves underneath one's own hand in the very letter one is writing."[34] But Kafkaesque ghostliness is only one way to classify the letter: if it is a shadowy text in one view, it is an embodied text in another. While letters require the impetus of literal physical absence, they also replace absence with a surrogate textual presence. Richardson expressed this function in a 1746 letter to Sophia Westcomb, to whom he extols the virtues of familiar correspondence: "And shall a modest lady then refuse to write?" he asks her, "Shall a virtuous and innocent heart be afraid of leaving its Impulses *embody'd,* as I may say?"[35]

The eighteenth-century's wish-fulfilling notion that epistolary language is naked and authentic perhaps argues for the exposure of voice fostered by the letter form; certainly, the idea that a pure act of communication takes place in letters was already bankrupt when it was put forward by the writers of classical letter manuals. Yet while the voice of a letter may be manipulative, cajoling, or sly, whatever its guise, its pretensions, or its motives, that voice remains always overwhelmingly present, and it demands a response in a way no other form of literature may. The pretense to sincerity in familiar letters, one critic has pointed out, functions as an "anti-rhetorical" stance, so that a letter implicitly denies its relation to other kinds of imaginative or documentary literature.[36] As a consequence, the letter is the only narrative form that can make a claim to that consummate eighteenth-century feminine virtue—artlessness. Letters present a fundamental paradox: their "artlessness" merges with their "true art" so that letters

become agents of control and containment. Burney's use of letters to
document painful experience makes clear her use of the form to regain hegemony and "authority" in her own life.

It is not surprising that Burney's first novel should have been epistolary. The letter is only one of many nonfictional modes appropri-
ated for the novel during the eighteenth century, a century whose
fictions tried relentlessly to achieve documentary status. J. Hillis Miller
asserts that these presentations of the novel as something other than
fiction — as collections of letters, found manuscripts, legal depositions,
journalism, edited documents — are "forms of counter-displacement,"
adding that "a novel is in various ways a chain of displacements —
displacement of its author into the invented role of narrator, further
displacement of the narrator into the lives of imaginary characters whose
thoughts and feelings are presented in that odd kind of ventriloquism
called 'indirect discourse.'"[37] The authors of epistolary novels displace
themselves into editors, then displace their editorial voice into a letter-
writing voice. This double displacement permits the author to invent,
select, and shape a fictional world without ever claiming to be a conscious creative force. Authorial creativity emerges only in its role as
arbiter in a medium dependent upon the intersubjective fluctuations
of privately expressed relationships.

A high degree of duplicity is inherent in the narrative form of the
letter. The tricks of voice this duplicity allows invade and control the
"innocent" and "artless" self-presentation of eighteenth-century heroines such as Pamela, Clarissa, and Evelina. Their letters seem intimate, and pretend to a discourse capable of exhibiting the interior
complexities, confusions, and contradictions of a private mind. However, the experience of reading epistolary fiction, from the *Lettres por-
tugaises* to the modernist burlesque return to the eighteenth century
in works as disparate as Viktor Schklovsky's *Zoo; or, Letters Not About
Love* (1923) and John Barth's *Letters* (1979), suggests that fictive letters
are usually vehicles for deceit or seduction, coy manipulation or sinister subversion, of which the quintessential examples remain Choderlos
de Laclos's *Liaisons dangereuses* and Jane Austen's *Lady Susan.* These works
demonstrate that epistolary discourse can provide an ideal structure
for the most elaborately duplicitous rhetorical performances. *Evelina,*
I shall argue in chapter 3, demonstrates this as well.

Burney's nonfictional narrative letters also participate in the sophisticated rhetorical potential of their form. Burney used her correspondence to dramatize private experience, and thereby to take retrospective control over it. She seized on epistolary discourse as a mode of
writing delimited by what is left unsaid and what is implied in the

lapses of time and space built into the letter exchange. These blank spaces—the unwritten and the between-written—organize the letter-text and empower it to repossess even what it cannot express about the writer's experience. Burney deliberately used the formal proper-ties of letters—margins, cross-writing, interior dialogue within the text; postal delays and paper shortages without—to elicit meaning and to turn her private letters into writerly objects. She is also always con-scious of audience, aware that as she writes her experience moves from a private to a public sphere. She spent years editing, revising, and collating both her father's and her own manuscripts, mindful of pub-lication possibilities and dangers. So, unlike Alexander Pope, Burney dispensed with the trappings of authenticated privacy and surprised intimacy so common to published collections of eighteenth-century letters.[38]

The "true art of letter-writing," as Jane Austen ironically called it, in fact relied in the eighteenth century upon the letter's concealing its nature as a written artifact. A letter is an anomalous text, occupy-ing the margins of literary discourse, and its writer, therefore, may remain uncommitted, as Burney wanted to seem to be, to the profes-sion of writing. The activity of letter writing suggests a fluid wit, but allegedly remains merely a private act of communication, even an ir-responsible act. Letters wear the mask of unelaborated vocal authen-ticity, of artifice forestalled, in their twin pretenses to spontaneity and to not writing (or to automatic, unconscious writing).

Burney took full advantage of the mutability of epistolary writing. Her letters are documents that reveal the modes by which she con-verted control over subjectivity and language and representation into female power. Indeed, in her manipulation of epistolary voices she firmly grasped the nightmare "pen of iron" and domesticated it into a household instrument for women. The strategies she used in her letters, appropriating pain, violation, and suffering into fictive nar-ratives of control as well as dramatizing intimate relationships through the pen's filter, mirror the strategies she employed in her novels and plays in more studied form and cogently demonstrate both Burney's discomfort about authorship and her rebellious, courageous commit-ment to locating, refining, and broadcasting her literary voices. Whether "private" or "public," Burney's narrative voices always both privilege and mask a central female consciousness engaged in a fully realized struggle for power as woman, as social critic, and as artist.

2

Writing the Unspeakable

In speaking of the final agonies of the Comtesse de Vercellis, whose valet and amanuensis he was for three months, Jean-Jacques Rousseau remarked in the second book of his *Confessions,* "J'ai suivi sa dernière maladie; je l'ai vu[e] souffrir et mourir sans jamais marquer un instant de faiblesse, sans faire le moindre effort pour se contraindre, sans sortir de sa rôle de femme" ("I was with her during her last illness. I saw her suffer and die without ever showing signs of weakness, even for a moment, without making the least effort to control herself, without doing anything unwomanly"). The comtesse suffered, as Frances Burney was diagnosed sixty-odd years later to suffer, from cancer. Her stoicism and self-command resemble Burney's in the face of life-threatening and body-violating illness. Here is Rousseau's description of the comtesse's last moments: "Sa mort fut celle d'un sage. . . . Sur la fin de sa maladie, elle prit une sorte de gaieté trop égale pour être jouée, et qui n'était qu'un contrepoids donné par la raison même contre la tristesse de son état. Elle ne garda le lit que les deux derniers jours, et ne cessa de s'entretenir paisiblement avec tout le monde. Enfin, ne parlant plus, et déjà dans les combats de

l'agonie, elle fit un gros pet. Bon! dit-elle en se retournant, femme
qui pète n'est pas morte. Ce furent les derniers mots qu'elle prononça"
("her death was that of a philosopher. . . . Towards the end of her illness, she assumed a sort of gaiety which was too regular to be unreal,
and which was only a counterpoise to her melancholy condition and
was the gift of her reason. She only kept her bed the last two days,
and continued to converse quietly with everybody to the end. At last,
speaking no more, and already in the agonies of death, she broke wind
loudly. 'Good!' she said, turning round, 'a woman who can fart is not
dead!' Those were the last words she uttered").[1] Burney, unlike Rousseau's comtesse, did not die of her disease; indeed, she survived for
almost thirty years after the surgical removal of her right breast. And
if she broke wind at the last in a singularly immodest and therefore
highly unBurneyan gesture, defying the demeanor of self-effacement
and tenacious reserve to which her life had been a monument, certainly no one had the temerity to report it. But Burney shared a number of things with other women of her time who endured cancer: she
lived and wrote in pain. Pain was the element that nurtured and sustained her, that tested her, that produced her drive, her desire, and
her art.

On 30 September 1811, in Paris, Burney underwent a simple mastectomy of the right breast to remove a growth her surgeons believed
to be a cancerous tumor. A wine cordial, possibly containing lauda-
num, served as the sole anesthetic agent. During the months that followed, Burney slowly and painfully composed a detailed narrative of
her illness and operation for her family and friends in England.[2] This
narrative appears at first reading to represent an oddly paraliterary
document: its nonprofessional descriptive history encapsulates the psychological and anatomical consequences of cancer in a text that is part
medico-surgical treatise and part sentimental fiction. While its wealth
of detail makes it a significant document in the history of surgical technique, its intimate confessions and elaborately fictive staging, persona-
building, and framing make it likewise a powerful and courageous
work of literature in which the imagination confronts and translates
the body. The formal, stylized operation and intimately encoded response retold in Burney's letter constitute two approaches to the same
timeless human need: the need to avoid pain and suffering.

Burney's letter is preoccupied with that need, and is preoccupied
as well with the narrative possibilities for representing violence. Can
this story be told? Burney's letter asks. By questioning the narratability
of her medical experience and bodily violation, Burney's mastectomy
document also questions the very nature of narrative representation,

in the private story of painful experience as well as in the highly codified genre of the medical case history. Writing, like the act of surgery, is an invasion of privacy that can be simultaneously wounding and therapeutic. Burney insists on narrating the violence and pain she found to be pervasive in the late eighteenth-century European social world. Her extraordinary letter, the circumstances of its composition and later revision, and the literary, medical, and cultural context of her experience serve as paradigms for Burney's inscription of herself into this world. The letter presents a fictive iconography of the body in narrative representation. The way Burney presents the embattled female body in this familiar letter maps the iconography as well of her embattled fictional heroines. That mapping itself—the careful inscription of a trapped female (body) in the world—empowers the female voice in all Burney's writings.

The composition history of the narrative describing Burney's breast disease illuminates part of the circuit of violence in her writing. For Burney, the physical act of writing, both before and after her mastectomy, was not only an act of social defiance but also a self-inflicted violent act, literally physically painful. Unlike the Comtesse de Vercellis, who obtained the services of Rousseau, Burney could not afford to employ an amanuensis. She was right-handed; it had become extremely uncomfortable for her to write long before the mastectomy itself. Immediately before the surgeons arrived, she took up a pen with effort to make a will and to write notes to her husband and son, but she wrote later that "my arm prohibited me" from writing to other friends to exorcise her dread while the surgery was in preparation. Holding and using a pen remained painful and difficult for her until at least 1815. She referred to being "still but *convalescente*" from "a dangerous & almost desperate illness" a year later, in a letter to Dr. Burney dated 18 September 1812 (*JL* 7:20), and in the winter of 1813 she complained of the effects of nasty English weather and inappropriate activity on her health. "I have cruel fears," she wrote to her brother in January, "as I am a slave to care & precaution, or an instant sufferer: for the least cold—damp—extension of the right arm, bending down the chest,—quick exertion of any kind,—strong emotion, or any mental uneasiness, bring on either short, acute pangs, or tolerable, yet wearing & heavy sensations" (*JL* 7:72). To her friend Mrs. Waddington, she lamented that "the oppression upon my breast makes all talking so fatiguing, so painful in its effect" and remarked that "you can difficultly conceive how I am forced to shut myself, from a cough that tears me to pieces when I talk" (*JL* 7:102). She also remarked to her husband, in two letters written in July 1812, that writing fatigued and pained her as she was required to rely entirely on wrist rather than shoulder muscles (*JL* 6:643).

A drawing of a woman with a mechanical arm, included with the Burney family papers in the Berg Collection of the New York Public Library and perhaps done either by Burney's friend Frederica Locke or, more likely, by her artist cousin Edward Francesco Burney (a portraitist, book illustrator, and caricaturist who produced occasional comic drawings and cartoons of the family), was probably executed some time after this surgery. The drawing may have been inspired by Burney's postoperative difficulties, and seems to comment on the ironic effects of surgical (and quasi-technological) intervention on the body (see figure 1). Although Burney claimed not to have reread or revised her mastectomy account at the time she originally composed it, her arm physically prevented her from dashing it all off in a blind heat. Indeed, in the letter itself she refers to "this miserable account, which I began 3 months ago, at least" (*JL* 6:613). Manuscripts reveal that Burney's handwriting changed markedly after 30 September 1811; the hand becomes larger, less steady, and erratic. Of physical necessity, the composition process was slow and laborious for her, as she often mentioned, and such a writing process, one can speculate, lends itself to self-consciousness of style rather than to spontaneity of expression.

Burney completed the last sheets of her letter to her sister Esther in June 1812 (the first sheets are dated 22 March), at a time when she was still convalescing, both physically and psychologically. The letter actually sent through the Napoleonic blockade to Burney's sister Esther is in an envelope marked "Account from Paris of a terrible Operation — 1812" and contains no apparent revisions or emendations, but the fact that Burney gave this letter a title when she returned to it for editorial work years later suggests a more studied text than the usual casually informative, familiar letter (though for Burney, letters were never casual anyway). Changes of ink corroborate Burney's own contention that it was not composed at one sitting. It contains only five paragraph breaks, and it does not appear to have been recopied (see figure 2). The whole is in Burney's own handwriting.

The second manuscript, however, is a fair copy of the original letter made before it left Paris (see figure 3). This copy omits the background to the operation and begins with "All hope of escaping being now at an end . . ." (*JL* 6:604). A sheet Burney marked herself with "Breast operation/Respect this/& beware not to injure it!!!" (*JL* 6:597) covers this version. Most curious, the fair copy contains several later emendations (almost certainly dating from the years 1820 to 1835

Figure 1. Ink drawing by a member of the Burney family. Courtesy Henry W. and Albert A. Berg Collection, The New York Public Library, Astor, Lenox and Tilden Foundations.

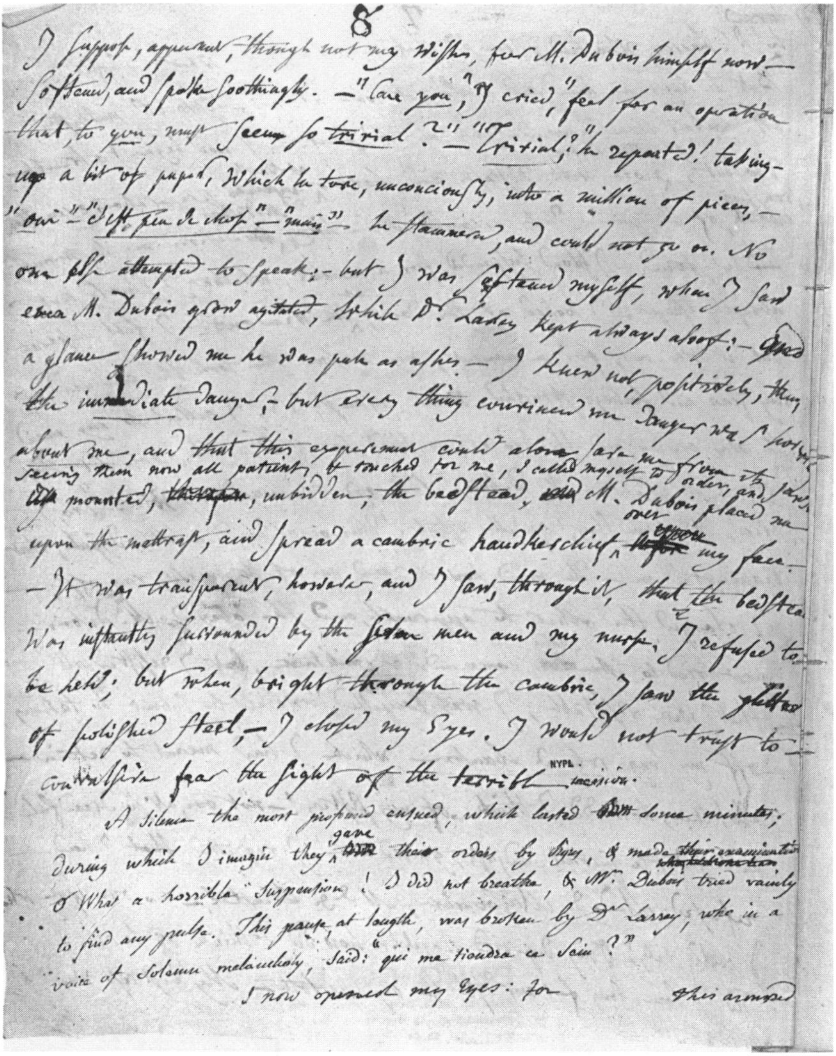

8

I suppose, appeared, though not my wishes, for M. Dubois himself now softened, and spoke soothingly. – "Can you," I cried, "feel for an operation that, to you, must seem so trivial?" – "Trivial?" he repeated, taking up a bit of paper, which he tore, unconsciously, into a million of pieces, – "oui – c'est peu de chose – mais –" he stammered, and could not go on. No one else attempted to speak, – but I was softened myself, when I saw even M. Dubois grow agitated, while Dr. Larry kept always aloof: – yet a glance showed me he was pale as ashes. – I knew not, positively, then, the immediate danger, – but every thing convinced me danger was hovering about me, and that this experiment could alone save me from its jaws.
Seeing them now all patient, & touched for me, I called myself to order, and I mounted, unbidden, the bedstead, & M. Dubois placed me upon the mattrass, and spread a cambric handkerchief over my face. – It was transparent, however, and I saw, through it, that the bedstead was instantly surrounded by the 7 men and my nurse. I refused to be held; but when, bright through the cambric, I saw the glitter of polished steel, – I closed my Eyes. I would not trust to convulsive fear the sight of the terrible incision.

A silence the most profound ensued, which lasted for some minutes, during which I imagine they gave their orders by signs, & made their examination – O what a horrible suspension! I did not breathe, & M. Dubois tried vainly to find any pulse. This pause, at length, was broken by Dr Larry, who in a voice of solemn melancholy, said: "qui me tiendra ce sein?"

I now opened my Eyes: for this aroused

Figure 2. Original letter to Esther Burney, dated 22 March 1812, p. 8. Courtesy Henry W. and Albert A. Berg Collection, The New York Public Library, Astor, Lenox and Tilden Foundations.

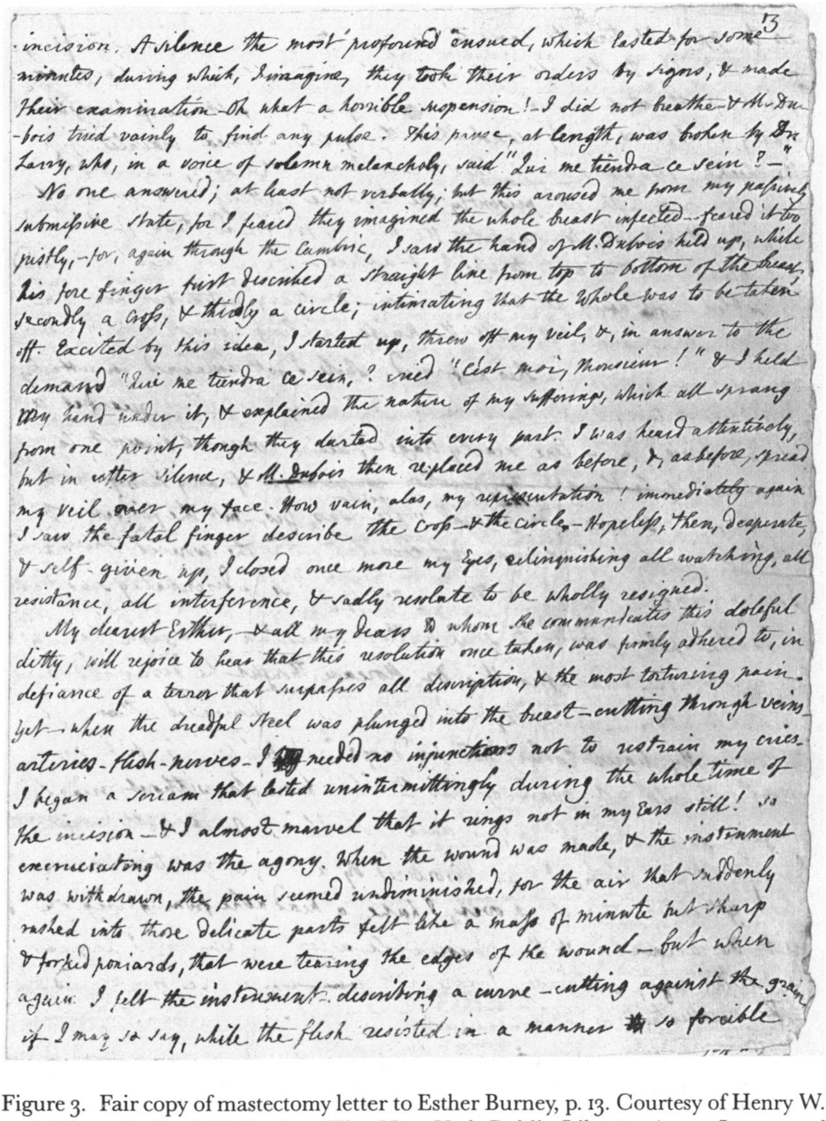

incision. A silence the most profound ensued, which lasted for some minutes, during which, I imagine, they took their orders by signs, & made their examination—Oh what a horrible suspension!—I did not breathe—& M. Du-bois tried vainly to find any pulse. This pause, at length, was broken by Dr Larry, who, in a voice of solemn melancholy, said "Qui me tiendra ce sein?—"

No one answered; at least not verbally; but this aroused me from my passively submissive state, for I feared they imagined the whole breast infected—feared it too justly,—for, again through the cambric, I saw the hand of M. Dubois held up, while his fore finger first described a straight line from top to bottom of the breast, secondly a Cross, & thirdly a circle; intimating that the whole was to be taken off. Excited by this idea, I started up, threw off my veil, &, in answer to the demand "Qui me tiendra ce sein?," cried "C'est moi, Monsieur!" & I held my hand under it, & explained the nature of my sufferings, which all sprang from one point; though they darted into every part. I was heard attentively, but in utter silence, & M. Dubois then replaced me as before, &, as before, spread my veil over my face. How vain, alas, my representation! immediately again I saw the fatal finger describe the Cross—& the circle—Hopeless, then, desperate, & self-given up, I closed once more my eyes, relinquishing all watching, all resistance, all interference, & sadly resolute to be wholly resigned.

My dearest Esther,—& all my dears to whom she communicates this doleful ditty, will rejoice to hear that this resolution once taken, was firmly adhered to, in defiance of a terror that surpasses all description, & the most torturing pain. Yet—when the dreadful steel was plunged into the breast—cutting through veins—arteries—flesh—nerves—I needed no injunctions not to restrain my cries. I began a scream that lasted unintermittingly during the whole time of the incision—& I almost marvel that it rings not in my Ears still! so excruciating was the agony. When the wound was made, & the instrument was withdrawn, the pain seemed undiminished, for the air that suddenly rushed into those delicate parts felt like a mass of minute but sharp & forked poniards, that were tearing the edges of the wound—but when again I felt the instrument—describing a curve—cutting against the grain, if I may so say, while the flesh resisted in a manner so forcible

Figure 3. Fair copy of mastectomy letter to Esther Burney, p. 13. Courtesy of Henry W. and Albert A. Berg Collection, The New York Public Library, Astor, Lenox and Tilden Foundations.

when she sorted through and edited her papers) in Burney's handwriting. Some examples of these additions to the text (in brackets)
reflect Burney's attitude toward her composition:

> —I affected to be long [deciphering] the note (*JL* 6:6o8)
> —Dr. Moreau, [the Magician] instantly (*JL* 6:6o9)
> —I now began to tremble violently, [or rather shiver,] more with dis-
> taste & horrour . . .
> —I began a [tortured] scream (*JL* 6:612)
> —I thought I must have expired [, in torments beyond] human life.
> (*JL* 6:612)
> — . . . the recollection is still so painful [so enfeebling—] my arm still,
> & always in a sling (*JL* 6:613)
> —However, [from the time the operation began,] I bore it with . . .
> (*JL* 6:613)

These revisions are neither extensive nor profound in themselves. They
prove, however, that Burney did reread the copy, if not the original,
and that she reread it ten or more (probably at least twenty) years
later with an ear to style and with an intention to preserve as dramatic a record as she could. Thirteen years later, in 1825, her Dunkirk
journal conveys the writer's postoperative sense of the experience in
a passage that refers to Mrs. Waddington: "She [Mrs. W.] little knew
my then terrible situation:—hovering over my head was the stiletto
of a surgeon for a menace of a Cancer—yet, till that moment Hope
of Escape had always been held out to Me by the Baron de Larrey—
Hope which, from the reading of that fatal Letter, became extinct"
(*JL* 6:707). Even in a passing reference, she remembers and renders
the event not merely as grim fact but as Gothic melodrama overlaid
with imaginative structure and symbol.

The revisions Burney later made in the letter when she edited her
correspondence suggest that she composed it with particular narrative
rhythms and pacing in mind. The long section leading up to the day
of surgery imitates and reenacts the drawn-out waiting period Burney endured, and the speeded-up, virtually out-of-control catapult-
ing prose that describes the surgery itself, periodically and abruptly
halted by the agonizingly repeated false sense that it was over, then
follows the slow, tense opening pages. Burney's family's participation
in the recopying (the handwriting of her son appears in the fair copy),
and briefly in the composing (General d'Arblay added his own inter-
polation), of the letter turn the work into a collective, participatory
act, a sort of confessional epistolary theater-in-the-round. All of these
acts of writing—revising, recopying, preserving, turning to familial

authorship—serve as coding mechanisms by which Burney translates surgical privacy into literature and the dread-provoking body into language. The obsessive intensity of the writing process, clear from the manuscripts, suggests that Burney endured the physical pain of writing to exorcise the remembered pain of surgery. This was not a new procedure for her; she had always turned to "scribbling" when under stress, as is demonstrated by her extraordinary statement that during the two hours before the surgeons arrived she would have liked to write to her sisters and friends as a means to pass the time had her weakened arm not prevented her. By treating the manuscript as a literary text, complete with all the appropriate editorial apparatus, Burney enables herself to experience it in memory as a literary event, and by reactivating her physical pain in the act of writing itself, she detaches herself from it.

Burney may have wanted to write before the operation, but afterward, she relates, she had to be coaxed out of silence by circumstance (she would later, as we saw in chapter 1, take copious "memoranda" about Ilfracombe and then not compose the story for six years). That she decided to convey the intimate experience of her illness and mastectomy to anyone at all came, she claims, from a concern for her family and friends. She wanted to keep inflated or misinformed rumors from reaching and alarming those she cared about in England: "I would spare, at least, their kind hearts any grief for me," the letter begins (*JL* 6:598). But, she claims, "nothing could urge me to this communication" except learning that someone ignorant of her intention to be secretive had written about it. She had not planned that any of her family, and especially her father, should ever learn of her illness. "But to You, my beloved Esther, who, living more in the World, will surely hear it ere long, to you I will write the whole history, certain that, from the moment you know any evil has befallen me your kind kind heart will be constantly anxious to learn its extent, & its circumstances as well as its termination" (*JL* 6:598). Thus, this "whole history" has for its inspiration a goal: to document and prove Burney's "perfect recovery." She presents it almost as a legal brief, a piece of evidence that the "whole history" metonymically authorizes a newly unwhole body. Though addressed to her sister, the letter is not intended solely for one correspondent, as she ends with instructions for its distribution and consumption by an extensive public: "Let all my dear Brethren male & female take a perusal," as well as Mrs. Angerstein, she commands, singling out her father, Mrs. Locke, Miss Cambridge, and Miss Baker for exclusion and asking Esther to use her

own judgment about "all others" (*JL* 6:614–15). Finally, Burney exhorts her sister to "read, therefore, this Narrative at your leisure, &
without emotion—for all has ended happily" (*JL* 6:615).

Burney presents her mastectomy letter as a confession of an event
kept secret, but she also presents it as a medical case history, a chronological ordering of symptoms and signs, a presentation she repeated
many years later when she came to write of her childhood inability
to read. By writing her experience as a public history, however costly
the effort for her, she divests it of some of its power of intimacy and
veils herself as well as her audience from the full impact of the agony
and fear her story simultaneously embodies and disembodies. Yet afterwards she disclaims the "history" she has composed: "I fear this is all
written—confusedly, but I cannot read it—& I can write it no more"
(*JL* 6:614). She suggests an odd, and oddly powerful, version of herself as writer here, refusing to reread her own work but obsessed with
how it will be received, offering it to others as absolute truth because
unadulterated by revision yet revealing her own ambivalent and fearful relation both to its writing and to its subject matter. In many
ways, she thus presents herself as both physician and patient.

Two weeks after the birth of her first and only child in 1794, when
she was forty-two, Burney had suffered from an abscess caused, she
thought, because the infant Alex had contracted thrush and "communicated it to my breast." The lump disappeared but, Burney wrote,
"they have made me wean my child! . . . What that has cost me!" (*JL*
3:94). Many seventeenth- and eighteenth-century explanations of carcinoma of the breast did connect the disease with complications from
breast-feeding immediately following childbirth. Burney probably understood a remote causal connection between the 1794 illness, which
had been painful though not dangerous, and the discomfort she began to notice in her right breast in August 1810. Her understanding
of the illness, in any case, was that it was cumulative and progressive;
Marianne Francis expressed that notion in a letter written to Hester
Thrale Piozzi in late September 1811: "A year ago—near two, now—she
had a lump in her left breast, which at first she neglected but which
afterwards encreased so much, the french surgeons, who are very skillful
told her that if it was not speedily extracted, it would become a *cancer.*"[3] It is impossible to speculate with any accuracy at this remove,
but modern physicians have questioned the validity of the diagnosis
made of Burney's illness. Her twenty-nine-year postoperative survival
—she lived to the age of eighty-seven—suggests that the amputated
breast had probably not contained a malignant tumor in the first place.[4]

Most of Burney's letter to Esther organizes the events that led up to her mastectomy, from the first awareness she had of discomfort in 1810 to the preparations she made for the surgery itself. At first, she avoided and ignored the problem, refusing to see a surgeon. She was not, however, an ignorant patient. She had done extensive medical research in preparation for the smallpox episode that begins *Camilla,* and she had been most attentive to health matters in raising an only son who was never terribly robust. Finally, she consented to see Antoine Dubois, a well-known surgeon, anatomist, and obstetrician who was attending the empress. Although neither Dubois nor Burney's husband d'Arblay confronts her directly after the first consultation, she knows immediately their implied diagnosis: "I had not . . . much difficulty in telling myself what he [her husband] endeavoured not to tell me — that a small operation would be necessary to avert evil consequences!" (*JL* 6:600). Already, Burney uses euphemism and circumlocution ("small" and "evil consequences") simultaneously to conceal and to represent her horror, and that subversion of professional medical discourse undercuts this document as case history at the same time that the novelistic, veiled language breaks through the letter's objective surface. Dubois's treatments, however, only made the symptoms worse, and the d'Arblays next consulted Baron Dominique-Jean Larrey, surgeon to Napoleon and now best remembered for his battlefield inventions of the "flying ambulance," the mobile field hospital, and the technique of amputation at the hip joint. Larrey's ministrations helped for a time, and Burney, become hopeful, felt both admiration and affection for him. Larrey called in François Ribes, a surgeon and anatomist who had served under him, and they consulted Jacques-Louis Moreau de la Sarthe. Happily for Burney, these surgeons had not yet been called to join Napoleon's Russian campaign; she was attended by the most eminent medical practitioners then in Paris.

From the moment when the doctors agree on the diagnosis, the mastectomy letter begins to rattle with contradictions, with rhetorical concealment, and with Burney's brilliant and courageous attempt to detach herself as narrator from the patient (and the body) under the knife in her story. Her detachment comes from both layers of the text's discourse: its case-history language and its "feminine" narrative of euphemism and disguise. Both mediating elements lead Burney to the narrative options of fiction. The doctors, she writes, "formally condemned me to an operation" (*JL* 6:603) after a joint consultation. Indeed, much of this account uses the terminology of criminal sentencing. The doctors "pronounced my doom" (*JL* 6:604); Burney twice refers to the operation itself as "the trial" (*JL* 6:604, 607). When the decision to perform surgery is made, Burney writes, "After sentence thus passed, I was in hourly expectation of a summons to execution" (*JL* 6:606). And when the surgeons finally arrive, Burney's readers are invited to witness an execution, complete with "the glitter of polished Steel" (*JL* 6:611) and an ineffectual blindfold.

Before the day of execution, however, there is a good deal of suspenseful waiting around, and a struggle for power occurs that involves Burney's access to information about what is to be done to her. At every turn, those around Burney try to reassure her, to mask the real danger she quite well knows she is in, and to keep her in ignorance. Her doctors treat her like a child who must be shielded from the truth because she would be capable neither of understanding nor of enduring it. Even Larrey, a family friend whose respect Burney, by then a famous novelist, valued, patronizes her with incomplete candor. They never inform her that they mean to amputate the entire breast; she comprehends the extent of the surgery only when she watches the doctors' sign language (used instead of speech because she was fully conscious) while the knife is poised above her.[5] Burney's writing, however, makes it clear that she understands her own justified resentment and sees through attempts to keep her from the facts. Dubois, for example, "uttered so many charges to me to be tranquil, & to suffer no uneasiness, that I could not but suspect there was room for terrible inquietude." D'Arblay, she says, "also sought to tranquilize me — but in words only; his looks were shocking! his features, his whole face displayed the bitterest woe" (*JL* 6:600).

The most telling irony in this letter comes from the fact that Burney herself shields and pities both doctors and husband in the end, getting the latter out of the way on the day of the operation and, during the surgery, helping the surgeons by steadying her breast with her own hands, and apologizing for causing Larrey emotional distress: "'Ah Messieurs! que je vous plains! —' for indeed I was sensible to the feeling concern with which they all saw what I endured" (*JL* 6:613). Yet earlier she had reproached Dubois: "Can *You*, I cried, feel for an operation that, to *You*, must seem so trivial? — Trivial? he repeated — taking up a bit of paper, which he tore, unconsciously, into a million of pieces, *oui — c'est peu de chose — mais —*' he stammered, & could not go on." She relents in her resentment only when "I saw even M. Dubois grow agitated" (*JL* 6:611). Even those nineteenth-century critics, like William Hazlitt and Thomas Babington Macaulay, who have been most harsh in granting Burney talents as a writer have agreed that she was one of the most observant and perceptive women ever to take up a pen; she is not reassured by these efforts to "tranquilize" and console her. In fact, the tables completely turn in her relationship with

her husband, who becomes the one in need of protection: "My poor
M. d'A was more to be pitied than myself though he knew not the
terrible idea I had internally annexed to the trial—but Oh what he
suffered!" Her son, then sixteen, she "kept as much as possible, and
as long, ignorant of my situation." Burney controls her husband here
precisely as she herself is being controlled by her physicians. As soon
as the alternative of surgery has become a certainty, a curious apparent
shift occurs in the narrative. From repugnance, concern for herself,
and anxiety about the prognosis, Burney turns all energy to her family in order to remove and defuse her own fears and to establish her
autonomy in an ordeal that she ultimately had to endure alone: "All
hope of escaping this evil being now at an end, I could only console
or employ my Mind in considering how to render it less dreadful to
M. d'A" (*JL* 6:604).

The doctors explain that Burney's suffering will be intense, and
Moreau asks whether she had screamed during the birth of her son:
"Alas, I told him, it had not been possible to do otherwise; oh then,
he answered, there is no fear!—What terrible inferences were here
to be drawn! I desired, therefore, that M. d'A. might be kept in ignorance of the day till the operation should be over" (*JL* 6:605). That
sequence of sentences moves swiftly from its starting point: the efforts of the doctors to stay her fears while still meeting their obliga-
tion to warn her of the severity of the physical pain she would have
to tolerate. The "terrible inferences" she understands them to be masking are immediately evident to her, and they are made more fearsome by the doctors' transparent effort to downplay them. No sooner
does she sense this dynamic of condescending and hiding, which of
course reveals to her the real horror of her situation, than she converts her reaction into concern for her husband—"therefore," because
a procedure of sidestepping "terrible inferences" is at work, she instantly switches roles and does for her husband what the doctors fail
to do for her.

Burney is not for a moment confused by the reassurance she receives; it makes her fears more vivid and makes her angry as well.
But she does successfully protect her husband. D'Arblay's interpolated
comment at the end of the letter to Esther, a document finally completed nine months after the operation and from which he first learns
its details (so that his participation becomes literary—as reader and
commentator) shows that Burney was correct in her impulse to keep
him from witnessing the surgery. He writes:

No language could convey what I felt in the deadly course of these
seven hours. . . . Besides, I must own, to you, that these details which

were, till just now, quite unknown to me, have almost killed me, &
I am only able to thank God that this more than half Angel has had
the sublime courage to deny herself the comfort I might have offered
her, to spare me, not the sharing of her excruciating pains, that was
impossible, but the witnessing so terrific a scene, & perhaps the re-
morse to have rendered it more tragic. for I don't flatter my self I could
have got through it—I must confess it. (*JL* 6:614)

It was not, however, easy to get advance notice. The surgeons do
not want their patient to have any knowledge of the time set for the
operation, a plan to which Burney vigorously objects—"I obtained
with difficulty a promise of 4 hours warning, which were essential to
me for sundry regulations" (*JL* 6:605). The doctors refuse to tell her
what preparations to make and will not inform her of what to expect
beyond their cryptic, and appalling, "Vous Souffrirez—vous souffrirez
beaucoup!" (*JL* 6:604). They tell her only to provide an armchair and
some towels. Still, she senses danger and makes her will, a gesture
she concealed from d'Arblay. She refuses the attendance of friends,
and retains only two servant women to stay with her.

Three weeks passed from the time Burney agreed to the operation
until the date it was performed. D'Arblay, finally, wrote to ask that
no further delay occur. It turned out, as Burney discovered two months
later, that the doctors had given up her case as hopeless. Larrey, at
last, takes Burney's wishes seriously: "I had said, however, he remembered, once, that I would far rather suffer a quick end without, than
a lingering life with this dreadfullest of maladies" (*JL* 6:607). When
the letter announcing the day arrived—"Judge, my Esther, if I read
this unmoved!" (*JL* 6:608)—her first thought is to keep it from her
husband.[6] She contrives to have him called away on urgent business—
"yet I had to disguise my sensations & intentions from M. d'A! . . .
such was my terror of involving M. d'A. in the unavailing wretched-
ness of witnessing what I must go through, that it conquered every
other, & gave me the force to act as if I were directing some third
person" (*JL* 6:608). This "third person," of course, represents both
the husband become "other" and the omniscient narrator, the pseudo-
objective observer who encircles the surgery patient in this text, the
physician taking a history. Burney becomes both novelist and physician, narrative and historiographical roles that transform her into an
outsider who witnesses her own most private experience, the only position from which she will be able to recount the operating scene. By
so composing her account, Burney repackages the experience both
for her readers and for herself. Fiction and case history here intersect.

The persona of the outsider-narrator remains during the hours of preparation. Burney made the room ready and supervised the folding of bandages—"Business was good for my nerves." Then, another delay. For two hours, she waited for all the surgeons to return—"a dreadful interval"—"I had no longer any thing to do—I had only to think— TWO HOURS thus spent seemed never-ending. . . . I strolled to the Sallon—I saw it fitted with preparations, & I recoiled—." That repugnance is her first direct confrontation of the reality to come. "But I soon returned; to what effect disguise from myself what I must so soon know?" (*JL* 6:609). The mistress of disguise and of feigned innocence in the heroines her novels celebrate now faces a physical reality that "artlessness," the consummate eighteenth-century virtue for "proper ladies," cannot alleviate. It is now that she writes, "I would fain have written to my dearest Father—to You, my Esther—to Charlotte James —Charles—Amelia Locke—but my arm prohibited me." When she returns to the scene, "the sight of the immense quantity of bandages, compresses, spunges, Lint—Made me a little sick" (*JL* 6:609). She gets through the waiting period by pacing herself into a catatonically detached absence of emotion.

The final four pages of Burney's letter recount the actual operation, a narrative that again weaves fiction with medical history, novelistic setting and suspense with surgical data. First, the doctors arrive —"7 Men in black." She had not been warned about their numbers and is briefly outraged: "I was now awakened from my stupor—& by a sort of indignation—Why so many? & without leave?—But I could not utter a syllable." What follows is a careful description whose tension makes it nearly unbearable to read. The tension comes, not simply, as might be expected, from the horror and gore of the event described in such detail, but from the curious dual quality with which Burney depicts her own behavior. She is indignant but mute. Dubois orders her to a bed, when she had been told an armchair would suffice—she is "astonished." Her fear and powerful anger now come from her helplessness; she will be supine, denied all dignity: "I now began to tremble violently, more with distaste & horrour of the preparations even than of the pain" (*JL* 6:610), because those preparations underline her powerlessness, her acquiescence, and the role her body has taken of an objectified entity over which she has lost control, or, rather, can only control afterwards by narrating this history. They disagree about whether her maids can remain with her; one is dismissed. Dubois "now tried to issue his commands *en militaire*" and, Burney writes, "I resisted all that were resistable" (*JL* 6:610).

Another indignity follows when the doctors compel Burney to dis-

robe. Like her first heroine, Evelina, Burney is here functioning without a rulebook—should she sit or lie down? what should she wear?—
in an unchoreographed dance. She focuses her attention in this retelling on her effort to take charge, to survive the ordeal without humiliation, to become one of the physicians. Indeed, the entire letter depicts
and metonymizes a dynamic of male-female power relations, a play
of professional authority against female autonomy as symbolized by
the sacrosanct female body here to be defiled. She now would have
wanted her sisters near, not for moral support, but "to protect—ad-
just—guard me" from the intrusion of these black-robed men who out-
number her.

The first part of the struggle ends when Burney confronts the medical men with their inability to understand what she feels, with the
fact that for them this is a clinical, routine, impersonal event. She
retrieves some ironic measure of control by getting on the bed "unbidden," as though the gesture were her will. Dubois spreads a transparent cambric handkerchief over her face. The handkerchief shields
her from nothing; in fact, it serves to emphasize the image she paints
of being converged upon, overpowered, ganged up on—"the Bed stead
was instantly surrounded by the 7 men & my nurse." Literally surrounded, she refuses to be held, in another attempt to maintain autonomy and dignity, and "Bright through the cambric, I saw the glitter of polished Steel"—she becomes quite literally here the prisoner
awaiting execution. "A silence the most profound ensued, which lasted
for some minutes. . . . —Oh what a horrible suspension!" (*JL* 6:6n).
Throughout, Burney emphasizes the hovering terror, the waiting, the
anticipation, the continuous effort to detach herself and to become
a clinician and historian.

Through this suspense comes an extraordinary courage—the prisoner turns out to have more stomach for what is to come than do her
executioners. Larrey breaks the silence with "Qui me tiendra ce sein?"
and the response comes from the patient herself: "I started up, threw
off my veil, cried 'C'est moi, Monsieur!' & I held My hand under it."
The sexual violation implicit throughout this scene is thus counter-
posed with a gesture of sexual display in Burney's proffering of her
own breast. Her "veil" is only symbolic, as the choice of term for the
cambric handkerchief makes clear. But the presence of a "veil," a gauzy
swaddling cloth through which she discerns her fate, makes the blurred
scene more vivid: "Through the Cambric, I saw the hand of M. Dubois held up, while his fore finger first described a straight line from
top to bottom of the breast, secondly a Cross, & thirdly a circle; intimating that the WHOLE was to be taken off." She had not known

the extent of the surgery, and this pantomime of a priest blessing a penitent or administering last rites "aroused me from my passively submissive state" (*JL* 6:6n).

Her protests meet with silence, and the veil is replaced: "How vain, alas, my representation! immediately again I saw the fatal finger describe the Cross — & the circle — ." She resigns herself, "self-given up," and closes her eyes. Then a curious thing happens. Now begins the operation itself — "the dreadful steel was plunged into the breast — cutting through veins — arteries — flesh — nerves" — and although Burney says her terror "surpasses all description," she gives us a marvel of detail. The ability so closely to observe, habitual with her, may itself have been a defense mechanism, an absorption into the trauma in order to control it, to become the historian during the making of the history. An eighteenth-century American patient, undergoing an amputation, remarked on that quality of surgical experience: "During the operation, in spite of the pain it occasioned, my senses were preternaturally acute, as I have been told they generally are in patients under such circumstances. . . . I still recall with unwelcome vividness the spreading out of the instruments, the twisting of the tourniquet, the first incision, the fingering of the sawed bone, the sponge pressed on the flap, the tying of the blood-vessels, the stitching of the skin, and the bloody dismembered limb lying on the floor."[7] Burney remains resolute; she defies her own fear and pain and does not resist, though she obeys the injunction to cry out with "a scream that lasted unintermittingly during the whole time of the incision — & I almost marvel that it rings not in my Ears still! so excruciating was the agony" (*JL* 6:612). The explicit description that follows is one of the most astonishing, and bravest, medical passages in literature.

This, the climax, Burney describes with the powerfully ironic phrase, "this doleful ditty":

When the wound was made, & the instrument was withdrawn, the pain seemed undiminished, for the air that suddenly rushed into those delicate parts felt like a mass of minute but sharp & forked poniards, that were tearing the edges of the wound — but when again I felt the instrument — describing a curve — cutting against the grain, if I may so say, while the flesh resisted in a manner so forcible as to oppose & tire the hand of the operator, who was forced to change from the right to the left — then, indeed, I thought I must have expired. I attempted no more to open my Eyes, — they felt as if hermettically shut, & so firmly closed, that the Eyelids seemed indented into the Cheeks. The instrument this second time withdrawn, I concluded the operation over — Oh no! presently the terrible cutting was renewed — & worse than ever, to separate the bottom, the foundation of this dreadful gland from the parts to which it adhered—Again all description would be baffled—yet again all was not over,—Dr Larry [*sic*] rested but his own hand, &—Oh Heaven!—I then felt the Knife <rack>ling against the breast bone—scraping it!—This performed, while I yet remained in utterly speechless torture, I heard the Voice of Mr. Larry [*sic*],—(all others guarded a dead silence) in a tone nearly tragic, desire everyone present to pronounce if any thing more remained to be done; The general voice was Yes,—but the finger of Mr. Dubois—which I literally *felt* elevated over the wound, though I saw nothing, & though he touched nothing, so indescribably sensitive was the spot—pointed to some further requisition—& again began the scraping!—and, after this, Dr. Moreau thought he discerned a peccant attom—and still, & still, M. Dubois demanded attom after attom—My dearest Esther, not for days, not for Weeks, but for Months I could not speak of this terrible business without nearly again going through it! I could not *think* of it with impunity! I was sick, I was disordered by a single question—even now, 9 months after it is over, I have a head ache from going on with the account! (*JL* 6:612-13)

This literally bonechilling account makes clear that *all* description was not, after all, "baffled." The sickness and "head ache" engendered by the writing itself suggests that, for Burney, to represent her surgery in language was to undergo it again—mediated this time through words instead of silence and screams—but this time because she is the writer she is also the surgeon. "Speechless agony" finds words; the patient becomes her own surgeon and medical historian.

Burney's biographer Joyce Hemlow, citing her subject's "realistic powers of description," warns readers that they should be prepared "either to enter the gruesome operating-theatre, feel the cutting and hear the screams, or to turn over the leaf and choose another tale."[8] Burney does transport us, with the novelist's skill, to the scene. More than that, she writes an itemized chronicle of this surgery that reads very much like a surgical treatise of the period; from it, we learn details about the procedures used to perform her mastectomy, and the implicit theories behind them. She may have been in screaming agony during the twenty minutes it took Larrey to complete his task, but she nevertheless took careful notice of each turn of the knife, including the operator's appalling shift of hand.[9] The combination of surgical particularity and personal trauma gives this letter its energetic ambivalence.

The term "doleful ditty" raises some intriguing questions about Burney's view of herself as both woman and writer when she composed this narrative. The phrase itself, often in the form "dismal ditty," is, according to Francis Grose's *Classical Dictionary of the Vulgar Tongue*, a colloquialism for "a psalm sung by a criminal just before his death at the gallows," and Burney had used the phrase in *Camilla*.[10] It is, indeed, "dicté"—an account written down as it might have been spoken and, Burney claims, unreread and never revised. Yet that alliterative phrase undercuts the power of the written performance. In fact, Burney seems determined to diminish the message here—an image of unswerving strength and endurance. She claims to have fainted twice—"at least, I have two total chasms in my memory of this transaction, that impede my tying together what passed" (*JL* 6:613), and it is not unusual for a traumatic event to cause memory loss. However, the loss of consciousness is conveyed only insofar as it might have caused a break in narrative continuity. We can only imagine what that "single question" was that "disordered" her mind during the ordeal—the trauma of losing her breast? of mutilation and disfigurement? or the fear of dying under the knife? At the end, while her own face, she says, "was utterly colourless" and her strength "totally annihilated," she finds time to worry about Larrey, become a gory specter in a Gothic denouement, "pale nearly as myself, his face streaked with blood, & its expression depicting grief, apprehension, & almost horrour" (*JL* 6:614).

Many writers have used the composing process as a means of coming to terms with the terror of their illnesses. Samuel Pepys's canonization of his bout with the kidney stone in his *Diary* is probably the most famous example, and recent writers as diverse as Norman Cousins and Audre Lorde have made their private medical ordeals public by composing confessional narratives.[11] Kidney stones seem especially to have inspired early writers to take up their pens. Along with Pepys, Cicero, Montaigne, Horace Walpole, David Garrick, and Benjamin Franklin were sufferers who turned their illnesses into prose. Montaigne justified his medical journalizing thus:

À faute de mémoire naturelle j'en forge de papier, & comme quelque nouveau symptôme survient à mon mal, je l'écris. D'où il advient qu'à cette heure, étant quasi passé par toute sorte d'exemples, si quelque étonnement me menace, feuilletant ces petits brevets décousus comme des feuilles sibyllines, je ne faux plus de trouver où me consoler de quelque pronostic favorable en mon expérience pasée.

(For lack of a natural memory I make one of paper, and as some new symptom occurs in my disease, I write it down. Whence it comes that at the present moment, when I have passed through virtually every sort of experience, if some grave stroke threatens me, by glancing

through these little notes, disconnected like the Sibyl's leaves, I never
fail to find grounds for comfort in some favorable prognostic from my
past experience.)[12]

Writing itself can provide a "favorable prognostic," can have medici-
nal properties. Burney's therapeutic strategies in writing about her
mastectomy are neither so straightforward nor so cheerful as Montaigne's. Her narrative detaches Burney the writing voice from Burney the physical body in a paradoxical attempt at once to disembody
the surgical event and to fuse bodily experience with the writing self,
to novelize her terror and to take her own medical history.

Literary critics have had little to say about Burney's mastectomy letter since its publication in 1975, and historians of medicine mention
it only in passing. Curiously, however, practicing physicians and surgeons have celebrated Burney and what she has to teach them about
a patient's experience. One such surgeon argues that Burney offers
a lesson in the humane practice of medicine, and that her letter presents sound advice about the following: diagnostic suspense; the dangers of excessively reassuring a patient; the torture involved in waiting and the cruelty of operative delay; the concern for family; and
the anxiety about mutilation.[13] Burney does not directly approach the
question of disfigurement either in this letter or in her subsequent
correspondence and diaries. Like her contemporaries, Burney never
approached her sexuality in any but oblique ways. The letter itself,
however, offers some hints. She speaks of "a conquest over my repugnance" (*JL* 6:598) to consent to a medical examination in the first
place. About her first reaction to the idea of an operation, she writes,
"Ah, my dearest Esther, for this I felt no courage — my dread & repugnance, from a thousand reasons *besides* the pain, almost shook all
my faculties, &, for some time, I was rather confounded & stupefied
than affrighted" (*JL* 6:600). D'Arblay urges a friend to write Larrey
"the most earnest injunction that would use every exertion to rescue
me from what I so much dreaded" (*JL* 6:601). Yet when the verdict
comes, Burney is "as much astonished as disappointed" and does not
offer any opposition, though "from my dread he [Larrey] had expected
resistance" (*JL* 6:603). It is clear from this letter that Burney understood and feared a great deal beyond mere physical pain from this
experience.
   A document of this sort could only have been written by someone
with a capacity to observe by detaching herself even from events in
which she plays the central role, by an accomplished narrator and jour-
nalist whose imagination overlays her own life to such an extent that

any experience becomes material for its own retelling as story. Burney's "doleful ditty" reveals a woman whose choreographer's sense of visual impact allows her to displace herself from her own body. Burney channeled her fear and anger into a medical history, reenacted her own "case," and thereby defused the framework of dominance and submission that she found as oppressive as the physical pain. Rendered as fiction, complete with a narrator's self-characterization, a coherent set of images and themes, and a constant concern for audience response, her written account permits Burney to domesticate the experience through its representation simultaneously as historical and as imagined narrative.

Burney's mastectomy letter offers an approach to one moment in the history of surgery by starting from the patient and her experience with her body and with physicians and surgeons.[14] The patient is the pivotal but elusive figure in the history of medicine, a discipline that has traditionally focused on practitioners and institutions and has treated patients only as the given precondition for medical knowledge rather than as its central concern.[15] As a medical narrative, Burney's letter emphasizes the *reception* of surgery rather than its *production*. As a literary artifact, the mastectomy letter also reveals the healing power of language, or "logotherapy."[16] Burney organizes and recasts her experience by transforming it into a historical text; she reopens, relives, and recloses her wound by representing it in writing.

Burney's deliberateness in opening her letter to both literary and medical interpretation derives from her narrative's relation to a form of clinical writing that has been called "a specialized literary form" and that follows absolute guidelines of structure, syntax, and discourse: the physician's medical history.[17] This document by definition is composed not only to be interpreted but to yield a particular type of interpretation: the differential diagnosis. If we examine the discrepancies between the official medical report and Burney's letter, an exchange of discourses emerges — the physician's depersonalized, authoritative, neutral history as against the patient's superpersonalized, nonprofessional, self-consciously angled narrative. Burney annotated this report, which is sewn to her letter to Esther and dated 1 October 1811, with this title: "Account of the Breast operation drawn up by the chief Pupil of the Baron de Larrey who passed the Night by the side of the Nurse to watch the still dreadfully suffering Malade":

Madame D'arblay à subi hier à 3 heures ¾ L'extirpation d'une tumeur Cancéreuse du Volume du poing et adhérente au muscle grand Pectorale et Dévelopée dans le sein droit.

L'opération faite par M^r Le Baron Larrey, assisté du Professeur

Dubois & des Docteurs Moreau, Ribes, <Hereau> & Aumont, a été très douleureuse & supportée avec un grand Courage.

La Squirre a présenté dans son centre un Commencement du dégénérescence Cancéreuse; mais toutes ses racines ont été enlevées & dans aucun Cas une opération aussi grâve n'a offert plus d'espoir de succès —

L'extrême sensibilité de la malade a rendu très violent le spasme qui a suivi l'opération, il n'a diminué que pendant la nuit et par l'emploi des potions calmantes anti-spasmodiques —

De 2 à 3 heures du matin madame a éprouvé quelques instans de sommeil très agitté à 4 des douleurs de tête des nausées et des vomissemens lui ont procuré beaucoup de fatigue & de faiblesse. Ces accidens que le Docteur Larrey avait indiqués comme devant terminer le spasme ont en effet été suivis de calme & de deux heures de sommeil paisible —

A 10 heures la malade est étonnée du bien être qu'elle éprouve — Mr Larrey la trouve sans fièvre, la douleur est presque nulle dans la plaie, lappareil [sic] n'offre pas même la transsudation sanguine ordinaire que l'exacte ligature des artères a empêché

On prescrit dans la journée quelques bouillons des crèmes de riz — de la gelée de Viandes

Pour boisson l'eau de poulet, & la décoction d'orge gommée & accidulée avec le citron, alternativement

Ce soir une Medicine avec la décoction de graine de lin & de têtes de pavôts (*JL* 6:615-16)

(Yesterday at 3:45, Madame d'Arblay underwent the removal of a cancerous tumor the size of a fist which had developed in the right breast adherent to the *pectoralis major* muscle.

The operation performed by the Baron Larrey, assisted by Professor Dubois and Doctors Moreau, Ribes, <Hereau> and Aumont, was very painful and was tolerated with great courage.

The scirrhus [hardened tumor] showed the beginnings of cancerous degeneration in its center; but all its roots were removed and no case of such a serious operation has offered greater hope of success.

The patient's extreme sensitivity made the spasm which followed the operation very violent, it did not diminish until during the night and with the administration of calming antispasmodic potions.

From 2 to 3 in the morning Madame experienced some moments of agitated sleep at 4 headache attacks of nausea and vomiting made her quite tired and weak. These events which Doctor Larrey had indicated would necessarily end the spasm were indeed followed by calm & by two hours of peaceful sleep.

At 10 the patient was surprised at the well-being she felt — Mr. Larrey found her without fever, the pain almost nonexistent in the wound, the precise ligature of the arteries had prevented even the ordinary transsudation of blood through the dressing.

We prescribe during the day boiled rice cream — meat gelatin
To drink chicken broth, and a potion of barley gummed and acidi-
fied with lemon, alternately
This evening a medication with a potion of linseed and poppy head
[My translation])

The medical student, like Burney herself, narrates a story in order
to represent the patient's postoperative medical condition. What story,
though, is available to him for narration? Burney's body, now an arena
of surgical intervention, becomes a text, one whose surface grammar
reveals symptoms and signs that require interpretation and prescrip-
tion. The student offers a chronology of events (the operation, the
spasm, agitated sleep, calm) and a firm postoperative diagnosis (almost certainly incorrect) on the basis of tissue analysis: a cancerous
tumor. He reports on her wound (nearly painless; bleeding under control) and prescribes a bland liquid diet.

The official medical report of Burney's breast disease, even in its
incompleteness, follows the basic outline for a medical history, whose
purpose is to narrow down the possibilities for disease by a rigidly
structured account that moves from first impressions to hypotheses
to firm diagnosis, and that carefully differentiates between symptoms
(the patient's complaints) and signs (the physician's objective findings).
The medical history is written in such a way as to "recapitulate the
steps in the process of thinking by which a physician reaches a diagnosis."[18] This recapitulation involves, first, a conversion of symptoms,
signs, and prior medical and other data into a narrative, and second,
the interpretation of that narrative, a process that involves analysis,
recognition, and extrication of the crucial detail. Clues may include
vocal inflection, facial expression, or posture, as well as specific complaints. The physician seeks a syntax in the patient's presentation and
records that syntax in the written medical history. The narrative reliability and storytelling skills of both patient and physician are called
into question in the patient history, and history writing in clinical
medicine — clinical records came into routine use around the time Burney was treated — has crucial implications for medical epistemology.

The patient's relating symptoms to a physician has often been hailed
as therapeutic in itself. While the patient's reliability as a narrator may
be called into question, that very unreliability can serve as a diagnostic clue, and a proper medical history includes a note on the history taker's impression of the informant's accuracy. Patients tell their
stories, to be sure, in order to seek relief from physical complaints,
but they may also want solace. The therapeutic or cathartic function
of giving (as opposed to taking) a history — cure through verbaliza-

tion, the talking cure—relates the patient history to a more recent model, the psychoanalytic dialogue. In its most extreme form, the patient narrates, like Scheherazade, in order to survive. But one psychoanalyst has recently pointed out that the physician's questions prompt a continuous retelling, a retelling as performance, by regulating for patients the narrative possibilities of their symptoms.[19]

That narration is enlisted in a scientific discipline as a major problem-solving technique itself raises questions. The right to narrate, Hayden White remarks, always hinges on some defined relationship to authority, but its use in science is suspect because science is "a practice which must be as critical about the way it *describes* its objects of study as it is about the way it *explains* their structures and processes."[20] Louis O. Mink draws a related conclusion, arguing that science, unlike inherently narrative disciplines such as history, can produce "detachable conclusions," whereas historical assertions are *"represented by the narrative order itself . . .* [and] *exhibited* rather than *demonstrated."*[21] The issue always returns to one question: What relation can narrative or narratability bear to historical truth?[22] We must ask this question in Burney's case, and understand the role of imaginative reenactment in her story in order to recognize her compulsion to tell this tale as well as the relation of its telling to her fictions. For physicians and patients, the narratable is curable disease, an event that intervenes in the course of health, then subsides into health again. Burney's illness and surgery represent for her violent interventions in the smooth order of everyday discourse. As events, they matched in narrative energy and possibility the stories she created in her fictions.

To write the medical history of her mastectomy was, for Burney, to detach and obscure the covert narrative her letter contains, the narrative of mutilation and disfigurement. Only recently has medical literature taken up the psychological, sexual, and social implications of breast cancer treatments; virtually no formal studies or discussions of this issue occur before the middle of the twentieth century. In the eighteenth and nineteenth centuries, the psychosexual implications of breast amputation are muted by the period's characteristic silence on the subject. The only direct reference I have located to the mutilating effects of mastectomy comes in Samuel Warren's *Diary of a Physician,* a series of sketches that first appeared in *Blackwood's Edinburgh Magazine* and were republished in 1832. In Warren's account, narrated from the surgeon's point of view, the following elliptical passage describes the patient's postoperative convalescence:

She was alluding, one morning, distantly and delicately to the personal disfigurement she had suffered. I, of course, said all that was soothing. "But, doctor, my *husband*—" said she, suddenly, while a faint crimson mantled on her cheek; adding, falteringly after a pause, "I think St— will love me yet!"[23]

Another nineteenth-century writer also glorifies, through a similar beatific disembodiment, a victim of breast cancer in an account of a mastectomy performed by Professor James Syme at Minto House, Edinburgh, in 1821. Syme was a conservative proponent of mastectomy; in his *Principles of Surgery* (1842) he notes that though the only efficacious procedure for defeating a cancer is to cut it out, "it would be subjecting the patient to useless pain and would bring surgery into discredit to attempt extirpation in cases where the extent or connections of the disease prevented its complete removal."[24] Unfortunately, many of Syme's patients died of infection following surgery, an all too common result of preantiseptic surgery, and this is the fate that befalls Ailie, the patient in a story by John Brown titled "Rab and His Friends." Brown shows her arranging herself on the table and turning pale but remaining still and silent through the procedure. Afterward, "she is dressed, steps gently and decently down from the table, looks for James; then turning to the surgeon and the students she curtsies,— and in a low, clear voice, begs their pardon if she has behaved ill."[25] She does well for four days before succumbing to sepsis and delirium. Like Dr. Warren's patient, Dr. Syme's is celebrated for maintaining, even to excess, feminine decorum and modesty despite the horrors of the knife. A character in Maria Edgeworth's novel *Belinda* (1801), Lady Delacour, also reflects this notion of feminine virtue when she confronts a breast injury she thinks to be cancer contracted from a blow received during a duel with a female rival. Lady Delacour refuses to see a physician: "That I would not do—I could not—I never will consult a physician—I would not for the universe have my situation known. . . . Why my dear, if I lose admiration, what have I left?"[26] These characteristics of submission, meekness, and vanity also appear in Burney's autobiographical account; they veil the sexual emblematization and symbolized (and actual) mutilation by mastectomy in early depictions of the ordeal and its aftermath.

The breast emblematizes both privacy and sexuality, and breast cancer, by intruding on the radical privacy of the body and thus medicalizing sexuality, threatens and breaks down that emblematization. Mary Astell, who died of breast cancer in 1731, is reputed to have reported of her mastectomy only that she "prayed to God and . . .

didn't cry out." She seems to have behaved very much as Rousseau
reports the Comtesse de Vercellis behaved. George Ballard, Astell's
first biographer (1755), described her final illness:

> She seemed to enjoy an uninterrupted state of health till a few years
> before her death, when, having one of her breasts cut off, it so much
> impaired her constitution, that she did not long survive it. This was
> occasioned by a cancer, which she had concealed from the world in
> such a manner, that even few of her most intimate acquaintance knew
> any thing at all of the matter. She dressed and managed it herself, till
> she plainly perceived there was an absolute necessity for its being cut
> off: and then, with the most intrepid resolution and courage, she went
> to the Reverend Mr. Johnson, a gentleman very eminent for his skill
> in surgery (with only one person to attend her) entreating him to take
> it off in the most private manner imaginable: and would hardly allow
> him to have persons whom necessity required to be at the operation.[27]

Ballard's strangely ambivalent syntax disguises Astell's theme: the disease and its cure represent a kind of sexual shame, and the rest of
Ballard's account emphasizes her stoic patience, her lack of struggle
or resistance, and her silent resignation in the face of pain. The whole
event, in this telling, smacks of duty answered. Yet it was precisely
during the century between Astell's ordeal and Burney's, an era whose
fashions promoted considerable breast display, that sexual emblems
such as the breast became medicalized and that medical and scientific
language became, concomitantly, sexualized.

Breasts had been symbols of fertility from antiquity, and represented
the radical sexual power women embodied, as the title of a 1678 treatise,
A Just and Seasonable Reprehension of Naked Breasts and Shoulders, demonstrates. The breast has received less attention than the uterus in studies
of anatomical representation, but it is as significantly tied to female
sexuality, motherhood, and natural morality, and it is, importantly,
the visible sign of femaleness. Late eighteenth-century medical writers
discussed the nutritional and moral functions of breast-feeding in the
same sentences as they proclaimed, in an interweaving of social ideology
with physiological destiny, the breast's beauty.[28] The body enfolds social as well as medical meanings and its efforts to maintain balances,
both visible and hidden, reflect this.[29] And the breast as a seat of natural morality and always imminent moral anarchy remains a theme
into the nineteenth century. One treatise counsels, for this reason, that
women curb their pleasure while breast-feeding:

> The mammary glands—which by their seat and form constitute the
> ornaments of the sex, become by their functions, the source of a new

existence, and are placed, by their structure, under the influence of
the moral activity. We cannot, then, too strongly recommend to mothers who suckle their children, to endeavour to acquire the calmness
and tranquillity necessary to the direction of a good education.[30]

That Mary Astell and Lady Delacour and Burney never explicitly
address the moral and sexual threat that breast disease and breast
amputation posed for them does not mean they were not morbidly
aware of that threat.

Galen's observation, still current in Burney's time, that breast cancer predominantly afflicts postmenopausal women produced some psychosocial theories that may help to connect Burney's complex response
to her illness and its treatment with the period's explanations of the
origins and processes of the disease.[31] The Galenic view held currency
into the nineteenth century, but one medical writer commented on
"the singular immunity from disease which is often observed after
[menopause]" and suggested that the "autumnal majesty" that accom-
panies this "vast improvement in health" can be turned to the cultivation of literary pursuits and salon society.[32] This observation speaks
to a complex of hormonal and chemical changes whose mechanisms
are still not fully understood. The observation, however, that more
women develop breast cancer (and certain other types of cancer as
well) after menopause resulted in the seventeenth and eighteenth centuries in a complicated "biological" blame tied not to the women themselves or their behavior (a separate issue altogether) but to female
anatomy. That is, women are more apt to develop breast cancer when
they have ceased to be reproductive beings, when they are no longer
sexually useful. Thus, a functioning reproductive system was thought,
with some medical justification, to protect women, both as healthy
physical entities and as participants in the social order.[33] An early explanation of this view as it pertained to breast cancer occurs in Nicho-
las Fontanis' *The Womans Doctour* (1652): "The Matrix [womb] hath a
Sympathy with all the parts of the body; . . . it hath likewise a consent with the breasts; and from hence proceed those swellings, that
hardness, and those terrible cancers that afflict those tender parts, that
a humour doth flow upwards, from the Matrix to the Breasts, and
downwards, again, from the Breasts to the Matrix."[34]

To conquer a cancer and live cured suggested a moral success on
the part of the afflicted woman. The first lay notice of a mastectomy performed in North America occurs in a curious announcement printed by Edward Winslow in the *Boston Gazette* of 21 November 1720:

For the Publick Good of any that have or may have Cancers—These
may certify, That my Wife had been labouring under the dreadful Dis-
temper of a Cancer in her Left Breast for several Years, and altho' the
Cure was attempted by sundry Doctors from time to time, to no effect;
And when Life was almost despair'd of by reason of its repeated bleed-
ings, growth & stench, and there seemed immediate hazard of Life,
we send for Doctor Zabdial Boylston of Boston, who on the 28th. of
July 1718 (in the presence of several Ministers & others assembled on
that Occasion) Cut her whole Breast off; and by the Blessing of GOD
on his Endeavours, she has obtained a perfect Cure.
    I deferred the Publication of this, least it should have broke out again.
Rochester, October 14, 1720[35]

The patient, Sarah Winslow, was thirty-six when she had surgery, and
had already borne six children; she died at the age of eighty-five. Her
medical triumph, like Burney's, was probably not, in fact, over cancer
—in both cases, the patient's multidecade survival more likely indicates a benign cystic disease. But both Sarah Winslow and Burney
triumphed morally over cancer and its attendant nightmares, over the
threat of sepsis, and over horrifying physical pain.[36]

Burney's mastectomy letter participates in a key historical moment
in the development of both literature and medicine as professional
activities, repositories of knowledge, and narrative disciplines. At issue
is a mode of perception and an underlying epistemology. How is the
body/self to be known and interpreted? And how is it to be represented
in narration? Michel Foucault, in his controversial book *The Birth of
the Clinic: An Archaeology of Medical Perception,* claims that Marie-François-
Xavier Bichat, as the first to reorganize the understanding of disease
processes, inaugurated "one of those periods that mark an ineradicable
chronological threshold," the moment at the turn of the nineteenth
century when clinical experience becomes a form of knowledge. "What
is modified in giving place to anatomo-clinical medicine," Foucault
writes, "is not . . . the mere surface of contact between the knowing
subject and the known object; it is the more general arrangement of
knowledge that determines the reciprocal positions and the connex-
ion between the one who must know and that which is to be known."[37]
Early physicians manually examined their patients only on rare occasions. They relied instead on patients' narratives and on observation
without touch, and the patient's narration of chronology and symptoms frequently was the sole basis for diagnosis, which was sometimes
even done by letter. Habitual physical intrusion upon the patient's body
for diagnostic purposes, by either physician or instrument, is a prac-

tice dating from the mid-nineteenth century. When autopsy became a common procedure in the eighteenth century, it inaugurated this shift from theory and word to observation and touch. The stethoscope on which Foucault focuses — and later the ophthalmoscope, the laryngoscope, the speculum, and, ultimately, the X-ray — distanced physicians not only from their patients' bodies but from their narratives as well — because one of the things these instruments exposed was narrative unreliability.[38] In literature, too, the question for writers became how to find a means to express the writing subject as written object, to test and codify narrative possibilities. This was Burney's specific dilemma in her diaries and letters, and in externalized form in her novels, and it is particularly acute in the mastectomy letter. How can she narrate this story?

Narrating stories, for Burney, served two related purposes. First, narration — writing the intimate and vulnerable self — represents an act of violence, a wrenching exposure that amounts to a self-inflicted incision, an aggressive attack on the writer's self. Second and concurrently, narration — exteriorizing the self's story — represents a therapeutic and healing process, a resolution and closure of wounds. In this sense, writing for Burney is like surgery: a deliberate infliction of pain in order to excise the pain, a violation of the body in order to cure the disease. Pen and scalpel, sharp objects both, coincide.[39] This connection had begun very early for Burney: at the age of fifteen, she made a bonfire of her juvenilia "to combat this writing passion" and "to extinguish for ever in their ashes her scribbling propensity." But to no avail; this was not surgery, but rather an alternative therapy: "This grand feat, which consumed her productions, *extirpated* neither the invention nor the inclination that had given them birth" (*Memoirs* 2:123) (my italics). The therapeutic function of writing for Burney is clearest when she writes about her own physical, emotional, and mental health: her imprisonment in a flooded cave and her husband's slow dying; her childhood reading problems and adult breast disease. The "conscious intellectual disgrace" of her youthful visual-perceptual difficulties yielded in late middle age to a bodily disgrace, an anatomical betrayal that had literally to be cut out. Burney wielded her pen on that occasion as Larrey had wielded his knife, as a natural instrument of aggression and necessary wounding that permitted her, by veiling and dissecting the body, also to construct and to take possession of a female self rendered finally invulnerable in writing precisely in response to its radical vulnerability in surgery. Her reading dysfunction had likewise promoted, in avenging response, a writing obsession in which one disability was overcome by an answering hyper-ability. To write her own medical history (as she used her novels to document her own social and political history) was to reundertake her own surgery: to control the probe, the knife, the wound, and the blood herself; to speak for the wound's gaping unspeakableness — the woman her own surgeon, both reopening and reclosing the incisions in her own body and in the body of her writing.

Burney's mastectomy letter presents, then, an intersection of medicine and the anatomized body with literature: it is a text that articulates medical reality by overlaying it with the imaginative and dramatic possibilities intrinsic to the aptly named operating theater, as it is a text that carves a writer's self-representation out of the body's encounter with the knife. Knowing the body as subjective experience merges with a knowing of the body as objective nature. In medicine, the body becomes spectacle; in imaginative prose, the writer's language repossesses the theater. Montaigne exemplifies this aggressive effort to repossess in his essay "Of Experience" when he writes:

> Je consulte peu des altérations que je sens, car ces gens ici sont avantageux quand ils vous tiennent à leur miséricorde: ils vous gourmandent les oreilles de leurs pronostics; &, me surprenant autrefois affaibli du mal, m'ont injurieusement traité de leurs dogmes & trogne magistrale, me menaçant tantôt de grandes douleurs, tantôt de mort prochaine. Je n'en étais abattu ni délogé de ma place, mais j'en étais heurté & poussé; si mon jugement n'en est ni changé ni troublé, au moins il en était empêché; c'est toujours agitation & combat.

> (I do little consulting about the ailments I feel, for these doctors are domineering when they have you at their mercy. They scold at your ears with their forebodings. And once, catching me weakened by illness, they treated me insultingly with their dogmas and magisterial frowns, threatening me now with great pains, now with approaching death. I was not floored by them or dislodged from my position, but I was bumped and jostled. If my judgment was neither changed nor confused by them, it was at least bothered. It is still agitation and struggle.)[40]

Burney's mastectomy letter exemplifies and enacts Montaigne's "agitation & combat." It is a historical text that narrates violence by organizing its language, its structure, and its strategies around the experience of surgery — bodily presence circumscribed by bodily violation — and that contains a narrative persona who emerges from a mind overseeing its body, a body circumnavigating its mind, a subject become object.

Burney's private voices — the compulsive therapies her writing embodied
for her — emerge fitfully from her letters and journals. These papers
were edited and expurgated by Burney before her death; they went
through another censor's hands when her niece and literary executor,
Charlotte Barrett, prepared them for their first publication in 1842.
But enough examples of Burney's unguarded prose have survived this
literary surgery to permit an analysis. Burney scholars do not have
to struggle against the wall of zealous protectionism erected by her
sister Cassandra to make of Jane Austen almost as mysterious a literary personality as is William Shakespeare. I have tried to argue in
these first two chapters that Burney's unpublished voices not only contain an autobiographical narrative and a plethora of historically intriguing tidbits, but that they also comprise examples of a narrative
strategy based on indirection and displacement and derived from repressed rage and repressed desire. Other impulses emerge in Burney's writings as well — she did write alongside as well as in resistance
to propriety; she meticulously recorded social experience out of wit
and lightheartedness as well as out of the darker materials of rage I
am tracing here. I focus on these materials — moments of trauma, conflict, resistance, and assault — because they best illuminate the suffocating atmosphere in the later novels. In Burney's private documents,
she reveals the same kind of narrative strategies she used in her fiction. In the four published novels, rage and desire are transformed
into rhetorical manipulation, madness, carnival: the volcanic spill-
age produced when female desire is yoked to the service of social
propriety.

Two

Fictions of Violation:
Women and Social Ideology

In imaginatively reenacting the anatomization of the writer's body, a private body violated and made public through the invasions of surgery, Burney's mastectomy narrative creates its writer's very selfhood as a response to violence. Long before her surgical ordeal in 1811, however, Burney's writings had already depicted physical and mental pain to satirize the cruelty of social and behavioral strictures, especially for women, and to pillory the sentimental conventions of eighteenth-century fiction. Burney showcased moments of endured violence and violation, both overtly physical and covertly psychological, in the three novels that predated her mastectomy as well as in the later journal-letters discussed in chapter 1. These moments serve as frameworks for her analyses of the varieties of female fear and of the forced loss of control that constantly lurk beneath society's polite forms and coerce women into self-suppression. Whether as medical catastrophe, social embarrassment, or criminal brutality, violence and violation fracture the surface of polite and acceptable social engagement and raise the specter of exposure from within as well as from without. This threat, the dread of public and publicized nakedness, informs each of Burney's novels.

It is not surprising that the narrative and rhetorical strategies Burney employed for the difficult mastectomy composition reflect techniques she had mastered in her fiction. Three of her novels had appeared by 1811 and their author had achieved popular fame and critical attention, though not fortune, for her literary efforts: *Evelina; or, A Young Lady's Entrance into the World* in 1778; *Cecilia; or, Memoirs of an Heiress* in 1782; and *Camilla; or, A Picture of Youth* in 1796. A fourth, *The Wanderer; or, Female Difficulties,* would be published shortly, in 1814, and had been partially composed earlier. The heroines Burney portrays share a problem that is also that of their creator's nonfictional surgical ordeal: how to remain a properly behaved, decorous eighteenth-century lady while burdened with legitimate, and terrorizing, anger at situations that limit her autonomy, and how to weigh the risks of rebellion against the humiliations of submission. Burney's four fictional heroines each, on occasion, find ingenious ways to subvert social constraints while they also each suffer from binding conventions. In the three novels composed prior to 1811, episodes of escalating violence and violation (nasty practical jokes and catastrophic social gaffes, accidents and illness, nightmares and madness) reveal a complicated relationship between decorous propriety and its potential for unexpected explosion.

Burney's novels encode struggles against forced loss of control in the way their apparently benign domestic settings turn out to foster potential and actual violence. In stunning episodes of unprepared, gratuitous brutality, violence repeatedly shatters the apparently conventional social economy the novels' settings appear to subscribe to and protect. The characters' obsessions with social appearances derive from the possibility that violence may break through surface behaviors at any moment. In *Evelina,* crude verbal and physical abuse is woven into the fabric of the dangerous social world in which Evelina seeks a place. One episode in particular demonstrates Burney's narrative uses of transformatory violence.[1] Captain Mirvan masquerades as a highway thief and attacks Madame Duval, who ends up wigless in a ditch with her feet tied together and the rope attached to a tree:

> Her head-dress had fallen off; her linen was torn; her negligee had not a pin left in it; her petticoats she was obliged to hold on; and her shoes were perpetually slipping off. She was covered with dirt, weeds, and filth, and her face was really horrible, for the pomatum and powder from her head, and the dust from the road, were quite *pasted* on her skin by her tears, which, with her *rouge,* made so frightful a mixture, that she hardly looked human. (148)

It is not primarily physical injury that is here sustained, though the physical attack is severe enough, but the violation of appearance. Madame Duval becomes a debauched witch; the Captain has literally undressed her. The victim's own description exaggerates the event's brutality while making clear the actual nature of the crime:

> He lugged me out of the chariot by main force, and I verily thought he'd have murdered me. He was as strong as a lion; I was no more in his hands than a child. But I believe never nobody was so abused before, for he dragged me down the road, pulling and hawling me all the way, as if I'd no more feeling than a horse. I'm sure I wish I could see that man cut up and quartered alive! . . . So, when I was got there, what does he do, but, all of a sudden, he takes me by both the shoulders, and he gives me such a shake! — *Mon Dieu!* I shall never forget it, if I live to be an hundred. I'm sure I dare say I'm out of joint all over. (149–50)

Madame Duval, never pacific herself in either language or gesture, internalizes the assault that has been made upon her and becomes from this moment forward "out of joint all over" in the narrative economy of Burney's novel. But the episode's final blow for her involves the loss of her "curls"; bald and naked because wigless, she cannot run for justice but must hide herself in the carriage. Captain Mirvan has removed her from the public sphere where justice resides and has rendered her not merely symbolically naked, but fundamentally private and forcibly enclosed as well. Justice thus becomes radically unavailable because the *appearance* of injustice — torn clothing, a bald head, a muddy wig — precludes seeking re-dress.

In *Evelina*, as this scene demonstrates, Burney concerns herself primarily with abuses of the facade rather than the edifice, the hair rather than the head. In this way, violation threatens social containment by subverting social decorum, underwriting a sort of brinksmanship diplomacy of the drawing room.[2] That edgy, precarious diplomacy continues to rule *Cecilia*, Burney's second novel, yet a more depraved atmosphere pervades there.[3] Cecilia's guardian Harrel's suicide at Vauxhall, for example, takes place, as do many of Burney's scenes of "terror," in an elegant public gathering place, a setting of leisure and ease that in and of itself encloses fearful dangers for Burney's heroines. Drunk and stupefied, Harrel shoots himself to avoid the debts that have decimated Cecilia's inheritance and humiliated his family. Burney's description of Harrel's death introduces a connection between physical pain and silence, horror and speechlessness, that permeates the rest of *Cecilia,* dominates *Camilla,* and reappears in inverted form, as we saw, in the mastectomy letter:

> He had lingered, she found, about a quarter of an hour, but in a condition too dreadful for description, quite speechless, and, by all that could be judged, out of his senses; yet so distorted with pain, and wounded so desperately beyond any power of relief, that the surgeon, who every instant expected his death, said it would not be merely useless but inhuman, to remove him till he breathed his last. (*Cecilia* 1:407)

Violence here takes on a characteristic it retains from 1782 on in Burney's writings: whereas in the comic *Evelina* of 1778 violations induce volubility, in the later writings violence is more overtly physical and is always accompanied by muteness, inarticulateness, "speechless agony." Pain is inarticulate, the body cannot speak.

Cecilia's climactic scene occurs when "grief and horror, next to frenzy, at a disappointment thus unexpected, and thus peremptory, rose in the face of Mrs. Delvile, who, striking her hand upon her forehead, cried, 'My brain is on fire!'" She bursts a blood vessel, an episode that may have been on Burney's mind when she composed her court directions in 1785, three years after *Cecilia*'s publication: a sudden, involuntary gush of blood signifies the ultimate loss of control for Burney, the incapacity to stanch passion. Cecilia and Mortimer find his mother "extended upon the floor, her face, hands and neck all covered with blood" (2:219). The physician's instructions for Mrs. Delvile's cure are that "she should be kept extremely quiet, and on no account be suffered to talk" (2:224). For Mrs. Delvile as for Mr. Harrel, emotional and financial violation results in violence to the body, whose therapy (or curse) is speechlessness: "speechless agony"—"too dreadful for description," much less narration. Later, Cecilia's own madness takes the form of distracted speech and confused cries in a sequence that anticipates the fragmented delirium and absolute silence of Camilla's similar madness (2:428–41). This silencing power of violence — its capacity to render language inaccessible and thereby to make narration impossible — particularly controls Camilla's delirium as well.

These paradigmatic sequences of violence in Burney's novels engage a subterranean discourse of suppression and expose normally hidden social pain by moving beyond the limits of physical endurance and hence beyond those of social convention. The sequences themselves become a discourse that defines the outer limits of language through the difficulty and necessity of narrating brutality, whether as social or emotional violation or as physical violence. The conventional social themes of Burney's surface plots — orphanhood, inheritance, courtship — are not themselves available for narrative representation, her writing suggests, except through abrupt interventions of violence. Burney needs to get beneath the facades of politeness, decorum, and propriety in order to tell her story. Writing and violence operate together for Burney: she continually ties language to eruptions of dread, delirium, and the tyrannies of social convention.

Burney's compulsion to write, demonstrated by her repeated references to a writing "mania" in her journals and letters and by her sense that to write was to defy convention, emerges in covert and coded ways in her first and third novels. I have grouped them together because both the epistolary *Evelina; or, A Young Lady's Entrance into the World* (1778) and the third-person *Camilla; or, A Picture of Youth* (1796) can be interpreted as treatises on the appropriate uses of language for young women in the late eighteenth century, and on the methods by which that apparent appropriateness may be rechanneled into female empowerment. Paradoxically, both *Evelina* and *Camilla* comment on the linguistic fabric of suppression for eighteenth-century female adolescents by metaphorizing silence and misunderstanding. Both novels map the terrain of eighteenth-century social protocols, in relations between the sexes and between youth and age, as a minefield waiting to explode. They contain tongue-tied and sabotaged conversations, misread gestures, and unfinished communications. In the epistolary *Evelina,* the heroine's letters represent an expressly feminine art: the art of coaxing, flattering, and mystifying; the art of requesting and granting permission or forgiveness; and the verbal ingenuity of the woman whose survival depends upon her appearing to remain ingenuous and innocent, and whose only tool of power lies in her use of language to manipulate both her situation and the way it is presented to others. *Camilla* also focuses on its heroine's imperiled efforts to communicate. By reading these two novels together, we can excavate beneath the eighteenth-century social virtues of "feminine" decorum and artlessness professed by their heroines to unearth a gritty language that controls both propriety and rebellion against it.

3

Evelina: Protecting
the Heroine

In 1778, the year *Evelina* was anonymously published (Burney's brother Charles had smuggled the manuscript to the London bookseller Thomas Lowndes), Burney wrote a little fantasy in her private diary:

> This year was ushered in by a grand and most important event! At the latter end of January, the literary world was favoured with the publication of the ingenious, learned, and most profound Fanny Burney! I doubt not but this memorable affair will, in future times, mark the zenith of the polite arts in this island! (*DL* 1:1)

Burney was twenty-five years old when *Evelina* appeared, and this self-aggrandizing fantasy belies the fact that she responded ambivalently to authorship. In the same year she revealed her dread of the publicity authorship conferred: "Let them criticise, cut, slash without mercy my book, and let them neglect me; but may God avert my becoming a public theme of ridicule!" (*DL* 1:76). This language makes clear that at some level the equation between text and body already existed for Burney long before her mastectomy.

Careful at first to keep her authorship of *Evelina* a secret, Burney was relieved and pleased, although she continued to accept praise with embarrassed modesty, when she was found out. *Evelina*'s publication history illustrates Burney's ambivalence. Because her handwriting was known to publishers — she had been her father's amanuensis for his *General History of Music* — she disguised it for the first two volumes her brother delivered to Lowndes (James Dodsley had earlier refused to look at an anonymous text). Charles used disguises — calling himself "Mr. King" and "Mr. Grafton" at the Orange Coffee House and muffled up in scarf and overcoat (as Camilla's brother Lionel would appear to her) to present the rest of the manuscript. When Lowndes decided to publish, Burney had to find time and space for secretive composition, not an easy task in her bustling household. Though she kept her father in ignorance of her authorship until the novel's success was assured and Samuel Johnson had exhorted her "to fly at the eagle!" (*DL* 1:68), her urge to print the work was clearly more than the "frolic" she claimed it to be. Burney lived in her imagination and she was committed to her writing and to its publication. Burney's heroines, as she herself, cared very much, nonetheless, to stand guard over their connections to family, society, and propriety. For her, overt rebellion against established norms by making public what ought to remain not merely private but utterly unspoken must be conducted by subtlety and subversion, by anonymous publication.

At the age of sixty, the Marquise de Lambert inaugurated one of the most important literary salons in Paris, and in "Advice of a Mother to her Daughter," she speculated on the education available to women in the eighteenth century:

> Nothing is . . . so much mistaken as the education which they give to young women; they design them to please; they give them no instructions but for the ornament and graces of the body; they flatter their self-love; they give them up to effeminacy, to the world, and to false opinions; they give them no lectures of virtue and fortitude. Surely it is unreasonable or downright madness to imagine that such an education should not turn to their prejudice.[1]

In her later "New Reflections on the Fair Sex," she angrily remarked:

> Let me, in the name of my whole sex, put these questions to the men. What is it you require of us? You all are desirous of seeing yourselves

happily united in the society of women of character, of an amiable turn
of mind, and of an upright heart: Allow women therefore the use of
such things, as contribute to the improvement of their reason. But are
you for such graces only as are subservient to pleasure? If this be the
case, don't murmur if women devote some few moments to the improvement of their outward charms.[2]

Burney's first heroine shares these concerns as she describes her progress from relative poverty and an uncomfortably ambiguous social
standing to the acquisition of an acceptable identity and status in the
social world. Evelina has not been appropriately educated for her task.
"Dearly, indeed," she tells her guardian, "do I purchase experience!"
(*Evelina,* 341). Yet, despite her claim to worldly experience, critics have
tended to view Evelina as a complacent and naïve victim of circumstances conveniently contrived by her creator. Evelina has been called
a "priggish mouse,"[3] a "nervous filly," and a "flustered goose."[4] It is
precisely her circumstances, however, that require her to be neither
pathetic nor docile, in fact require her to be none of these domesticated
barnyard creatures. Burney's *Evelina* is more than merely a comedy
of manners and errors. It should be read, instead, as a feminist novel
of education, and as the story of a young woman whose nefariously
ambiguous position forces her to learn how to keep others from making decisions for her. It is a story, then, of private sovereignty and
self-determination. Burney became much more adept at writing a
feminist ideological critique as her art matured and her voice gained
narrative and political confidence. But already in 1778, she displayed
her talent at quiet insurrection against a world that required women
to submit to authority beyond their control and to suppress their most
fundamental desires.

The major clue to how Evelina understands and responds to her
situation lies in the epistolary documents the novel presents us with.
Letter writing in *Evelina* is a synecdochic gesture: it stands, in minia-
ture, for the tenuous and danger-fraught communication process between authority and its charge, between the empowered and the powerless. A well-behaved young woman, Evelina knows, must be innocent
and artless, and the "art" of letter writing—that accomplishment for
cultured ladies we looked at in chapter 1—should reflect this. But innocence and artlessness get Evelina continually into trouble, so self-
preservation demands that she replace those traits with experience as
fast as she can. Her guardian, the Reverend Arthur Villars, affects
not to understand this exigency (though Evelina's grandmother Madame Duval knows and promotes it), so as Burney herself had not

wanted to appear studious in public, Evelina also must disguise her
burgeoning intelligence of the ways of the fashionable world. Letters
are the vehicles for this deceit, as we have seen them to be vehicles
for rhetorical repossession through Burney's private epistolary voices.
Letters became an especially licensed mode of writing for eighteenth-
century women writers and their heroines precisely because letter
writing was a sanctioned female activity. Because it was licensed, the
letter also presented a potential arena for subversion. As a narrative
form, letters pretend to spontaneity and absolute sincerity. But they
can never be utterly sincere, as no crafted piece of writing can be without artifice. Evelina makes sophisticated use of this potential, as did
Burney herself.

The mere gesture of signing her letters is complicated for Evelina,
because her rhetorical problems begin with her name, which has been
given her by Villars. It is a version of her dead mother's maiden name,
Evelyn, and Villars also gives her the anagrammatic made-up surname of "Anville." From birth, then, Evelina's names are absurdist
constructions, neither fully given nor fully family names. Names in
a Burney novel both bestow and withhold identity; they are absolute
signs for the slipperiness of female selfhood and the conflicted play
of female dependence and autonomy in a culture that infantilized its
women. Indeed, the resolution of *Evelina* can come about only when
the complex kinship and authority systems of family and education
are sorted out, and the heroine legally becomes Evelina Belmont Orville, shedding "Anville" altogether as she achieves at last a legitimate
and publicly sanctioned name. Evelina turns out, of course, *not* to be
the poor orphan girl: she is the daughter of a wealthy aristocrat, Sir
John Belmont, who had married and then abandoned her mother.
But even after Belmont belatedly recognizes Evelina as his daughter,
no sooner can she claim the Belmont name, fortune, and social status,
than she trades in all three for the parallel sanctions of marriage to
Lord Orville (who has, significantly, no given name). In fact, although
the entire plot seems to involve intricate ploys to earn back her rightful name and birth identity, only one of the novel's letters is signed
"Evelina Belmont" precisely because Evelina's quest to regain her family and legitimate "name" is paralleled by a quest to replace those original blood ties, the instant they are legalized, with ties of her own choice
and determination. But self-determination for eighteenth-century
women derives first and foremost from social legitimation.

Throughout, it is Evelina's connections to key men that matter most,
because only in accordance with those connections can her social status be ratified. She replaces these men one by one, and quite systematically: first, her biological father replaces the surrogate affective par-

ent Villars; then her husband takes over for both father figures. Indeed, Evelina seeks Villars' initial approval of Lord Orville by comparing the two men. "I sometimes imagine, that, when his youth is flown, his vivacity abated, and his life is devoted to retirement, he will, perhaps, resemble him whom I most love and honour," she writes of the hero to her guardian (72), so the lineage (and the circularity and circulation) of mentors is clear ("Orville," after all, is another version of "Anville"—and/or an equivalence). The anxiety Evelina expresses throughout the narrative about how to "sign" her letters—and letters depend upon their signatures for authenticity, a fact dramatized by her libertine persecutor, Sir Clement Willoughby, with his forgery at the end of volume 2—provides, then, the impetus she requires to undertake and to complete her search.

Evelina's "signature," the authority by which she signs the correspondence that constitutes her narrative, also prefigures the problematic naming of Burney's other heroines, especially Cecilia Beverley, whose protofeminist need not only to keep her own name upon marriage but also to impose it on her husband so embroils her romance with Mortimer Delvile, and Juliet Granville of *The Wanderer,* whose disguised name (L. S./Ellis) is as "made up" as is Evelina's initial appellation. When Evelina sheds her superfluous false surname Anville to take on a public name, it does not matter whether she goes by the legitimating "Belmont" whose respectability the novel's plot wins her. She needs that only momentarily in order to sanction her marriage and yet another name change. Belmont and Orville, fashionable names both, are interchangeable. The name, indeed, serves metonymically as a sign for social propriety; Madame Duval, for example, "told them, that she had it in her head to *make something* of me, and that they should soon call me by another name than that of Anville, and yet that she was not going to have the child married, neither" (121). The fashionable Mrs. Beaumont embarrasses Evelina with a barrage of questions about which of the Anvilles—those in the north or those in Lincolnshire—she is related to. And her worst mortification, when her uncultured cousins the Branghtons finagle the use of Lord Orville's carriage in a rainstorm, comes most acutely from the misuse of her *name,* which she had urged them not to speak aloud (if she had simply remained silent, she points out later, the embarrassment would never have occurred, as these people call her only "Cousin" or "Miss" and never refer to or address her by proper name). She upbraids Tom Branghton with particular zest when he gains access to Orville by mentioning "Miss Anville." "Good God," she expostulates in fury, "and by what authority did you take such a liberty?" (248).

Evelina's mother had had her own obsessions with names and titles, though she did not hesitate to sign her posthumously delivered letter to her profligate husband "Caroline Belmont": "Shall I call you by the loved, the respected title of husband?" she asks him. "No, you disclaim it! — the father of my infant? — No, you doom it to infamy! — the lover who rescued me from a forced marriage? — No, you have yourself betrayed me! — the friend from whom I hoped succour and protection? — No, you have consigned me to misery and destruction!" (338). Caroline negatively defines each of the titles she rejects for Belmont. And when her father beholds Evelina for the first time, he identifies her with the exclamatory "My God! does Caroline Evelyn still live!" (372). Both Evelina and Polly Green, the imposter Belmont has raised as his own daughter, are married within a week of Belmont's recognition, prompting Mrs. Selwyn, Evelina's chaperone at Bristol, to remark, "If either of you have any inclination to pull caps for the title of Miss Belmont, you must do it with all speed, as next week will take from both of you all pretensions to it" (377). Lord Orville introduces Evelina as Miss Belmont to his sister Lady Louisa, then immediately announces, "I hope shortly . . . to have the happiness of presenting [her] to you by yet another name" (381). Captain Mirvan greets her with "So, Miss Belmont, I wish you joy; so I hear you've quarrelled with your new name already?" (392). In the midst of all this name changing, Evelina writes a curt letter to Willoughby, and "not knowing by what name to sign, I was obliged to send it without any" (389). To this point, Evelina's letters have gone partially unsigned, as "Evelina ---- -----," on the grounds, she writes Villars in her initial letter to him, that "I cannot to *you* sign *Anville,* and what other name may I claim?" (24). Only one letter to Villars is signed "Evelina Belmont," and with this closing: "Now then, therefore, for the first — and probably the last time I shall ever own the name, permit me to sign myself" (404) — a strange fate (ownership as both admission and possession) for the name whose acquisition has been the novel's driving force.

The crucial issue in *Evelina*'s use of letters and signatures is reader- and writer-context. The recognized conventions of eighteenth-century epistolary fiction and the general tone of comedic benevolence cultivated by Burney in *Evelina* make it too easy to forget that the Reverend Arthur Villars, the primary reader of Evelina's letters as well as her guardian, has decision-making along with moral power over her. He represents the source of all permission. If she angers or offends him, all is lost — on his approval rests her tenuous foothold in polite society. We cannot expect, then, that her letters to this guardian, to whom she writes most regularly and frequently, will be straightforward. She has no choice but to edit them carefully. This represents a crucial facet of Evelina's narrative strategy. She is a storyteller with an ulterior motive. The covert distortions that her self-editing necessarily prompts control the narrative Evelina's letters ultimately produce.

The epistolary format of the novel, an expected enough fictional mode in 1778, allows Burney to play on problems of tone, sincerity, and narrative truth. Evelina uses her letters as emissaries to her guardian: they plead her case without offending her judge. Each volume of *Evelina* presents a problem of education—both in how to behave and in how to phrase and organize an account of one's behavior—and this education ultimately serves to train Evelina in the procedures for conducting a search for a father, a husband, a name, and a proper and publicly sanctionable social status. In volume 1, she learns aristocratic manners: how to refuse to dance at an assembly without creating gossip; what to wear and where to sit at the opera; how to distinguish the fashionable from the vulgar. In volume 2, she joins the London middle class, learns the dangers of the city and its pleasure gardens for an unescorted woman, and applies her new knowledge of social rules, now sometimes to her own advantage. By volume 3, she actually controls the behavior of others toward her and determines her own social position. From the outset, however, she has a facility with words and their arrangement, though her education also makes her more adept with language's tyrannies and its argumentative potential.

In Villars' initial account of Evelina to Lady Howard, he describes her as "this artless young creature, with too much beauty to escape notice, . . . too much sensibility to be indifferent to it; but . . . too little wealth to be sought with propriety by men of the fashionable world" (18). Villars seems most concerned with the "female difficulties" articulated by Burney's last heroine, Juliet Granville of *The Wanderer,* who represents a radically politicized and economically extreme evolution of Evelina's character. Juliet concludes of the woman alone: "Her honour is always in danger of being assailed, her delicacy of being offended, her strength of being exhausted, and her virtue of being calumniated" (*Wanderer* 5:395). These statements quite succinctly express the problem for Burney's heroines. But Villars focuses on a side issue: though not wealthy before Belmont accepts her, Evelina is never poverty-stricken, and with the addition of Madame Duval's considerable worth to the legacy Villars intends for her, financial exigency does not plague her—for Tom Branghton or the dull Mr. Smith (Samuel Johnson's favorite character in the novel), for example, she is seen as a highly desirable match. What does make Evelina an unacceptable marriage partner for a man of fashion is her ambiguous family connection and lack of a legal name, a problem Villars consistently evades. Evelina must maintain her sensibility and apparent artlessness, and slip around the social problems her pseudo-illegitimacy poses.

Evelina's relation to her guardian of her adventures in the "world" remains deliberately incomplete. Sometimes she uses Richardson's "writing-to-the-moment" stance, writing with one arm while the other is up to its elbow in social crises to achieve this ("I can write no more now. I have hardly time to breathe" [*Evelina,* 25]); letters get lost, crossed, or abandoned ("I could not forbear writing a few words instantly on my arrival; though I suppose my letter of thanks for your consent is still on the road" [26]); she apologizes for her lack of "style" and rhetorical polish ("pray excuse the wretched stuff I write, perhaps I may improve by being in this town, and then my letters will be less unworthy your reading" [28]); long intervals are left blank and unaccounted for ("The first fortnight that I passed here, was so quiet, so serene, that it gave me reason to expect a settled calm during my stay; but if I may now judge of the time to come by the present state of my mind, the calm will be succeeded by a storm, of which I dread the violence" [273]); and, finally, in the ultimate disclaimer of overwrought emotion and rhetorical intensity, she writes of the plot's climactic romantic confrontation: "I cannot write the scene that followed, though every word is engraven on my heart" (352) — for the first time taking the female prerogative of private sentimental discretion to announce to Villars just what it is she is concealing in a procedure that makes a text of the heroine's body. Letter writing itself becomes one of Evelina's chief activities: "I have a vast deal to say, and shall give all this morning to my pen. As to my plan of writing every evening the adventures of the day, I find it impracticable; for the diversions here are so very late, that if I begin my letters after them, I could not go to bed at all" (28). Although Evelina claims to be sending her guardian a minutely detailed journal, a comprehensive account of her "entrance into the world," in fact, she maintains the selective privilege of the creative artist throughout her narrative. She writes from the angle from which she chooses Villars to view her adventures; she adopts a discourse of innocence arrested and then tutored; and he reads ultimately only what she wants him to know.

One sign of the careful editing process Evelina uses in her letters to Villars is the difference in tone and style between these letters, which make up the bulk of the narrative, and the several others she has occasion to write during the course of the novel. The most important of these other letters are addressed to her friend, confidante, and alter ego Maria Mirvan, whom Evelina calls "my second self" (122) and "the friend of my heart" (159). They contain hints about Evelina's analysis of the journal she has been deliberately and self-consciously composing for Villars. The letters to Maria mark tonal shifts in the narrative, and serve as meditational breaks from the newsy, fast-paced yet discursively bloodless letters Evelina sends to her guardian. She never tells *him*, for example, that London is "where I lately enjoyed so much happiness," a "gay and busy" place (172). She divulges her real thoughts and feelings only to Maria, even confessing to Villars, "I conceal nothing from her, she is so gentle and sweet-tempered, that it gives me great pleasure to place an entire confidence in her" (157).

Evelina writes to Maria mostly from Berry Hill, Villars' country home (there is one transcribed letter from London, along with one from Bristol Hotwells — more from Bristol are alluded to but not included in the novel). Evelina is, quite simply, bored and restless at Berry Hill in Villars' company. She needs a female friend, and Villars, she admits, filial tenderness notwithstanding, will no longer do. "Perhaps," she writes to Maria, "had I first seen *you*, in your kind and sympathizing bosom I might have ventured to have reposed the secret of my soul" (254). Villars, clearly, does not have all of Evelina's confidence, and it is not surprising that a seventeen-year-old girl should withhold some of her feelings from the apparently kindly but dangerously ineffectual and naïvely judgmental elderly country parson who has raised her. This lack of complete trust in Evelina's account to Villars, understandable or not, must temper our critical reading of the novel. Most critics have, like Villars himself, been duped by Burney into believing that Evelina has presented us with the whole historical truth, when the narrative discourse of the novel offers clear evidence to the contrary.

The letters to Maria, unlike those to Villars, are direct, their style colloquial and forthright, their tone unstudied. Explaining her mood to Maria in one of the Berry Hill letters, Evelina writes: "I blush for what I have written . . . but I restrain [my gravity] so much and so painfully in the presence of Mr. Villars, that I know not how to deny myself the consolation of indulging it to you" (255). And to Villars, before recounting yet another social faux pas, Evelina explains with feigned contrition: "Will you forgive me, if I own that I have *first* written an account of this transaction to Miss Mirvan?" (249). The forged letter from the scheming Willoughby, on which one of the plot's love complications turns, is indeed communicated to Maria and concealed from Villars. To Maria, Evelina admits that she questions and doubts her own feelings, those same feelings whose purportedly absolute definition constitutes her journal to Villars. To Maria, she explains her masquerade at Berry Hill: "All my thoughts were directed to considering how I might dispel the doubts which I apprehended Mr. Villars had formed, without acknowledging a circumstance which I had suffered so much pain merely to conceal" (263).

At the end of her story in Berry Hill, however, Evelina repents of having concealed her disillusionment about Lord Orville's letter, and vows "an unremitting confidence" to Maria *and* to Villars in future, a vow that validates the novel's third volume. On arrival in Bristol, she tells Maria, "I will continue to write to you, my dear Miss Mirvan, with as much constancy as if I had no other correspondent; tho' during my absence from Berry Hill my letters may, perhaps, be shortened on account of the minuteness of the journal which I must write to my beloved Mr. Villars" (269). The compelled "must" still urges us to weigh Evelina's discourse to her guardian, especially as the final volume witnesses his double displacement by Belmont and Orville. But in fact we do not read another letter to Maria from this point on. The novel refers to replies from Maria which inspire Evelina to unburden herself, but these are never transcribed. And we read only one of the letters to Maria from London, which Evelina mentions to Villars: "She [Maria] made me promise to send her a letter every post. And I shall write to her with the same freedom, and almost the same confidence, you allow me to make use of to yourself" (165). When the two friends are reunited at Bristol Hotwells in the last sequence, Evelina writes especially elliptically to her guardian, "I say nothing of our conversation, because you may so well suppose both the subjects we chose, and our manner of discussing them" (392) — a calculated silence. So there is a second novel here, over which *Evelina* rests like a palimpsest: the novel that Evelina's letters and conversations with a peer, another young woman, would comprise.

The opening narrative pretext for the journal to Villars, then, already engages a problem of vocal sincerity, as Evelina appears to participate reluctantly, at least at first, in the production of this narrative. In her initial letter to Villars, she writes: "I am half ashamed of myself for beginning this letter" (23), the first of a series in which she asks his sanction for her plans. The Mirvans, she pretends, have put her up to it, and her opening missive has an express and specific purpose — to secure permission from Villars to accompany the Mirvans to London, an apologetic gesture of request that Evelina repeats throughout the novel. "Decide for me," she tells her guardian here, and later, ". . . think for me, . . . my dearest Sir, and suffer my doubting mind, that knows not which way to direct its hopes, to be guided by your wisdom and unerring counsel" (123). Her manipulations in these apologies and in her effort to appear helplessly dependent upon her guardian's judgment, however, are hidden surely only to Villars. We can hardly be taken in when, for example, she writes of the London trip, "Pray don't suppose that I make any point of going, for I shall hardly sigh to see them depart without me; though I shall probably never meet with such another opportunity" (24).

This is Evelina's most apparently ingenuous, even childish, letter, and it employs an oblique address to its recipient. "Well but, my dear Sir," writes Evelina, "I am desired to make a request to you. I hope you will not think me an incroacher; Lady Howard insists upon my writing! — yet I hardly know how to go on; a petition implies a want, — and have you left me one? No, indeed" (23). Guilt manipulations are overt here: "What a happy party! Yet I am not *very* eager to accompany them; at least, I shall be very well contented to remain where I am, if you desire that I should." And she ends, "You will not, I am sure, send a refusal, without reasons unanswerable, and therefore I shall chearfully acquiesce. Yet I hope — I hope you will be able to permit me to go!" Evelina's subsequent letters all bear expressions of affection for Villars, and some also close with elaborate signatures, but none again matches the fawning and cunning cultivation of this first, which she signs as follows: "Adieu, my most honoured, most reverenced, most beloved father! for by what other name can I call you? I have no happiness or sorrow, no hope or fear, but what your kindness bestows, or your displeasure may cause" (24). She never calls him "father" again, but it can be argued from this rhetorical overkill that the plot for Evelina depends upon her speaking past the Reverend Mr. Villars. She pretends to act, always, with his implied consent.

"By what other name can I call you?" Villars fits ambiguously into Evelina's world: his surrogate role as her dead mother's champion is an awkward one for both of them. What kind of man orders this heroine's world? Villars' character and his motives are perhaps the least examined in the novel, and critics have ignored him precisely because they have assumed his benignity. We meet him directly only in his letters to Lady Howard, instead seeing him primarily through the prism of Evelina's address to him, through his admittedly and openly censored responses of instruction to her, added to the handful of business reports he dispatches to Lady Howard. If he reveals himself at all, it is in these last. At first, he seems to oppose any project to secure Evelina her rightful name and inheritance, an odd stance for one who claims to have her best interests at heart. He disapproves of a lawsuit on the rather prim grounds that such an enterprise is "so violent, so public, so totally repugnant to all female delicacy" (127): it is clear to whose delicacy the procedure is repugnant. He does not weigh the possibility that poverty, dependency, namelessness, and placelessness might be even more repugnant to a young woman who has been raised breathing the headily mysterious romantic ether of aristocratic pretensions and abandonment. Villars remarks of his scheme for Evelina: "My plan . . . was not merely to educate and to cherish her as my own, but to adopt her the heiress of my small fortune, and to bestow her upon some worthy man, with whom she might spend her days in tranquillity, chearfulness, and good-humour, untainted by vice, folly, or ambition" (127–28). But if Evelina calls him initially her "father" for lack of a more suitable title, he fails to provide her with the first gift of an avowed father: legitimacy. Villars claims her as his property to "bestow" without being able to install her in the patriarchal family system such a bestowal demands and presupposes.

Evelina's anagrammatic namelessness denies her even minimal social respectability, the thing Villars claims most to desire for her protection. Lady Howard accuses him, politely, of "so carefully concealing the birth, name, and pretensions of this amiable girl" that he thereby diminishes her chances for a good marriage (or any marriage at all) because of the "mystery in regard to her birth" (124). Villars refuses, in fact, to aid in any design to convince Sir John Belmont to recognize his daughter: "As to myself," Villars writes petulantly, "I must wholly decline *acting*, though I will, with unwearied zeal, devote all my thoughts to giving counsel: but, in truth, I have neither inclination nor spirits adequate to engaging personally with this man" (128–29). In other words, he is all talk and no action. Yet when Madame Duval threatens to cut Evelina from her will, we get another story from Villars: "To me, I own, this threat seemed of little consequence . . . but the incertitude of [Evelina's] future fate, deters me from following implicitly the dictates of my present judgment. . . . In short, . . . I was obliged . . . to compromise with this ungovernable woman, by consenting that Evelina should pass one month with her" (163).

Villars' charge, unlike her difficult grandmother, can be "governed." To justify his concession of a month in London with Madame Duval, Villars sanctimoniously writes, "But, alas, my dear child, we are the slaves of custom, the dupes of prejudice, and dare not stem the torrent of an opposing world, even though our judgments condemn our compliance!" And we read in the version of this explanation sent to Lady Howard that Villars has, in fact, obeyed custom rather than conscience, and been motivated by a concern for wealth over righteous behavior. He tells his ward to do as he says rather than as he does ("you must learn not only to *judge* but to *act* for yourself") and charges her with his famous threat, "Remember, my dear Evelina, nothing is so delicate as the reputation of a woman: it is, at once, the most beautiful and most brittle of all human things" (164). Samuel Crisp made a similar observation to Burney (and indeed the "Daddy"/"Fannikins" correspondence of Burney's youth reads at moments like that between Villars and Evelina; Villars has been assumed to be modeled on Crisp): "I will never allow you to sacrifice a grain of female delicacy for all the wit of Congreve and Vanbrugh put together" (*DL* 1:104), Crisp told Burney of her comedy writing. Burney herself more knowingly presented this view in an oft-quoted remark from a letter to Crisp: "I would a thousand times rather forfeit my character as a writer, than risk censure or ridicule as a female" (*DL* 1:102).

"The reputation of a woman" receives its severest setbacks from the behavior and social presentation of Evelina's assertive grandmother, a character who is never permitted to compose her own letters and is thereby barred from participation in the production of this narrative. Madame Duval is a woman Villars calls violent, vulgar, ignorant of propriety, and in general "by no means a proper companion or guardian for a young woman" (13). If he is unwilling to deprive Evelina of this dubious woman's fortune, why does he so readily refuse to help her get the much larger one to which she is legally entitled? In fact, Evelina's economic situation is not as lean as the pathetic adjectives attributed to her would make it seem. Though Madame Duval threatens and expostulates, her contrition over abandoning Evelina's mother makes it unlikely that she will really cut off her granddaughter, and her money, bourgeois and inelegant though its owner may be, is not an inconsiderable sum, its provenance Evelina's cowardly but economically correct grandfather. Villars, too, if he sincerely intends Evelina to inherit from him (and he has no other visible heirs), has a respectable country parson's income to bestow, certainly at least the income of Mr. Tyrold in *Camilla*. The problem, as Villars understands it, is not how to claim Evelina's rightful material possessions; rather, it turns on how to possess the aristocratic status and titled pretensions and equipages Belmont's name and wealth can confer.

To solve this problem, Villars passes Evelina to the authority of four successive women, a curious gesture in itself from a man who has argued that approaching Belmont would be "repugnant to all female delicacy"—Lady Howard, Mrs. Mirvan, Madame Duval, and Mrs. Selwyn. It is through their delegated power that Evelina eventually makes her plea to her biological father. Lord Orville describes Mrs. Mirvan as "a true feminine character" (289). Madame Duval, in contrast, is a splendid creation of surliness and good-natured ill-breeding. Finally, it is under the guidance of Mrs. Selwyn, whose manners and understanding Evelina dubs *"masculine"* (268), that she wins both her father's recognition and the hand of Lord Orville. Villars passively leaves Evelina to the counsel of women, and women are the agents in all the novel's major events. Even Lady Belmont, long dead, speaks forcefully from the grave on Evelina's behalf through her posthumous letter to her husband. Only Villars, of all her elders, abandons Evelina entirely to her own devices by refusing to run direct interference for her.

What has Villars taught Evelina to prepare her for adult womanhood and to arm her against the deceptions of the fashionable world, and how does he react to her independent decisions? He rebukes her, from the outset, for her efforts to survive in the London social jungle. Yet the only weapon he arms her with is a knowledge of courtly-genteel language, the sign of her inherited social class.[5] Of her two assembly fiascos, he writes: "I am sure I need not say, how much more I was pleased with the mistakes of your inexperience at the private ball, than with the attempted adoption of more fashionable manners at the ridotto. But your confusion and mortifications were such as to entirely silence all reproofs on my part" (55). That is not reassuring, and when Villars does get around to giving advice rather than reproaching, his pronouncements are not of much practical use. "Alas, my child," he laments, "the artlessness of your nature, and the simplicity of your education, alike unfit you for the thorny paths of the great and busy world" (116). When Belmont appears to disown Evelina in his first letter to Lady Howard, Villars consoles her with exhortations to refrain from claiming her birthright while warning her with just the opposite admonition — to avoid passivity — with regard to Sir Clement Willoughby: "You cannot, my love, be too circumspect; the slightest carelessness on your part, will be taken advantage of. . . . It is not sufficient for you to be reserved; his conduct even calls for your resentment" (161). Nevertheless, having commanded Evelina to inaction toward her father and vehemence against Willoughby, Villars himself capitulates with open cowardice and venality to Madame Duval, by far the most unsettling of Evelina's tormentors because the most legitimate and the most perspicacious about the younger woman's position as a statusless woman; Evelina's plight in some ways resembles that of her grandmother, who is a foreigner traveling with a man to whom she is not married.

So how does Evelina acquire an education in the course of the novel? Some of her most telling because least well guarded reflections come before her schooling has quite begun. Needless to say, what she learns, to Villars' chagrin, are the rules of fashionable social behavior and coquetry. Burney uses her initial innocence about these rules as an effective cover for recounting social engagements with biting satire. Here, for example, is Evelina at her first ball, describing her outrage at being on display and powerless, an outrage that occasions her first social blunder when she acts instinctively on it without regard for what is "proper":

> The gentlemen, as they passed and repassed, looked as if they thought we were quite at their disposal, and only waiting for the honour of their commands; and they sauntered about, in a careless indolent manner, as if with a view to keep us in suspense. . . . I thought it so provoking, that I determined, in my own mind, that, far from humouring such airs, I would rather not dance at all, than with any one who should seem to think me ready to accept the first partner who would condescend to take me. (28–29)

Shortly after this scene, the egregious but put-upon fop Lovel minces forward, and not only does Evelina refuse to dance with him, setting up her first major gaffe, but she is also at pains to conceal her laughter. This is more than merely a comment on the social ineptitude of an innocent country girl in the city, and more than mere harmless social satire. Burney, too, is outraged that a woman should not be at liberty to turn down a man, and while she makes her heroine initially ignorant of the complex implications of saying no to a man who is merely unappealing to her, she does not make her stupid. Evelina's assessment that she has been displayed as merchandise is accurate, and her resentment justified. And the merchandising of Evelina, though less overtly unfolded, comprises the novel's central subject: both Evelina and her creator recognize that.[6]

Lovel himself, the offended suitor here, receives his belated come-uppance in the violent climactic final scene of the novel. One of Burney's best realized surface characters, Lovel undergoes an undressing at the end of *Evelina* that parallels the undressing of Madame Duval already discussed and is perpetrated as well by Captain Mirvan and his malevolent practical joking. The Lovel scene answers Evelina's humiliation at the ball, because it skewers the play of appearance and social meaning that Burney criticizes in *Evelina,* a novel in which problematically false exteriors of self-containment are penetrated through frequently cruel physical exposure, and self-imposed behavioral discipline is continually threatened. Captain Mirvan introduces into a polite drawing-room gathering a "full dressed and extravagantly *à-la-mode*" (400) monkey meant to parody Lovel. Lovel attacks the creature with his cane, whereupon the monkey springs onto his assailant's neck and bites his ear:

> Mr. Lovel was now a dreadful object; his face was besmeared with tears, the blood from his ear ran trickling down his cloaths, and he sunk upon the floor, crying out, "Oh I shall die, I shall die! — Oh I'm bit to death!" (401)

The discussion that ensues focuses entirely on Lovel's appearance. "[I]t is but a slit of the ear, it only looks as if you had been in the pillory," jokes the Captain. "[A]nd who knows but it may acquire you the credit of being an anti-ministerial writer," adds Mrs. Selwyn, with vintage Burney wit.[7] But Lovel's own concern is more immediate: "'I protest,' cried Mr. Lovel, looking ruefully at his dress, 'my new riding-suit's all over blood!'"; "Mr. Lovel then walked to the glass, and looking at the place, exclaimed, 'Oh Heaven, what a monstrous wound! my ear will never be fit to be seen again!'" He meets the suggestion that he cover the wound with a wig in outrage: "'A wig!' repeated the affrighted Mr. Lovel, '*I* wear a wig? — no, not if you would give me a thousand pounds an hour!'" (402). And, finally, Lovel declines advice to "save face" by challenging Mirvan to a duel, not wanting to call a professional fighter to account, and is ultimately forced to shrug off the incident as "a trifle" (403).[8] This havoc-wreaking threat to a character who resides entirely on the surface, a man of form alone, makes him as much an object of merchandise as Evelina had been at the ball, and avenges her. But she is no longer threatened by him, so feels compassion now for his plight, a plight that parallels her own: "I was really sorry for the poor man who, though an egregious fop, had committed no offence that merited such chastisement" (401).

How to avoid being condescended to as a formal object — which for a young woman in the eighteenth century amounts to how to say "no" — becomes a pressing issue for Evelina. By her second assembly, a ridotto, she has learned that she will not be able to make her own choices, to get away simply with saying "no" to one man and "yes" to another. So this time she claims to have been previously engaged. When this too (a bald lie: the other side of straightforward truth is straightforward falsehood) gets her into trouble, and turns Sir Clement Willoughby into her persecutor, she recognizes both the ridiculousness and the rigidity of the proper forms she is expected to follow, and of Willoughby's claim to offense: "I turned away from this nonsense," she writes, "with real disgust" (41). She goes on to remonstrate: "'Indeed, Sir,' said I very seriously, 'I must insist on your leaving me,'" and finally, "You have tormented me to death; you have forced me from my friends, and intruded yourself upon me, against my will, for a partner" (44), though she does not yet know how to prevail against this male assertion of forced control in Willoughby's manipulation of the rules of public manners. Evelina concludes this sequence by telling Villars, "I am too inexperienced and ignorant to conduct myself with propriety in this town, where everything is new to me, and many things are unaccountable and perplexing" (48).

Oddly, neither Evelina nor Villars takes responsibility for this ignorance: she has never had access to simple social customs that concern public relations between the sexes. Camilla Tyrold, in contrast, though also raised in the country, is in complete command of public rules of behavior before she appears at a ball for the first time (though she too becomes trapped by these rules despite her training in them). Villars' passivity on this issue makes him a co-conspirator, under the guise of protecting her, in the blindfolding of Evelina. She needs to learn for herself, which she does. In volume 2, faced with Madame Duval's insistence that she go to the Hampstead assembly with the importunate and self-absorbed Mr. Smith, she puts her hard-won knowledge to use and avoids having to dance with this crude, would-be beau: "Mr. Smith teazed me till I was weary of resistance; and I should at last have been obliged to submit, had I not fortunately recollected the affair of Mr. Lovel, and told my persecutor, that it was impossible I should dance with him, even if I wished it, as I had refused several persons in his absence" (223). In fact, Mr. Smith serves as a kind of inspiration to Evelina. She tells Villars that "the extreme vanity of this man makes me exert a spirit which I did not, till now, know that I possessed: but I cannot endure that he should think me at his disposal" (225). She had used the same word at her first ball — "disposal." Willoughby, too, who compromises Evelina in his carriage in volume 1, comes in for his rebuke from her in volume 3. When he tries to use fashionable rhetoric to seduce her, she replies, "'Sir Clement,' cried I, angrily, 'you have no right to make any conditions'" (357). It is possible, finally, to say "no," at least momentarily, and get away with it. But, as Evelina herself has put it, "dearly, indeed, do I purchase experience!" (341), and her purchases are made, ultimately, in the marketplace of the eighteenth-century's gender economy.

The most problematic of these coded social transactions occur at public assemblies that involve actual or metaphorical dancing. From the first private ball to Ranelagh, the Pantheon, Vauxhall, Marylebone Gardens, and the Hampstead Ball, Evelina must either dance with an unwanted partner, entrap a desired partner, or choreograph a circuitous retreat through dark pathways. When she dances, her partners hold on to her by force, with a grip that causes physical pain. This is as true of the prostitutes who each bruisingly grasp one of her arms as it is true of Willoughby. In Vauxhall's "dark walks," Evelina and Polly and Biddy Branghton are forced into a group "dance" with a gang of drunks who "formed a kind of circle, that first stopped our proceeding, and then our retreating, for we were presently entirely inclosed." When Evelina breaks out of this prison by thwarting an iron grip, she soon finds herself "running into the arms" of another set of men, with "both my hands, by different persons, caught hold of" (196). The dance, thus, represents not merely the "disposal" of women; it is also literally imprisoning. When Evelina refuses to "dance," she finds herself against her will in a carriage whose driver conveniently loses his way, or standing on a raised platform (at the fireworks display; in Mrs. Beaumont's primate-invaded drawing room) alone and terrified above the crowd.

Even when Evelina dances with Lord Orville, she does so under tainted circumstances: she has previously refused another eligible partner or she has dishonestly told a suitor that she was previously engaged. Only when she creates another couple — Madame Duval and Mr. Smith — and then contrives to refuse other partners while she remains inappropriately alone, can she properly avoid dancing altogether. The dance — its oppressive nonchoice of partners for women and the complacent "disposal" of women by unself-consciously possessive men — serves as a metaphor for the female condition throughout *Evelina*. The fashionable and public places of dancing represent labyrinthine symbolic prisons for the unescorted and unidentified woman: absolute danger lurks everywhere in these locations.

In a cunning appeal to Lord Orville, Evelina announces:

> There is no young creature, my Lord, who so greatly wants, or so earnestly wishes for, the advice and assistance of her friends, as I do; I am new to the world, and unused to acting for myself, — my intentions are never wilfully blameable, yet I err perpetually! — I have, hitherto, been blest with the most affectionate of friends, and, indeed, the ablest of men, to guide and instruct me upon every occasion; — but he is too distant, now, to be applied to at the moment I want his aid; — and *here*, — there is not a human being whose counsel I can ask! (306).

When she needs a man's advice — when the counsel of Mrs. Mirvan or Mrs. Selwyn is unavailable or incomplete — she must cajole, flatter, and manipulate, all with apparent innocence and real charm, to get it, as she does here. We have to remember a number of things as we read this double-edged speech. Evelina transcribes it in a letter to Villars, and her impressive achievement here is that she manages to flatter Villars and Lord Orville simultaneously while all along cultivating the appearance of artless ingenuousness and charming pathos in her own self-presentation. Evelina is, among other things, quite a mistress of rhetorical seduction.[9] It seems clear that she requires all the verbal art of which she is capable to tell the tale of her adventures in search of a father and husband to a man who wishes to play both roles for her without formally taking on either one and who has deliberately, therefore, absented himself from participating in her welfare, yet to whom she feels indebted. The duplicity this situation breeds and demands must be continually taken into account in reading Evelina's letters.

Susan Staves has analyzed the dangerous world Evelina's situation places her in, and perceptively writes that Evelina "begins as a delicate young girl and seems to think her problem is principally that she will be thought to be indelicate, rather than that she will actually become so."[10] That expresses the crux of eighteenth-century morality and sensibility, especially for women: it does not matter what Evelina actually must become to get past the difficulties her denied birth and wealth present her with. She seeks social respectability, and what matters for that is what people think. What people think and gossip about frequently depends upon the success of disguises and subterfuge and does not bear any necessary relation to the truth. So one observation we can make is that the accepted prefeminist critical interpretation of "poor, dear, innocent Evelina" both within and outside the margins of this text — the image of the diminutive, flustered, silly, nervous, and naïve domestic pet — represents Evelina's success in controlling public opinion and maintaining the outward forms of modesty and artlessness against all odds.

Evelina's brief encounter with the Marylebone women of pleasure underscores this principle of appearance: what frightens her about these women is that they are so transparently what they are, that they offer no attempt at disguise. Mary Wollstonecraft put it well: "It is vain to expect virtue from women till they are, in some degree, independent of men. . . . Whilst they are absolutely dependent on their husbands they will be cunning, mean, and selfish."[11] And Patricia Meyer

Spacks has pointed out that "female innocence . . . is male oppression"[12] — the innocent woman makes social blunders because she is forced to act out her innocence in a world where the crucial element for social survival, particularly for women, derives from Lord Chesterfield's notion of "decorum," a notion that in the eighteenth century shifts away from the Horatian idea of the "fitting" and becomes ferociously repressive. The need to appear innocent is coerced: the eighteenth-century feminists who wrote about education for women — Mary Astell, Lady Mary Wortley Montagu, Catherine Macaulay, Mary Wollstonecraft—all make this point. When Cynthia's parents in Sarah Fielding's *David Simple* (1744–53), for example, whisk a book out of their daughter's hands, it is with the admonition, "Miss must not enquire too far into things, it would turn her Brain; she had better mind her Needle-work, and such Things as were useful for Women; reading and poring on Books, would never get . . . a husband."[13] The chief complaint, made repeatedly by violated and resisting women, was that women were deliberately kept in ignorance and then primed to behave as though that ignorance were a virtue.

There are two portraits, however, of fully autonomous women in *Evelina*. The first portrait of female free agency in the novel, ambivalently negative, concerns the two prostitutes at Marylebone, described at first simply as "two ladies" to whom Evelina appeals for "protection" when she loses her companions after the fireworks display and finds herself publicly alone. The women laugh at this request, as well they might: throughout the novel Evelina is mortified by being seen by Lord Orville either with the "wrong" people (her bourgeois relations), or in inappropriate conversation with a man, but this situation causes the hero the greatest concern. Like Juliet in *The Wanderer,* Evelina learns that men are not to be trusted for help in an emergency, hence her selection of these women rather than "some bold and unfeeling man" (233). While their primary speech is laughter, the prostitutes indeed rescue Evelina from her imprisoning circumstances and conduct her safely to her friends. Only when Lord Orville raises his eyebrows at them does the heroine realize her error; afterwards, when Madame Duval remarks that they are "two real fine ladies," Evelina knowingly tells Villars, "Indeed it is wonderful to see how easily and how frequently she is deceived" (236). The joke, though, turns out to be on Evelina and her imposed-upon companions, and on Lord Orville, who misunderstands the nature of this acquaintance. He even confesses that he wanted to inquire into Evelina's connection with "those women" before he made his proposal (389), in a gesture that unites him with the watchful Edgar Mandlebert of *Camilla*. The women themselves are publicly circulating agents in a novel in which free agency for women represents a radical departure from social norms. Burney never otherwise judges or condemns them.

The novel's other and more primary portrait of a female free agent depicts Mrs. Selwyn, the fast-talking country gentlewoman who teases as nastily and laughs as loudly as any of the men in her set. She occasions a series of discussions of acceptable public behavior for women. Willoughby complains of "the unbounded licence of her tongue," which he finds "in a woman . . . intolerable" (343); her biting quips humiliate both Lord Merton and Lovel, who despise her without being able to get the better of her. But despite outright contempt from the novel's fashionable people, Mrs. Selwyn remains a woman to reckon with. Unlike Evelina, who puts up with social slights and self-deprecatingly calls herself "Nobody" in an echo of Lovel (35, 289), Mrs. Selwyn asserts her presence, her wit, and her will on the company and on Sir John Belmont and the plot's resolution. While most of the characters, including Evelina and indirectly Villars, remark her behavior in degrees ranging from affectionately raised eyebrows to outright contempt, Burney uses her to present a woman who is kind and compassionate to those who deserve it and who achieves independent status without compromising herself either socially or personally. Mrs. Selwyn is a foil for Madame Duval, who also keeps her own counsel but does not know as well how to maneuver successfully through the rules and forms of polite society, and for Mrs. Mirvan, who is socially impeccable but inexorably tied to a loutish husband she cannot stand up to or control. Evelina portrays all three of these older women who chaperone her — none ever speaks or writes in her own voice except through the heroine's transcribed dialogue.

Burney's assessments of Mrs. Mirvan, Madame Duval, and Mrs. Selwyn are complicated. If Mrs. Selwyn is, as I have suggested, a voice for female self-acceptance and independence (as Mrs. Arlbery is in the later *Camilla*), the other two represent opposing poles on either end of the female social spectrum. Mrs. Mirvan is an oppressed wife married to an abusive husband who orders her around and removes all options from her, freeing her only when he is away at sea. Madame Duval, by contrast, is matched against Captain Mirvan as a character whose roughhewn sensibility makes it impossible for her to empathize with others. Mrs. Mirvan and Madame Duval are present at many of the novel's sites of violence: the entrapping dances and the fashionable parade grounds. If we read these three women together and take Mrs. Selwyn to be the most sympathetically portrayed — adept at fashion and manners like Mrs. Mirvan, yet unoppressed by social allegiances; forthright and self-assured like Madame Duval, yet astute and compassionate — then it is hard to overlook the fact that she is the one character whose navigation through the waters of fashionable society is unanchored and therefore unimpeded by a male companion.

Another pair of incidental but apparently unaffiliated women in *Evelina* fare considerably less well than do the Marylebone prostitutes, and raise more complex questions about the circulation of women in the novel. These are the two eighty-year-old women who appear in an odd interpolated sequence in the novel's final volume. The interchangeable fashionable men at Bristol endlessly present wagers to one another, involving everything from phaeton races to competitive bowing to extempore couplet-composing contests. In these scenes, failure to compete draws the charge of womanishness. Jack Coverley, for example, accuses Lord Orville of being "as careful as an old woman" (288) when he tries to prevent a phaeton race, and when the gentlemen are given pause by Mrs. Selwyn's proposal of a contest based not on physical prowess but on who can recite from memory the longest ode of Horace, she asks, "Come, Gentlemen, why do you hesitate? I am sure you cannot be afraid of a weak *woman*?" (290). The dispute, in the end, will be "settled by a race between two old women" (295), as though by that metonymic means the issue of gender identity, social status, and competition could be "settled" by focusing the debate on figures who are in every way outside the social conditions for competition in any market at all. When the race begins, and a horrified Evelina describes the racers as "two poor old women" who, "[t]hough they seemed very healthy for their time of life, they yet looked so weak, so infirm, so feeble, that I could feel no sensation but that of pity at the sight," Orville merely "looked very grave during the whole transaction." "Doubtless," Evelina speculates, "he must be greatly discontented at the dissipated conduct and extravagance" of one of the wagerers, his brother-in-law to be (311).

This footrace, one of the novel's infamous scenes, pulsates with violence. The women first run into each other and fall bruised on the gravel track. Then they "hobbled . . . , stumbled and tottered" until one slips and "with great force, she came again to the ground," where she remains "too much hurt to move." Evelina rushes to help, but is stopped by a cry of "No foul play!" from Lord Merton, and Coverley, for whom the injured woman is running, "was quite brutal; he swore at her with unmanly rage, and seemed scarce able to refrain even from striking her" (312). Historical and sociological explanations for this scene have been proposed, and certainly the frequent physicality and brutality of eighteenth-century popular entertainments finds a reflection and commentary here.[14] In addition, the footrace represents the apotheosis of both physical violence and social violation against women. Rendered sexless by their age, these octogenarian women have no individual identities. They compete, like dogs or horses, on behalf of and for the profit and esteem of their sponsors. This scene in many ways renders Burney's most acute fictive representation of the fate of feminine beauty and the attention it fleetingly commands, and of the social place of women as figures for the self-aggrandizement of men. They have only use-value and counter-value in competitions between male interests.

Evelina fails to save these elderly victims from ignominious torture, but her own independent moment arrives when she rescues the sentimental, Wertherish Macartney in the novel's most melodramatic episode. Though she faints, falls to her knees, and bursts into tears periodically (for Villars' benefit, at least) throughout her trials, including in this scene, Evelina here sustains a physically courageous presence of mind. She rushes into Macartney's room and grabs his pistols; she tricks him into accepting a gift of money; she makes a secret appointment with him and writes to him. And finally, she shares her inheritance with this illegitimate brother and his imposter wife (though Polly Green, who has passed as and been raised as Miss Belmont, is deemed more deserving of this inheritance, though she has no blood ties to the family, than is Macartney, who asks Belmont to "own" him, but not to "portion" him). Evelina behaves courageously in this subplot, and acts without counsel from anyone, maintaining Macartney's secret until the end even from Lord Orville, who questions the propriety of their meetings.

"Propriety," indeed, is one of Burney's key words in *Evelina*, and the conjunction in Evelina between propriety and property informs much of the plot: the heroine must struggle for self-ownership. When Lord Orville inquires of Evelina late in the novel to whom she owes allegiance and to whom he should address his proposals, she confesses, "I hardly know myself to whom I most belong" (353); in Villars' first account to Lady Howard, he speculates of Sir John Belmont, "Is there any probability that he will properly own her?" (19). Yet, despite these conditions that apparently present Evelina as a kind of currency to be exchanged from one man to another, she is also valorized as a participant in the negotiations for her name. Nancy Armstrong has argued that in *Pamela*, Richardson alters the exchange and contract rules between the sexes by "inserting Pamela's voice into the field" and thereby revising political relationships in a "version of consensual exchange with the male."[15] Though Pamela is Mr. B's servant and hence under

his aristocratic control — she already "belongs" to him — Evelina is paradoxically less empowered than her predecessor. While Orville consults her will, his ultimate concern is to learn who "owns" her and who
can therefore "give her away," bestow her upon him as the primary
symbolic property in a marital transaction.

Samuel Johnson offers eight definitions of *property* in his *Dictionary
of the English Language* (1755), among them "Right of possession" and
"*Property* for *propriety.* Anything peculiarly adapted." Johnson cites Locke:
"*Property,* whose original is from the right a man has to use any of the
inferior creatures, for subsistence and comfort, is for the sole advantage of the proprietor, so that he may even destroy the thing that he
has *property* in." *Propriety* Johnson defines as "peculiarity of possession;
exclusive right" and "accuracy; justness," while *proper* means to Johnson, among ten definitions, "fit, accommodated; adapted; suitable;
qualified."[16] *The Oxford English Dictionary* points out the common root
of these words in the Latin *proprietate.* The *OED* cites Burney's 1782
Cecilia as its first source for one sense of the word *propriety* — "confor-
mity with good manners or polite usage; correctness of behavior or
morals; becomingness, decency." "The proprieties" are "the things that
are considered proper; the details of conventionally correct or proper
conduct." Burney's use in *Cecilia* is cited from this phrase: "Such propriety of mind as can only result from the union of good sense with
virtue." The *OED* also cites Hannah More's 1799 fourth edition of her
Female Education: "The decorums, the proprieties, the elegancies, and
even the graces, as far as they are simple, pure, and honest, would follow as an almost inevitable consequence." To behave well and to "belong" to someone are synonymous for Burney's women, so it is no
wonder that their names — the external designations of ownership —
and their attempts at independent action are so fraught with problems.

Burney places her heroines repeatedly in predicaments that require
them either to unmask themselves and risk social censure or to be
disastrously misunderstood, yet their challenges to the social order
can never be fully open or direct. In the dedicatory epistle that pref-
aces *The Wanderer,* Burney provides some clues about her analysis of
the distortions in narrative voice that Evelina, of necessity, must em-
bed in her letters. She asserts that the novel

> is, or it ought to be, a picture of supposed, but natural and probable
> human existence. It holds, therefore, in its hand our best affections; it
> exercises our imaginations; it points out the path of honour; and gives
> to juvenile credulity knowledge of the world, without ruin, or repen-
> tance; and the lessons of experience, without its tears. (*Wanderer* 1:xvi)

Although that statement has not become as canonical as Samuel Johnson's "numbering the streaks of the tulip" pronouncement in *Rasselas* (1759), it derives from the same universalizing and moralizing neoclassical impulse, and it adds a social importance to the Johnsonian view of literary form.

Evelina purchased her experience dearly; Burney wants to provide it to others at the simple price of a printed book. Evelina writes that "there ought to be a book, of the laws and customs *à-la-mode* presented to all young people, upon their first introduction into public company" (83). *Evelina* serves as such a book: lacking a guide to the confusing byways of social etiquette for unmarried women, Evelina composes one for herself as she goes. Walter Allen, disparagingly and quite unfairly, calls this social element in Burney's theory of the novel a "femininization," a term that he uses to mean "a diminution of range" in relation to what he terms the "masculine" and "expansive" works of novelists such as Fielding and Smollett. The only world open to Burney's heroines, Allen says, is the world that is "accessible to a conventionally brought up upper-middle-class young lady constantly chaperoned."[17] Johnson had made the same observation, but in the form of a compliment. "No writer so young and inexperienced," he wrote, "had ever seen so deeply into character, or copied the manners of the time with more accuracy."[18] And Burney herself answered that charge (a similar one has been leveled over and over again against Jane Austen) in a 1778 diary entry:

> Perhaps this [writing *Evelina*] may seem a rather bold attempt . . . for a female whose knowledge of the world is very confined, and whose inclinations, as well as situation, incline her to a private and domestic life. All I can urge is, that I have only presumed to trace the accidents to which a "young woman" is liable. I have not pretended to show the world what it actually *is,* but what it *appears* to a girl of seventeen: — and so far as that, surely any girl who is *past* seventeen may safely do? (*DL* 1:2)

Such a "restricted" world, in any case, imposed as it was on large segments of the reading populace, was of interest in itself. But the accusations of narrowness and limitation, accusations that have crippled Burney criticism as until recently they crippled Austen criticism, also explain why Burney's and Evelina's narrative art must be duplicitous, and why expanding the range and locating and inscribing alternative kinds of power are so crucial to a character as circumscribed in options as is Evelina "Anville" Belmont Orville.

Evelina does not, of course, triumph fully over the patriarchial social order that commands her submission and her duplicity. She does
not manage to overturn that order; what she achieves is a measure
of personal autonomy and control *within* the confines of "acceptable"
social behavior for women in the last third of the eighteenth century.
Burney's first heroine is decorous and polite on the surface, but beneath it she strains against the bonds her decorous behavior implies.
The older models before her of possible situations for women are unacceptable ones: Mrs. Mirvan has not so much "dwindled into a wife"
as she has been trapped for form's sake into union with a virtual sadist;
Madame Duval encounters ridicule wherever she goes for her scorn
of social convention; and Mrs. Selwyn, though independent, witty,
and fashionable, is fundamentally alone. Evelina feels understandable
anxiety with respect to the role she is expected to play, and she must
disguise this anxiety, the product of a challenge to convention, from
her guardian Villars. As Lady Mary Wortley Montagu complained
in 1710 in a letter to Gilbert Burnet, " 'tis look'd upon as in a degree
Criminal to improve our Reason, or fancy we have any."[19]

In 1778, silence was still the most attractive quality in women and
the notion of modesty, despite intermittent calls for educational reform from writers of an earlier period such as Mary Astell and Daniel
Defoe, was still almost as powerful as it had been in 1697, when *The
Whole Duty of a Woman* was published containing this passage:

> Modesty confines itself not to the face only . . . but spreads itself in
> life, motions, and words. . . . Your looks, your speech, and the course
> of your whole behaviour should own a humble distrust of yourselves;
> rather being willing to learn and observe, than to dictate and pre-
> scribe. . . . As you value your reputation, keep us to the strictures of
> this virtue. . . . Give no occasion for scandal or reproach; but let your
> conversation set an example to others. . . . In all public assemblies be-
> have yourselves with all reverence and modesty and becoming decency.
> *Let neither your thoughts nor eyes wander.*[20]

It is clear that had Evelina set out openly to communicate a social
critique, to "dictate and prescribe," as the novel itself ultimately does,
the Reverend Villars and Lord Orville both would have thought her
mad. Unlike her more politically mature younger sisters Cecilia,
Camilla, and Juliet, who risk censure from their lovers and are abandoned by those lovers at every crucial juncture, Evelina deliberately
minimizes her risk taking. Nevertheless, we watch Burney's first heroine
successively manipulate the emotions of all the men in the novel, from

Villars, Sir John Belmont, and Lord Orville, who make her "thrice-happy" (and give her three names), to Sir Clement Willoughby and Lovel, Mr. Smith, the melodramatic Macartney, and Monsieur Du Bois. We can recapitulate the progress Evelina makes in assertive independence: at her first ball, she is incensed that the men "thought we were quite at their disposal" and that disposal humiliates her; at a later ball she says of an unwanted suitor that he inspires her to "exert a spirit which I did not, till now, know that I possessed . . . [and] I cannot endure that he should think me at his disposal"; she writes of the seduction ploys of another leering pursuer, "I turned away from this nonsense with real disgust"; and finally, she tells off her worst persecutor in no uncertain terms: "'Sir Clement,' cried I, angrily, 'you have no right to make any conditions.'" These are the words of a woman who speaks not meekly but in anger, not innocently but with sophisticated and knowing rebellion, not ingenuously but with calculatedly sharp-tongued cunning.

As the novel evolved at the end of the eighteenth century, it became more and more parodically conscious of its own conventions. Patricia Meyer Spacks has written that eighteenth-century women novelists "employ the writing of novels to affirm the social order that limits them."[21] Yet over time, the frail and swooning heroine became the butt of the joke, overreaching and finally exploding in Jane Austen's juvenile send-up, *Love and Freindship*. By 1813, when Eaton Stannard Barrett published *The Heroine; or, Adventures of Cherubina*, we get a tongue-in-cheek lament about the protagonist's failure to qualify for the role of "heroine," despite the fact that *The Heroine*'s epigraph is "L'histoire d'une femme est toujours un Roman."[22] "Cherubina" starts out as "Cherry" ("It reminds one so much of plumpness and ruddy health. Cherry—better be called Pine-apple at once. There is a green and yellow melancholy in pine-apple, that is infinitely preferable." The alteration is minimal: "'Tis only changing y into ubina, and the name becomes quite classic").[23] When her governess is dismissed for kissing the butler (she is "not even permitted to take and receive a hysterical farewell"),[24] Cherry begins an epistolary narrative addressed to her, and complains of her circumstances:

> I am doomed to endure the security of a home, and the dullness of an unimpeached reputation. For me, there is no hope whatever of being reduced to despair. Alas, I must waste my health, bloom, and youth, in a series of uninterrupted prosperity.
> It is not, my friend, that I wish for ultimate unhappiness, but that

I am anxious to suffer present sorrow, with the hope of securing future felicity. . . . Now my ambition is to be a Heroine, and how can I hope for success, unless I, too, suffer privations and inconveniences? Besides, have I not far greater merit, in getting a husband by sentiment, adventure, and melancholy, than by dressing, gadding, dancing, and singing? For heroines are just as much on the alert to get husbands, as other young ladies; and in truth, I would never voluntarily undergo misfortunes, were I not certain that matrimony would be the last of them. But even misery itself has its consolations and advantages. It makes one, at least, look interesting, and affords an opportunity for ornamental murmurs. Besides, it is the mark of a refined mind. Only fools, children, and savages, are happy.[25]

When Cherry's father burns her vast collection of novels and romances in order to purify the house, she apostrophizes:

Adieu, then, ye dear romances, adieu for ever. No more shall I sympathize with your heroines, while they faint, and blush, and weep, through four half-bound octavos. Adieu, ye Edwins, Edgars, and Edmunds; ye Selinas, Evelinas, Malvinas: ye inas all adieu! The flames will consume you all. The melody of Emily, the prattle of Annette, and the hoarseness of Ugo, will all be confounded in one indiscriminate crackle. The Casa and Castello will blaze with equal fury; nor can the virtue of Pamela save you; nor Wolmar charmed to see his wife swooning; nor Werter shelling peas and reading Homer, nor Charlotte cutting bread and butter for the children.[26]

Barrett satirizes a tradition that begins with Richardson's *Pamela* in 1740, moves to Rousseau's *Nouvelle Héloïse* in 1760 and to Goethe's *Die Leiden des jungen Werthers (The Sorrows of Young Werther)* in 1774, and culminates, in this parodic account, with the works of Ann Radcliffe in the 1790s. But in the comic Cherubina's vision of heroism, as in this sentimental tradition, there is one end in view. The only way out of tragedy and suicide is to find novelistic closure and social enclosure within conventional heterosexual marriage, and thereby to establish a space within the dominant ideology of bourgeois domesticity.

Instead of affirming a social order that restricts them, as Spacks suggests, women writers subvert that order by employing its own tactics to undercut and ridicule it. In Burney's *Evelina*, the prize — marriage to an aristocratic and wealthy lord — may be conventional. But Evelina's social identity is secure because of that prize, and never for a moment does she forget the risks she runs if she refuses it, or the price she must pay to substitute true security for the fickle coin of coquetry.

Evelina is the story of how an individual denied her rightful access to power, money, title, family, and name manages to get all those things in the end without openly breaking any of the rules of decorum. As Catherine Macaulay wrote of the power of women in her *Letters on Education* in 1790: "Such is their use in the system of mundane creation, and such their natural influence over the male mind, that were these advantages properly exerted, they might carry every point of any importance to their honour and happiness."[27]

Evelina's comedy, akin to that of Burney's plays *The Witlings* and *Love and Fashion* in its dramatic choreography, introduces the themes and metaphors of violation Burney pursues in darker colors and more physical guise in her next three works of fiction. The comedy here comes from the heroine's (and her creator's) youthfully impetuous and sly inversion of powerlessness into power, as Evelina learns to manipulate social manners and fashion so that she gains the greatest possible control over her life without offending those who seek to "guide" her. She compares Lord Orville to Villars (in letters to the latter, be it noted) and her eventual husband indeed shares some of her guardian's dour tendencies, but he also consults her will and bows to her judgment of her own behavior on occasion, and it does not take a great leap of the imagination to conjure up an older, married Evelina consciously managing her pliable husband. Cecilia Beverley and Camilla Tyrold may have less success with their complicatedly arranged marriages, as they face more insidious dangers than does Evelina, but we can postulate that Burney's last heroine will achieve total control over the melodramatically persecuted Albert Harleigh.

Name, family, kinship, and public acknowledgment are all undertows that swirl recurrently in Burney's novels, and especially in *The Wanderer*, where a multinational French-English identity also appears as an ideological crux (Burney herself had a French grandmother named Dubois, and of course later a French husband and a long-term temporary residence in France). But the most powerful rhetorical experiment and thematic center in all the novels, most carefully integrated in *Evelina* and *Camilla*, is the heroine's silence when she is violated. Evelina's silence is never as radically threatening or as dangerous as Camilla's, but it is all-pervasive (in her own account) at key moments of danger. When with Lord Orville, Evelina is rendered totally or virtually speechless: "I hardly ventured to say a word all the time we were walking" (*Evelina*, 61). When with nastier companions, she stammers, or speaks in monosyllables, or is entirely mute, in a paralysis of language: "I was quite silent, having too much apprehension to make reproaches, and too much anger to speak without"

(99), she says of the breaches of propriety that stifle her with Willoughby. And she remains both "speechless" and "motionless" in her first encounter with her father (373). Evelina's ambiguous signatures, her speechlessness, her "I hardly know myself to whom I most belong!" (353), define both her unwillingness to reveal all to Villars and her entrapment by propriety. This circumstance appears in comic light in *Evelina*. In *Camilla*, silence reigns over the dark possibilities of madness.

4

Camilla: Silencing the Heroine

The harrowing climax of Burney's third novel, *Camilla,* renders a scene that embodies Burney's fierce and fiercely defensive attitude toward her own composing process. Camilla's nightmare confrontation with Death, examined at the beginning of chapter 1, dramatizes the insistent violence from which Burney's literary *oeuvre* derives: it serves as her most stunning fictional analysis of the nature of writing, both as a physical and imaginative activity and as a way to claim authority of perception. Camilla's visionary "writing" contains a paradigm for the vocal structure of female literature. Burney's heroines—and she herself in the conscious role of heroine in her letters and journals—prefer to remain silent. For Burney, the female voice speaks only when spoken to, its words always defensive, challenged, and challenging. This vocal structure inscribes itself in Burney's writing as the graphic expression of a continuous splitting between rebellion and uncontrollable imaginative necessity.

Camilla's dreamed confrontation with language made concrete yet effaced, menacingly alluded to, and always out of reach, completes the complicated matrix of speech and silence that Burney casts in

Camilla. Her heroine's problematic muteness dominates the nightmare episode. When she tries to pray, she utters "incoherent ejaculations"; she approaches the bleeding corpse of the novel's villain with "speechless apprehension" (*Camilla,* 874). Even as Camilla fights against the sharp, forked, chilling hand of Death on her breast, its hollow voice speaks to her, so that it seems as though her struggle itself activates the threatening words. In the dream, Camilla attempts in vain to silence her voice and her iron pen; yet when she recognizes Edgar Mandlebert, the sentimental hero, she is struck dumb, able only to "put forth her feeble hand" through the bed curtain in response to her lover's imploring "Camilla! Camilla! — your silence rends my soul!" (877).

Throughout the novel, Burney privileges moments in which a necessary communication fails and her protagonist confronts silences in the white space of an empty page. In particular, Burney repeats one paradigmatic sequence. A plot crux demands that Camilla compose a difficult, revelatory letter; she becomes paralyzed, fusses at her pen and toys with the blank paper, and crumples a series of false starts, finally abandoning the attempt. On one such occasion, Camilla "began twenty letters without proceeding in any one of them beyond two lines" (502), finally leaving the abortive epistles on the table with an explanatory note; a major plot upheaval occurs when an unintended addressee finds this collection of paper. Another such episode immediately precedes Camilla's nightmare. She composes and dispatches a letter to her parents that, it develops, will never be delivered. She then tries to write a letter for Edgar, but succeeds only in putting one incomplete sentence on the paper and adding "Not to be delivered till I am dead" (870). This scrap of paper falls unheeded to the floor — its inadvertent retrieval and delivery ultimately bring about the novel's resolution. In this way, *Camilla* is a tapestry woven of misdirected scraps of paper, misinterpreted half sentences, misapprehended gestures, unwritten and undelivered letters. Camilla either cannot write at all, her language paralyzed, or she produces a disordered writing that is more confusing than silence. For Burney and for her alter-ego creation, loss and salvation, embarrassment and forgiveness, all reside within the writing process.

Camilla is a better developed, more aesthetically sophisticated narrative than *Evelina,* and its more fluid situations continue to echo and elaborate the conditions for young women that had trapped Burney's first heroine. By her third novel, Burney was able more frankly to articulate the social ideology she critiqued, as she does, for example, in the letter Camilla receives from her father in which he raises (though does not advocate) "the equity of that freedom by which women as well as men should be allowed to dispose of their own affections" (358). Far more independent and experienced and far better educated for the world she encounters than was Evelina, Camilla still wears the shackles of social rules. Nevertheless, Burney, herself older now and more mature as a novelist, advocates defiance far more clearly in *Camilla.* Her heroine's chief tormentor here, ironically, is the hero-lover who is so seduced by the world's outward forms and courtesies that he becomes an officious, judgmental authoritarian who, like Miss Bydel in *The Wanderer,* believes the world's gossip, reads surface appearances without sounding depths, fails to check his sources or his interpretations, and ultimately imprisons himself in his own "punctilio" and fussy gallantry.

In *Camilla,* Burney goes far beyond the witty, though sharp, critique of manners presented in *Evelina.* Using many of the same materials as had made up the earlier work—public assembly scenes and stock characters such as the fop, the powerful society lady who flouts social convention, the meddling, irritable governess, and the pedant—Burney creates a complex psychological novel in *Camilla* as well as a critique of social ideology. As *Evelina* had measured the abstract and sometimes dangerous arbitrariness of social rules and their tyranny for women, so *Camilla* measures the impact of the world *Evelina* had charted on individual human beings. Camilla Tyrold, unlike Evelina "Anville," enters the world with the conventional social cards (birth, beauty, intellect, charm, education, family, talent) all stacked in her favor. But precisely that situation and her youthful "free spirit" make her an ideal candidate to test against the stifling requirements of eighteenth-century social forms and ideologies.

The canvas of *Camilla* in some ways is smaller than that of the other three novels, and more like Jane Austen's concentration on "3 or 4 families in a country village" in its focus on the Tyrold family in Hampshire. But *Camilla* attempts far more than *Evelina* in its expansive plot, its "Udolphish" mass and inclusion of elements of Gothic terror, and its transformation of the heroine's key attractions from innocent forthrightness into playfulness, energy, and "dawning archness of expression" (13) and of the hero's from exemplary "parfit gentil homme" manners to watchful, fretful distrust. Indeed, *Camilla* begins where *Evelina* stops: its heroine already knows the rules and has a relatively comfortable social situation. "The reigning and radical defect of her character," Burney's narrator says of Camilla, is "an imagination that submitted to no control" (84). While Evelina learns to manipulate the control she submits to with a rhetorical facility that allows her to disarm authority, Camilla, initially less aware of the precariousness of

female selfhood in relation to the systematic degradation wrought by
social rules, gives her imagination free play and looks to her friend
Mrs. Arlbery, who possessed "wit . . . at will, . . . a raillery so arch,
a spirit of satire so seasoned with a delight in coquetry" (89) and "a
perfect indifference to what opinion she incurred in return" (78), as
a model for independent womanhood. As Mrs. Arlbery is a Mrs. Selwyn with added beauty and panache, Camilla is an already experienced and fashionably trained Evelina who expects no treachery.

Camilla establishes its plot base early: through Sir Hugh Tyrold's
well-meaning carelessness with his niece, Camilla's sister Eugenia both
contracts smallpox and suffers a fall that deforms her shoulder and
makes one of her legs shorter than the other. To compensate the previously beautiful Eugenia for these permanent physical defects and
to assuage his own inconsolable guilt, Sir Hugh makes her his sole
heir, thereby disinheriting his other nieces and nephews. As a consequence, Eugenia becomes a target for fortune hunters who pretend
not to notice her scarred face and deformed body. At the same time,
the Tyrolds' hopes to marry Camilla to their neighbor Edgar Mandlebert undergo misunderstandings, complications, and setbacks. The
twin romantic dilemmas of Eugenia and Camilla establish the novel's
thematic and metaphorical structure in relation to the question of valid
interpretation: appearance challenges and belies truth (quite literally
in Eugenia's case), and behavior must be read and analyzed.

Camilla's initial romantic conflicts establish the crises of language
and gesture that most of the work explores. Mandlebert's tutor Marchmont counsels him to "study her" (159) until he is thoroughly convinced
of her worth before proposing marriage to Camilla:

> Whatever she does, you must ask yourself this question: "Should I like
> such behaviour in my wife?" Whatever she says, you must make your-
> self the same demand. Nothing must escape you; you must view her
> as if you had never seen her before; the interrogatory, Were she mine?
> must be present at every look, every word, every motion; you must
> forget her wholly as Camilla Tyrold, you must think of her only as
> Camilla Mandlebert; even justice is insufficient during this period of
> probation, and instead of inquiring, "Is this right in her?" you must
> simply ask, "Would it be pleasing to me?" (159–60)

Already possessing judgmental and priggish tendencies (Joyce Hemlow calls Mandlebert one of the two greatest prigs in English literature, the other in her view being Coelebs in Hannah More's 1809 didactic novel, *Coelebs in Search of a Wife*),[1] Mandlebert now becomes

a positive Cerberus at this instruction, even though he recognizes in Dr. Marchmont a classic misogynist ("I know you think ill of women" [161], he says to him). Mandlebert is exhorted to be more than minutely observant of Camilla's "value"; he is advised that "to be even scrupulous is not enough; to avoid all danger of repentance, you must become positively distrustful" (160). That distrust creates the centerpiece of the novel's conflict and, no great wonder, ultimately causes Camilla to go temporarily mad.

Burney explores in this novel the interplay of social expectations, discretion, privacy, embarrassment, and human communication. This is not the story of a courtship, though it incorporates its last phases of dawning realization. But making no declaration to each other, each lover remains ignorant of the other's regard and silent in their private encounters. Thus, *Camilla* tells the story of love postponed, thwarted, frustrated, misled, and deliberately unspoken and even disguised. Marchmont's cautions engender Mandlebert's suspicion; open treachery at first, then Mandlebert's suspicion itself, create Camilla's distance.

Whenever the Tyrold women appear in public — from the smallpox-ridden Northwick fair during their childhood to Mrs. Arlbery's public breakfasts — they encounter misconstruction and social danger. In *Evelina,* this danger is clear-cut and the heroine is aware of it as it happens. In *Camilla,* the conclusions drawn from public observation remain unspoken and fester, although the characters take scrupulous care to avoid "misapprehension." Flowers presented to Camilla are thought to signify her willful seduction of Edgar; because these flowers are extorted by her cousin Indiana and worn by her in public, Edgar believes Camilla to have disdained his gift. This kind of confused and miscoded information controls the novel's plot. Financial crises also fuel a plot in which, in fact, none of the principals lacks substantial assets; this paradox represents another of the novel's set of metaphors for mismanaged and misinterpreted communications. Camilla's world is one in which all meaning is fluid, all signs ambiguous, all apparently definitive readings open to revaluation.

A powerful paradox in *Camilla* derives from its insertion of a central voice of moral authority, the voice of Camilla's father, into the novel's world of moral erosion. Unlike the harsh and finally self-defeating Marchmont, Mr. Tyrold takes account of the deformation of women required by established social conventions even as he embodies the received conduct doctrines of the age. The "little sermon upon the difficulties and the conduct of the female heart" (353) that he composes for his daughter — a set piece that was extracted from the novel and widely anthologized — epitomizes the institutionalized discourse of authority against which Burney writes. Indeed, Burney's efforts to write against such discourse provide the novel with much of its tension, and prompt one critic to argue that "*Camilla* reads like a response to [Mary Wollstonecraft's A] *Vindication [of the Rights of Woman].*"[2]

Sermonizing and its tyrannies figure prominently in the rhetoric of *Camilla.* Mandlebert preaches to Camilla throughout, offering himself as her "monitor" and moral guide and most happy with her when he finds himself "enchanted that he was authorized, once more, to inform himself with openness of the state of her affairs, and of her conduct" (437). Frequently described as "austere" and "vigilant," Mandlebert has inherited the principled rigidity of his two guardians, both of whom are professional clergymen renowned for their sermons, but has not leavened that rigidity with much compassion or grace. But the centerpiece sermon of Augustus Tyrold, Camilla's father and the rector of Etherington, comes precisely at the novel's midpoint. When he writes this letter of advice and admonition, Tyrold believes his daughter to be unrequitedly in love with Mandlebert, believes Mandlebert to have no matrimonial intentions toward her, and believes Camilla's emotional openness to expose her potentially to public censure. He composes a sermon for her, therefore, and tells her to "read it alone, and with attention" (353).

Tyrold's sermon became the best-known section of *Camilla* when it was published and, like the Savoyard vicar's profession of faith in Rousseau's *Emile* before it, was excerpted and reprinted separately. With some abridgments, it appeared in an anthology that went through five printings between 1809 and 1816 and included one of the eighteenth century's most popular conduct treatises: *A Father's Legacy to his Daughters* by John Gregory (1774).[3] Augustus Tyrold's letter repays careful attention: it encodes in the father's discourse the ethos of a society that entraps Burney's women (and some of her men) with its rules not so much about conduct itself, but about the public interpretations of conduct. This kind of moral education from the father figures similarly in Ann Radcliffe's 1794 *Mysteries of Udolpho,* a novel Burney may have had in mind as she composed sections of her "Udolphish" *Camilla.* Radcliffe's heroine Emily St. Aubert receives her instructions at the outset of the action:

> St. Aubert had too much good sense to prefer a charm to a virtue; and had penetration enough to see, that [Emily's] charm was too dangerous to its possessor to be allowed the character of a blessing. He endeavoured, therefore, to strengthen her mind; to enure her to habits

of self-command; to teach her to reject the first impulse of her feelings, and to look, with cool examination, upon the disappointments he sometimes threw in her way. . . . He instructed her to resist first impressions, and to acquire that steady dignity of mind, that can alone counterbalance the passions.[4]

Traits that make young women "interesting objects" also endanger them; the more charming the woman, the more danger she is in. Situated at the center of *Camilla,* Tyrold's sermon might be taken, as editors Edward A. Bloom and Lillian D. Bloom conclude, as "the moralistic essence of the novel, setting forth an ideal of ethical conduct."[5] It is certainly the essence of established social ideology in relation to women. But it is not only a moralistic distillation of received wisdom; it represents, both literally and structurally, the language of the patriarch that Camilla must learn to translate, to speak herself, and, finally, to erase. It is the rule book and conduct manual Evelina had lacked; having it, however, Camilla is no better prepared than was her predecessor to navigate through the world. She knows now what she has to resist. Evelina remained for a time ignorant of her own powerlessness; Camilla's father asks his daughter not merely to acknowledge her powerlessness but to seek "an accommodation to circumstances" (355) and to embrace it as "[t]he temporal destiny of woman" in her "doubly appendant state" (356).

Tyrold begins by posing a problem in order to absolve himself. A woman's parents, he writes, must educate her for her eventual husband, but not foreseeing who that husband might be to whom ownership of the daughter will pass, parents are without guidelines until "the station to which she [the daughter] shall belong" manifests itself. Unless the father can ordain an arranged marriage (as his brother Sir Hugh tries in vain to do for both Indiana and Eugenia), "the proper education of a female, either for use or for happiness, is still to seek, still a problem beyond human solution; since its refinement, or its negligence, can only prove to her a good or an evil, according to the humour of the husband into whose hands she may fall" (359). That sentence obliterates the "fallen" female: her education has no intrinsic value, no relation to her. Its pragmatic value depends upon her husband, according to his "humour," and "use" or "happiness" are terms a woman may carry to her husband as a fringe benefit in her role as wife. "A problem beyond human solution"? Beyond the father's solution, anyway.

The point, for Tyrold, is that whatever her education, a woman must remain "ductile to new sentiments and employments" so that she will submit to rather than resist the station (and the man) that offers her a place in society. Therefore, Augustus Tyrold writes to Camilla, "You have been brought up, my dear child, without any specific expectation" because of "the uncertainty of the female fate." The Tyrolds, he writes, attempted to inculcate three primary values in their daughters: simplicity, docility, and accommodation. Their lot unspecified and unspecifiable while they are growing up female, they must be trained for any eventuality, "to fit you for the world as you may find it." Women are not agents in their own lives. Camilla's predisposition for Mandlebert, apparently unreturned at the letter's writing, demonstrates her to be yearning for that agency, to desire not the world as she finds it but a world that she might participate in shaping. She must combat that desire, her father tells her, and the combat will require hard work ("It is now, Camilla, we must demand your exertions in return" [357]) to recompense her parents for their efforts during her "days of unconsciousness" (360).

Unlike Villars of *Evelina* and Marchmont, Tyrold is a good man who will suffer for his misjudgments and his daughter's desires. He raises here but then evades the question fundamental to Burney's enterprise as a novelist: "We will not here canvass the equity of that freedom by which women as well as men should be allowed to dispose of their own affections." "There cannot, in nature, in theory, nor even in common sense," he admits, "be a doubt of their equal right: but disquisitions on this point will remain rather curious than important, till the speculatist can superinduce to the abstract truth of the position some proof of its practicability" (358). This unnamed "speculatist" against whom Tyrold defends himself even before an attack might also argue that, had Camilla at any point fully unburdened herself to Mandlebert, the novel would not have needed to be written, as a marriage would have taken place before Burney could have filled even one hundred pages. The "speculatist," indeed, might be Camilla, or Burney, herself.

In fact, Burney's novels protest against the conflicts and unnecessary complications that arise because, as Tyrold puts it, "where there are two parties, choice can belong only to one of them" (358) and choice resides with men. Burney no doubt remembered here her own youthful efforts to reject the unwanted 1775 suit of Thomas Barlow.[6] Lacking choice, women must use subterfuge and coquetry, and Mrs. Arlbery's advice to Camilla to bait Mandlebert with her attention to other men and her apparent negligence of him counterpoints Tyrold's advice. Both counsel disguise; both counsel silence; both counsel struggle against inclination; both counsel amusement and diversion. But their underlying philosophies reflect mirror images of each other. Tyrold's precepts ("Delicacy is an attribute so peculiarly feminine, that were your reflections less agitated by your feelings, you could delineate more distinctly than myself its appropriate laws, its minute exactions, its sensitive refinements" [359–60]) become weapons of female empowerment in Mrs. Arlbery's discourse. As Tyrold himself points out, women are better than men at designating the borders and laws of appropriate female attributes.

Tyrold's fundamental goal in this sermon is to plead the virtues of discretion and silence: "What you would rather perish than utter," he argues, "can never, since untold, be suspected" (360). Camilla must willingly face, even seek, the "scrutiny" of others as she would face "the all-viewing eye of our Creator" (361). She must avoid "imprudence" and "indulgence" and embrace "modest propriety" (362). But discretion in this case, Tyrold knows, means concealment. He fears that Camilla's talents as an actress will be no better than those of the company that so execrably performs *Othello* in *Camilla*'s masterful comic sequence, a troupe of actors unable to shed their native dialects, clothing, gestures, and personalities. Bad acting will not do. "Discriminate, nevertheless," the sermon dictates, "between hypocrisy and discretion. The first is a vice; the second is a conciliation to virtue" (61). But not speaking is only one mode of silence — the self-censorship that silences gossip and "publication" — and Tyrold's advice about "acting" to disguise other discourses of revelation might well serve as this novel's epigraph: "There are so many ways of communication independent of speech, that silence is but one point in the ordinances of discretion" (360).

As it turns out, Augustus Tyrold need not have worried about his middle daughter's capacity to remain silent. "Speech and truth were always one with Camilla," the narrator informs us when her father questions her about her dejection, "who, as she could not in this instance declare what were her feelings, remained mute and confounded" (343). Evelina, similarly questioned by Villars, took refuge in letters to her friend Maria, and minded less the rhetorical gestures that implicate absolute truth. Camilla's sister Eugenia, who retreats from her childhood accident and illness by burying herself in the study of Greek and Latin, uses language to replace appearance. For Camilla, in contrast, the necessity for public revelation stuns her into muteness, as occurs in the nightmare scene that climaxes the novel. Another scene, however, prepares for that mute nightmare of the iron pen, a scene that also involves Camilla's inability to wield a pen that is thrust into her hands. Tyrold's sermon leads to the Tunbridge Wells mid-portion of *Camilla;* its ending concerns an unfinished episode of forced writing whose convolutions lead to one of the work's central misunderstandings.

Desperately in debt and demanding that she ask her uncle Sir Hugh Tyrold for money on her own behalf, Camilla's brother Lionel puts a pen into his sister's hand: "Camilla sighed, but let him put the pen into her hand, whence, however, the very next moment's reflection was urging her to cast it down" (501). Not an iron pen, this time, merely a normal quill: this is a waking nightmare. Left alone to compose the letter she has promised to send to her uncle, she does not know how to begin: "How represent what she herself so little understood as the necessity of Lionel? or how ask for so large a sum, and postpone, as he desired, all explanation?" Her father had warned her to distinguish carefully between her private and her public selves, and to merge the two into the public, yet now she is stymied by the bond of her promise to dissemble: "She was incapable of any species of fraud, she detested even the most distant disguise" (501). Even when she decides simply to ask straightforwardly, "she began twenty letters without proceeding in any one of them beyond two lines." Finally, she pushes herself away from the writing table in disgust, "determined not to write another word," but returns when she remembers her brother's threats of evil to the family should he fail to procure two hundred pounds. She decides in the end to tell Lionel she cannot write, but she fears his response, and decides to make her refusal in writing: "After considering in a thousand ways how to soften to him her recantation, she found herself so entirely without courage to encounter his opposition, that she resolved to write him a short letter, and then retire to her own room, to avoid an interview" (502).

Interrupted by someone at the door, Camilla does not complete this letter to Lionel, but "leav[es] her unfinished letter, with the beginnings of her several essays to address Sir Hugh, upon the table, to shew her various efforts, and to explain that they were relinquished" (503). The bell-ringer is Sir Sedley Clarendel, who, finding and reading the documents himself, tucks them into a blank cover along with a note to Camilla and a bank draft for the requested sum. When Lionel returns, she refuses his offered pen to write again and, finding Clarendel's draft, he refuses to relinquish it, thus indebting Camilla improperly to a foppish suitor. Worse, Lionel teases her about Clarendel's attachment and later writes a "sportive rhapsody" of a letter to thank her and addresses it to "my dear Lady Clarendel" (512). As both Mrs. Arlbery and Clarendel himself see this letter, Camilla's efforts to rectify matters prove fruitless. Mandlebert absconds before she can request a loan from him, her father's ward and thus a legitimate banker for her, and when she proposes to write to Clarendel to offer an explanation, Mrs. Arlbery points out the irony:

> "Ay, write by all means; there is nothing so prettily forwards these affairs, as a correspondence between the parties undertaken to put an end to them."
> She went, laughing, out of the chamber, and Camilla, who had seized a pen, distressfully flung it from her. (516)

She will not firmly grasp and tame "the pen" until she emerges from her nightmare. During the preceeding nine hundred pages, she picks it up only to put it down again, or begins but cannot finish her compositions, or refuses its proffered nib altogether.

The unfinished collections of letters to Sir Hugh on Lionel's behalf fail because they are instigated from outside rather than from within. Later, as Camilla's own situation becomes more and more compromised and as Mandlebert's relentless watchfulness tears at her reserve, Camilla repeats that crucial act of not writing again and again. Burdened by debts and guilt, Camilla leaves home for London, determined "to reveal the whole by letter" (791) to her father. But when she starts to "ruminate upon her purposed letter," she wavers. She cannot reveal all, first, without implicating and thereby betraying her brother. Yet if she omits Lionel's role, there is no way to explain the chain of events that has culminated in her own debts. To explain the ball dress at Southampton, she would have to confess to her flirtatious machinations to win back the offended Mandlebert and admit that she had been duped by a person as silly and transparently fraudulent as the social hanger-on Mrs. Mittin. Camilla's service to the poor is the only element she is willing to confess without shame. That creates a problem when she sits down to compose this letter and thus to exonerate herself: "Vainly she took up her pen; not even a line could she write" (794). The letter remains unwritten. Shortly thereafter, the adventurer Bellamy, a diabolical character whose very name ("bel-ami") ironically contrasts with his malevolence, abducts Eugenia and Camilla is forced to write, but can produce on that occasion only a brief note "in scrawling and distinct characters":

> O my Father—our Eugenia has disappeared! she was lost last night at the Opera—Mr. Bellamy was conducting her to Mrs. Berlinton's coach—but we have seen neither of them since!—What—what must we do? (799)

This stammered note is addressed by someone else, because "Camilla's hand could not make the address legible" (799). The legibility of the letter itself is also called into question: it telegraphs rather than narrates Eugenia's, and Camilla's, entrapped predicament.

Camilla also begins to have difficulty reading in addition to her writing problems. Her sister Lavinia's letter telling her not to return home when her debts have ruined the family, delivered two days late (postal services and private delivery systems break down repeatedly in *Camilla*), is read by Camilla "with a distraction that made it wholly unintelligible to her; yet [she] could not read it a second time; her eyes become dim, her faculties confused, and she rather felt deprived of the power of thinking, than filled with any new and dreadful subjects for rumination," and the letter falls to the floor as Camilla stares vacantly around her (519). When she is urged to write a note to her father in prison, "Camilla could not write: to kneel, to weep, to see, was all she could bear to plan; to present to him the sight of her hand writing she had not courage" (828), as though the mark of her hand, the utterance of her pen, could betray her. She writes only an "incoherent" letter to Lavinia "upon the distraction of her mind" (833). When she does write, delivery both of her letters and of responses to them presents insurmountable difficulties. The final crisis that precipitates Camilla's madness comes when a letter she believes (incorrectly) to have been delivered elicits no response: "Unused to transact any sort of business for herself, she had expected, in sending a letter, an answer as a thing of course" (865).

Camilla counts on the conventions of communication throughout this novel, and those conventions continually betray her. Letters represent contact; time passes at the inn yet "produces no loved presence, no letter, no summons" (866). She tries to write an explanatory and contrite account of her history to her mother "and rising, took up a pen to relate the whole transaction. But her head was confused, and the attempt shewed her she was more ill than she had ever herself suspected" (867). She grasps the pen a second time, but even before it touches paper the arrival of Bellamy's funeral procession interrupts her. Finally, Camilla manages two missives, a farewell to her family written "with infinite difficulty . . . every bending down of her head making it ache nearly to distraction" (869) and "one poor word" to Mandlebert:

> She again took her pen, but had only written "O Edgar! in this last farewell be all displeasure forgotten! — from the first to the final moment of my short life, dear and sole possessor of my heart!" — when

the shooting anguish of her head stopt her hand, and hastily writing the direction, lest she could write no more, she with difficulty added, *"Not to be delivered till I am dead;"* and was forced to lie down, and shut all light from her strained and aching eyes. (870)

The sign to her that she is dying comes when she realizes that she cannot read the prayer book she has requested: "Her eyes, heavy, aching, and dim, glared upon the paper, without distinguishing the print from the margin" (873). Edgar's letter, too, eludes her. When she attempts to read it, "the characters seemed double to her weak and dazzled eyes" (878). Writing and not writing, the print and the white space, speech and silence come together in Camilla's final nightmare, a dream sequence already examined as paradigmatic of Burney's approach to writing. In the dream, she initially refuses to write when asked, then loses control of her hand, grabs the "pen of iron" and writes "guilty characters"—letters that become embedded in the page as though stamped there by a branding iron. As she continues to write against her will, the pen suddenly ceases to mark the page, and she is left with a blank paper. She awakens just as voices demand that she read and the volume before her explodes.

Letters, words, sentences—the component parts of a written object—are fully transparent in Camilla's nightmare, first as sulfuric, biblical illuminations, and then as the radical transparency of empty space and blankness, the physical representation of Camilla's inability throughout the novel to speak or write clearly. Earlier, I suggested that this paradigmatic dream demonstrates Burney's own problematically ambivalent stance as a professional writer as well as her sense that writing—that act that requires an iron implement—might undermine her femininity, or at least the world's judgment of her as a woman. Camilla's familiar letter writing occurs only in moments of pecuniary crisis, to explain or arrange debts, and comes to represent for the heroine a metonymic version of herself as an amalgam of her expenditures, a marriage of vanity (the squandered money on baubles and fashions) and charity (the donations to the stricken poor). Both her parents and Mandlebert "read" Camilla's debts as signs of her value to them and theirs to her. But money in *Camilla* refuses to talk. While Camilla envisions a compensatory, exculpating composition to clear her name, ultimately, when she can confront the misreadings of the text of her world directly and offer a corrective, she becomes silent.

Burney's narrator describes Camilla as lively, vivacious, heedless, and open. But that portrait suggests a character capable of rebellion, and when Camilla feels most inclined to rebel, her muteness most overtakes her language. When Mandlebert criticizes a proposed visit to Mrs. Arlbery, a visit Camilla is keen to make, she is too torn to respond. "You will not speak? yet you do not deny that you have some uneasiness?" Edgar asks. "Ask nothing! suggest nothing! and think of it no more!" Camilla replies, stopping suddenly in the middle of a sentence with unspoken words "quivering on her lips, and leaving her sentence unfinished, abruptly walked away" (172). In wonderful contrast to Camilla's muteness when she cannot be straightforward is Sir Hugh's delightful double talk. On the subject of some starving beggars who have been convicted of stealing meat, he says:

> My little girl has been telling me all their history; and, God forbid, I should turn hard-hearted, because of their wanting a leg of mutton, in preference to being starved; though they might have no great right to it, according to the forms of law; which, however, is not much impediment to the calls of nature, when a man sees a butcher's stall well covered, and has got nothing within him, except his own poor craving appetite; which is a thing I always take into consideration; though, God forbid, I should protect a thief, no man's property being another's, whether he's poor or rich. (109)

Sir Hugh says all things at once, pleasing everyone and using language that slips and slides so that in saying all things, he has implicitly agreed with nothing: a consummate politician's tongue in a nonpartisan head. Camilla, however, has no facility with slippery diction; if she cannot speak out clearly, she stammers and remains silent. Eugenia and Mrs. Tyrold provide another kind of contrast — they mince no words. To her wayward daughter at the novel's conciliatory denouement, Mrs. Tyrold comes right to the point: "If Edgar has merited well of you, why are you parted? — If ill — why this solicitude my opinion of him should be unspoken?" And when Camilla hesitates in response: "Speak out, then, and speak clearer, my dearest Camilla. If you think of him so well, and are so sure of his good intentions, what — in two words, — what is it that has parted you?" (895). In two words: Mrs. Tyrold demands that Camilla recapitulate what has taken Burney nine hundred pages to recount. Eugenia, too, communicates lucidly and in simple declarative sentences. "Have you heard, my dear sister," she asks Camilla, for example, "that Clermont has refused me?" (630). Camilla, however, has not inherited her kinfolks' way with words.

Adjectives concerning silence and speech are used repeatedly to describe Camilla and Edgar Mandlebert. The heroine hangs her head "in speechless perturbation" (176); she is "in dismay unspeakable" at Lionel (525); Edgar's questions leave her "enchanted, affrighted, bewildered, yet silent" (539); she looks at Edgar "in speechless wonder" when he first declares his love (577) and when he sees Camilla next maintains a "mute distance" (616); when he breaks off their engagement, "he was mute" and Camilla "would not give him time to speak" (641); when he tries to approach her later, "his tongue became parched" (685); Camilla is unable to explain Edgar's departure to her father, telling him "in a voice scarce audible" that he should hear it from Eugenia (753); learning of her father's bankruptcy, Camilla "spoke not, heard not" (820) and reveals her incipient madness with "words of alarming incoherency" (824) at her father's imprisonment; unable to order a carriage, she "found herself deprived of the power of utterance, and looked a picture of speechless dismay" (825); at Winchester, she is "scarcely able to articulate her words" (829); she approaches Eugenia "in a speechless transport of sorrow" (840) but remains "beyond speech" (841); the corpse of Bellamy renders Camilla "nearly stiff with horrour, chilled, froze, with speechless apprehension" just before her nightmare (874); she is unable to speak when Edgar appears at the inn, until he cries "Camilla! Camilla! — your silence rends my soul" (877) and she takes his letter with "unspeakable amazement" (878); her mother's arrival leaves her "speechless, immovable" (881); at their reconciliation, Edgar asks Mrs. Tyrold to "plead for me where I dare not speak" (896). Only when Camilla is able to give Edgar a complete "ingenuous narration" (902) that serves retroactively to exonerate her are the lovers able to offer each other "a reciprocal confidence that left nothing untold, not an action unrelated, not even a thought unacknowledged" (901). Evelina, too, becomes occasionally mute in moments of crisis, but her silences pass quickly. The whole plot of *Camilla* rests on mutually misinterpreted silences. As Camilla summarizes for her mother, the lovers' separation derives from "accident, . . . deluding appearance, . . . and false internal reasoning on my part, — and on his, continual misconstruction!" (896).

Two of the abortive interviews between Camilla and Edgar Mandlebert deserve close attention. The first of these occurs after the crucial quay scene in Southampton, when Mandlebert escorts Camilla from the bathing house on the quay where she has been accused of shoplifting and trapped by strange men. In this scene, the townspeople place wagers on Camilla's honesty in a fashion reminiscent of the social wagering that surrounds the infamous footrace in *Evelina,* and importunate strangers imprison Camilla in this space of leisure and undress as Evelina had been imprisoned in the pleasure gardens. Mandlebert walks Camilla away from this humiliating scene:

> Edgar and Camilla continued their walk in a silence painful to both, but which neither knew how first to break; each wished with earnestness an opening to communication and confidence; but, mutually shocked by the recent adventure, Edgar waited the absence of Mrs. Mittin, to point out the impropriety and insufficiency of such a guard; and Camilla, still aghast with terror, had no power of any sort to begin a discourse. (616)

Mrs. Mittin, in contrast, talks incessantly to cover their silence (as frequently does Sir Hugh), though when she departs Camilla, instead of confronting Mandlebert with her intended announcement that he can have his liberty, only "stammered something upon every other subject, to keep that off" (617). Finally, she begins: "'I have something,' she cried, 'to say, . . .' but her voice became so husky, the inarticulate sounds died away unheard, and blushing at so feeble an opening, she strove, under the auspices of a cough, to disguise that she had spoken at all, for the purposes of beginning, in a more striking manner, again" (619). Eventually, she is able to ask him about Clarendel's letters, but their discussion does nothing to clear up Mandlebert's misreading of that correspondence. And as Mrs. Mittin had impeded their conversation at first, then interrupted it later, they are ultimately interrupted first by the delivery of a letter from Mrs. Berlinton to Camilla and then by a footman requiring an answer. As Mandlebert is beginning to speak conciliatorily, the servant enters "and the interruption was critical: it called him to his self-command: he stammered out that he would not impede her writing; and, though in palpable confusion, took his leave" (621). He has dropped hints that he still cares for Camilla, but no resolution emerges from this interview in which six pages of half-finished sentences, unspoken hopes and fears, and surprised facial expressions must bear the entire communication burden.

The second abortive interview takes place at the conclusion of the egocentric Lord Pervil's birthday yacht party, after Mandlebert has surprised Lord Valhurst proposing to Camilla and the two interpret that encounter in diametrically opposed ways. Camilla believes her refusal will prove her loyalty to Mandlebert; he assumes it shows that she has become a consummate dissipated coquette and decides to take permanent leave of her for a tour of the Continent:

> Is this, thought he, Camilla? Has she wilfully fascinated this old man seriously to win him, and has she won him but to triumph in the van-

ity of her conquest? How is her delicacy perverted? what is become
of her sensibility? Is this the artless Camilla? modest as she was gay,
docile as she was spirited, gentle as she was intelligent? O how spoilt!
how altered! how gone! (705)

Mandlebert requests a meeting before he departs, and opens it with
a long speech about the dissipations of Mrs. Berlinton and the haz-
ards for Camilla of her gaming and company—when given the chance,
Mandlebert always plays his chosen role of Camilla's moral monitor.
But again he begins to stutter at the end of his speech, and abandons
his final repetitive sentence unfinished: "All that, now, I mean to enter
upon, all that, now, I wish to enforce, a few words will comprise, and
these words will be my—."

Camilla does not speak in this "conversation," though her silence
does not prevent Mandlebert from interpreting her response:

He would have said my last but his breath failed him; he stopt; he
wanted her to seize his meaning unpronounced; and, though it came
to her as a thunderbolt from heaven, its very horror helped her; she
divined what he could not utter, by feeling what she could not hear.
(708)

After Mandlebert finds his voice again to speak of parting, Camilla
again fails to answer him:

Camilla turned aside from him; but not to weep; her spirit was now
re-wakened by resentment, that he could thus propose a separation,
without enquiring if she persisted to desire it. (709)

As he continues, relentlessly yet with less and less conviction, he begins a second time to truncate his sentences before he finishes them,
and to end them on a rising interrogative intonation that invites contradiction and request. Just when it appears, however, that the lovers
might haltingly arrive at an understanding, they are again interrupted:

His struggle here grew vain; his voice faltered; the resentment of Camilla forsook her; she raised her head, and was turning to him her
softened countenance, and filling eyes, when she saw Melmond, and
a party of gentlemen, fast approaching her from Mrs. Berlinton. Edgar
saw them too, and cutting short all he meant to have added, kissed,
without knowing what he did, the lace of her cloak, and ejaculating,
"Be Heaven your guard, and happiness your portion!" left her hand
to that of Melmond, which was held out to her, and slightly bowing

to the whole party walked slowly, and frequently looking back, away:
while Camilla, nearly blinded now by tears that would no longer be
retained, kept her eyes finally upon the earth, and was drawn more
dead than alive, by Melmond to the coach. (709)

Mandlebert leaves the country after this "interview"; during it, Camilla does not utter one word.

Other, more voluble characters serve as foils to Camilla's silence.
Mrs. Mittin and Sir Hugh talk incessantly, the former in order to
curry favor and defraud, the latter in order not to offend. Indiana's
governess, Miss Margland, also a talker when rhetorical manipulation can work to her advantage, as when she accuses Camilla of wrong-
ing Indiana, has other vocal talents as well, notably "a most capital
feminine accomplishment, screaming" (667). Camilla's cousin Clermont Lynmere castigates his uncle for his fluid tongue, saying, in the
affected style of the *ton*, "You descant too much upon words, sir; we
have left off, now, using them with such prodigious precision. It's quite
over, sir" (601). Tyrold's sermon, after all, had enjoined Camilla to
silence, echoing conduct book injunctions, and ordering Camilla not
only to refrain from speech, but to avoid as well other modes of in-
teraction that can be misinterpreted. Something always stays Camilla's
tongue. Language is forever confounded, stunned, or forced underground in *Camilla*.

The shift from Evelina's knowing manipulations of language to
Camilla's choking on words has to do in part with the radically differing narrative strategies and narrating voices in the epistolary *Evelina*
and the indirectly told *Camilla*. While not writing, not speaking, and
misinterpreting are arguably the central activities in *Camilla*, *Evelina*'s
energy grows out of the impulse to recreate experience by writing it
down. As we saw Burney herself changing her own letters and journals with retrospective and even retroactive self-control, so Evelina
renews her education as she translates it for her guardian, reenacting
it in a version that will win his approbation. Camilla, in contrast, rarely
speaks for herself even in dialogue, though Burney was one of the first
writers to experiment with *style indirect libre*, a mimicking entry into
the consciousness of her characters in order to record their thoughts.[7]

This mind-reading quality of *Camilla* subtly erases the choreographic
and authorial presence of the novel's narrator and seduces readers
into a belief that no single character in the work knows as fully as
they the particularities of mind and interpretation around the axis
of which the plot turns. This form of authorial mind reading, when
coupled with the self-effacement of the author/narrator, plunges the

reader into the character's own uncertainties. We must test Camilla along with Mandlebert; we must resent that testing along with Camilla.

Evelina's separate letters lend to Burney's first novel an episodic quality. Each adventure resolves back into the smooth, finished text of Evelina's correspondence with Villars. *Camilla* exfoliates at a more leisurely pace and its indirect style renders it more fluid and more unified than the earlier novel. Burney's narrator pontificates briefly in *Camilla*'s opening paragraph and again in the novel's final sentence ("What, at last, is so diversified as man? what so little to be judged by his fellow?" [913]), but in between the reader sees this Hampshire world shiftingly, but always through the eyes of one or another of its denizens. Here, for example, is an early description of Camilla's charms for Sir Hugh Tyrold:

> The sprightly little girl, thus possessed of the heart, soon guided the will of her uncle. He could refuse nothing to her endearing entreaty, and felt every indulgence repaid by the enchantment of her gaiety. Indiana, his first idol, lost her power to please him, though no essential kindness was abated in his conduct. He still acknowledged that her beauty was the most complete; but he found in Camilla a variety that was captivation. Her form and her mind were of equal elasticity. Her playful countenance rekindled his spirits, the cheerfulness of her animated voice awakened him to its own joy. He doated upon detaining her by his side, delighted to gratify her if she wished to be absent. She exhilarated him with pleasure, she supplied him with ideas, and from the morning's first dawn to the evening's latest close, his eye followed her light springing figure, or his ear vibrated with her sportive sounds; catching, as it listened, in successive rotation, the spontaneous laugh, the unconscious bound, the genuine glee of childhood's fearless happiness, uncurbed by severity, untamed by misfortune. (15)

A compound point of view emerges here, requiring that we ask whose voice speaks in order to understand Camilla's childhood portrait. Who privileges the sprightly, elastic, gay, sportive, playful, spontaneous, unconscious, uncurbed, and untamed qualities of this girl whose strong will leads her to need rescue from terror, abandonment, tragedy, and madness? Not the girl herself, whose very unconsciousness in this passage precludes its derivation from her own angle of vision. Instead, Burney combines Sir Hugh's voice ("He could refuse nothing to her endearing entreaty") with a narrative persona that emerges clearly only in the final phrases of foreshadow ("uncurbed by severity, untamed by misfortune").

Sir Hugh Tyrold, the perpetrator of Eugenia's troubles, has a good heart and is loved by all, but otherwise is not kindly treated in Burney's portrait. His naïveté, suffered by the family because of his affectionate nature and good intentions, is not so well tolerated by the narrative persona. Even apparently benign naïveté courts danger and causes harm to others, Burney's novels report, and it is useful to compare Sir Hugh to three of Burney's other unthinking but allegedly benevolent endangerers of women, Villars in *Evelina,* Giles Arbe in *The Wanderer,* and Lionel Tyrold in *Camilla.* Villars endangers Evelina by his passivity, his possessiveness, and his cowardice. He affects not to comprehend the ways of the fashionable world and refuses to teach Evelina that world's rules, mores, and customs. The Tyrold daughters are better taught by their parents (and they are the only young women in Burney's novels to be raised in a traditional nuclear family with a mother as well as a father, though the mother becomes crucially unavailable at key moments). Sir Hugh's naïveté is presented as good-hearted, but Burney's lack of patience with even that kind of fuzziness about the world emerges as she paints Sir Hugh as more childish than the children, and his thoughtlessness as unwittingly (or, rather, witlessly) corrupting and corruptible. Giles Arbe, similar to Sir Hugh in apparent benevolence of intention, talks too much and thinks too little, thereby insinuating himself into Juliet Granville's private affairs where he has no business, and causing her even greater financial embarrassment. Lionel, the high-spirited Tyrold brother, represents a malignant version of Sir Hugh's naïveté. His teasing machinations cause the Bellamy fiasco, imprison Camilla with the insufferable Dubster, and generally orchestrate many of the novel's mixed signals and misunderstandings.

Extolling forthrightness and assertive speech, Burney paints these characters—Villars and Giles Arbe as well as Sir Hugh and Lionel—as people who trigger, practice, and sustain habits of concealment. None of them is an outright villain (despite the homologic gesture of Villars' name), but all of them are more dangerous to the heroines than the openly condemned villains such as Willoughby and Clarendel, who at least have their charms. Lionel shares some of the villains' traits, though his conspiracies are not deliberately evil and we discover eventually that he is racked by both self-knowledge and self-hatred. Villars is simply weak, self-important, and self-centered. Sir Hugh Tyrold and Giles Arbe, presented as entirely well-meaning, cause enormous damage through their thoughtless goodwill. A little calculation, Burney suggests, is a good thing.

On the other hand, the characters who oppose naïveté and promote watchfulness and calculation are the mentors in *Camilla:* Tyrold, whose sermon on feminine virtues, female education, and discretion stands at the novel's center, and Marchmont, the misogynist tutor to Mandlebert. Like Villars, both are clergymen, and their role in the novel, as Villars' in *Evelina,* is to preach. Marchmont admits to his negative view of women: "I have not had reason to think well of them," he tells Mandlebert, and warns him, "Whatever is her appearance of worth, try and prove its foundation, ere you conclude it invulnerable; and whatever are your pretentions to her hand, do not necessarily connect them with your chances for her heart" (161). On this advice, Mandlebert becomes "the scrupulous, the scrutinizing, the delicate Edgar" (553). Mandlebert, more than Lord Orville, is a Villars-style hero. Where Orville's scruples have grace, elegance, and style, Mandlebert's merely mark him even at age thirteen as a "manly boy" (17) who by age twenty will be prematurely and permanently middle-aged. Only when he possesses Camilla's hand as well as her confidence does Mandlebert allow her "a gaiety so large to be feared" (913).

Female mentors also appear in *Camilla* in the form of the sensible, straightforward, but largely absent Mrs. Tyrold; the manipulative and insecure Miss Margland; the youngest sister, Eugenia, whose physical ineligibility for the conventional marriage marketplace makes her precociously wise at fifteen and available as one of the novel's mentors; and Mrs. Arlbery, the Mrs. Selwyn-like free spirit who combines the no-nonsense, no-illusions view of the world proposed by Camilla's mother with the knowing social power that a Miss Margland would like to orchestrate but cannot for lack both of skill and of influence. The description of Mrs. Arlbery at the Northwick ball, where the Tyrolds first encounter her, prepares us for her role as an antiromantic independent intellectual:

> A lady, not young, but still handsome, with an air of fashion easy almost to insolence, with a complete but becoming undress, with a work-bag hanging on her arm, whence she was carelessly knotting, entered the ball-room alone, and, walking straight through it to the large folding glass doors for the tea-room, there stopt, and took a general survey of the company, with a look that announced a decided superiority to all she saw, and a perfect indifference to what opinion she incurred in return. (73)

Navigating alone, dressed for comfort rather than for the appropriateness of the social occasion, and fully autonomous, Mrs. Arlbery announces herself as the novel's judgmental voice.

From Mrs. Albery's disquisitions come commentaries on the nov-

el's action that serve both as social critiques and as disguised soap-
boxes for Burney's analysis of the predicaments her heroine faces. For
example, Mrs. Arlbery teasingly castigates Camilla for refusing the
wealthy Lord Valhurst, on the grounds that their age difference would
ensure her outliving him into a moneyed freedom of choice. Camilla
demurs on moral grounds and Mrs. Arlbery defends women who make
marital selections with such thinking:

> This is all the romance of false reasoning. You have not sought the
> man, but the man you. You would not have solicited his acceptance,
> but yielded to his solicitation of yours. The balance is always just, where
> force is not used. The man has his reasons for chusing you; you have
> your reasons for suffering yourself to be chosen. What his are, you have
> no business to enquire; nor has he the smallest right to investigate yours.
> (780)

Mrs. Arlbery lives in fashionable society, but only because "if one
has not a few of [these *tonnish* people] in one's train, 'twere as well turn
hermit" (399), and she sees through the despicable affectations that
surround her: on "the dearth of character in the world," she remarks,
"Pope has bewailed it in women; believe me, he might have extended
his lamentation" (398). And it is Mrs. Arlbery who sees through
Mandlebert's plot to test Camilla and condemns it, in an astute character analysis:

> He is a watcher; and a watcher, restless and perturbed himself, infests
> all he pursues with uneasiness. He is without trust, and therefore with-
> out either courage or consistency. To-day he may be persuaded you
> will make all his happiness; to-morrow, he may fear you will give him
> nothing but misery. Yet it is not that he is jealous of any other; 'tis
> of the object of his choice he is jealous, lest she should not prove good
> enough to merit it. (482)

She speaks of Mandlebert's "fastidiousness" and of her "instinctive
aversion to those cold, haughty, drawing-back characters, who are
made up of the egotism of looking out for something that is wholly
devoted to them, and that has not a breath to breathe that is not a
sigh for their perfections" (483). No wonder Edgar would rather Camilla not visit this insightful woman. "Mandlebert is a creature whose
whole composition is a pile of accumulated punctilios," Mrs. Arlbery
warns Camilla. "He will spend his life in refining away his own happiness: but do not let him refine away yours" (484). One of Burney's
finest achievements in characterization, Mrs. Arlbery speaks for her

creator in an internal self-referential condemnation of Camilla, and of *Camilla*'s enterprise: to win this unappealing "monitor" of a man as a husband. Camilla would have been freer with a Lord Valhurst who openly coveted her for his self-serving need to possess a pretty young wife than with a Mandlebert who will look out forever for any break in her unconditional commitment to his welfare and happiness.

The metaphorical courtship dance that so eludes Camilla and Mandlebert—at a real ball early in the novel, the protagonists begin but then are thwarted from dancing no fewer than four times (63–76)—is analyzed within the novel by the one character whose "deformity" leaves her unauthorized to participate, Eugenia. Eugenia's medical catastrophe merits a close look, since Burney comments on the relationship between physical health and personality, body and intellect, with her portrait of this young woman whose blighted beauty causes her to turn to a life of the mind. As the youngest (and originally the prettiest) Tyrold child, and the frailest, Eugenia had not been inoculated against smallpox along with the other children. As a consequence, she contracts the disease when Sir Hugh allows the children to visit a local fair where they encounter a little boy whose face bears its recent ravages. Burney studied medical texts in order to write this sequence. When she had her own son Alex inoculated in 1797, the year after *Camilla*'s publication, she wrote to her father: "I had studied that misfortune so thoroughly under Eugenia, that I was prepared to meet it with philosophy" (16 March 1797, *JL* 3:291). She describes the inoculation in elaborate detail in this letter and in an earlier letter to her sister Susanna, calling it "the dreaded operation." Eugenia becomes "seamed and even scarred by the horrible disorder" of smallpox, which leaves her with "the dreadful havoc grim disease had made on her face, not a trace of her beauty left" (29). The later seesaw accident leaves her, in addition, with a hobbled gait, and she grows up with "her whole figure diminutive and deformed." Her parents agree to Sir Hugh's will alteration "since no other reparation could be offered to the innocent sufferer for ills so insurmountable" (33). Burney surely remembered Eugenia's fate when she underwent her own deforming medical catastrophe in 1811—the attitude toward physical beauty and bodily perfection expressed through Eugenia reflects Burney's notion that a failure in health and appearance represents irrevocable change for a woman. Tellingly, Eugenia compensates by turning to the study of classical languages and making herself a scholar. Unlike other blighted characters, such as Harrel and Mrs. Delvile in *Cecilia*, Eugenia becomes not mute, but the most eloquent character in the novel. For her, language replaces appearance.

Because Eugenia, unlike Edgar Mandlebert, is incapable of sus-
pecting that words and behavior can represent anything other than
what they state, Bellamy's plot to dupe her succeeds. This plot (not
so far from the actual complicated and incestuous elopements in the
Burney family) oppresses the Tyrolds and leads to the Gothicism of
the murdered corpse sequence at the inn that so deranges Camilla.
Eugenia herself, however, never romanticizes her situation nor pities
herself, though she falls in love with the romantic notions of Melmond
and subscribes to Melmond's literary tastes (Thomson's poetry) and
to those of his sister (Akenside's *Pleasures of the Imagination,* Rowe's *Letters from the Dead,* James Hammond's *Love Elegies,* and Madame de
Graffigny's *Peruvian Letters*).[8] Tyrold gives Eugenia a *Spectator* essay to
read on ugliness and takes her to see a physically beautiful but totally
demented woman who lives nearby as a lesson after Eugenia is publicly insulted for her defects.[9] But in inverse proportion to her physical charms, her intellect thrives, and Burney uses Eugenia's plight to
illustrate the eighteenth-century prejudice against learned women.

In *Camilla,* Burney mocks that prejudice. After Lionel plants misinformation about the inheritance and matrimonial arrangements of
the Tyrold sisters, the rumor circulates that Eugenia studies with a
Latin and Greek master:

> This, shortly, made Eugenia stared at still more than her peculiar ap-
> pearance. The misses, in tittering, ran away from the learned lady;
> the beaux contemptuously sneering, rejoiced she was too ugly to take
> in any poor fellow to marry her. Some imagined her studies had stinted
> her growth; and all were convinced her education had made her such
> a fright. (748)

Clermont Lynmere's argument for rejecting Eugenia's hand and her
inheritance also turns on this point. When his sister tells him that
Eugenia speaks Greek and Latin, he replies, "Does her so? then, by
the Lord! she's no wife of mine! I'd as soon tie myself to a rod. Pretty
sort of dinners she'll give!" (597). When Sir Hugh announces that
Eugenia has been "brought up in the style of a boy," Clermont asks,
"And what have I to do with marrying a girl like a boy? That's not
my taste, my dear sir, I assure you. Besides, what has a wife to do
with the classics? will they show her how to order her table? I suppose
when I want to eat, I may go to a cook's shop!" (592). Ironically, it
is Eugenia whose abduction enacts a conventional heterosexual sentimental plot, as does the melodramatic shooting accident that frees
her from her brutal husband. Her refusal (on principle) to fight her

marriage in court condemns her to imprisonment by the caustic Bellamy, but her stoicism also maintains Eugenia above the madding crowd of gossip and fashion.

Eugenia's literal entrapment in her deformed body and imprisonment in the house arrest Bellamy requires of her are only two of the kinds of prisons that enclose Burney's women in *Camilla*. Metaphors of imprisonment dominate much of Burney's writing. A claustrophobic sense of enclosure besieges Burney the surgery patient in her mastectomy letter; similar moments of airless panic also assail her fictional heroines. Evelina becomes trapped in Willoughby's carriage and locked within a surrounding phalanx of drunken louts. Camilla, too, finds herself threatened by enclosure, both literal and metaphorical, on crucial occasions. Seated in a box at the theater, she insinuates herself into a corner where she may be hidden from Mandlebert's judgmental eye. Mandlebert comes upon her in Mrs. Arlbery's garden where Clarendel forcibly holds her by the hand. Dubster's summerhouse, with whose ladder Lionel playfully disappears, serves as another prison: a place inappropriate for unchaperoned single women from which the Tyrold heroines cannot escape without outside intervention. Not perceiving her imprisonment, first by social rules, then by physical force, Mandlebert leaves offended rather than trying to rescue Camilla. The most literal prison for Camilla in the novel is formed by the bathing room in Southampton, in a scene that brutally extends the threat a woman alone endures from strange men that Burney first fictionalized in the Vauxhall sequence in *Evelina*. Here an empty room beckons as refuge, but when ducked into turns out to trap lone women in what appears to be an invitation to lasciviousness. Burney was to foreground this metaphor of continuous entrapment in *The Wanderer*, whose protagonist repeatedly seeks asylum in enclosures that metamorphose into prisons at the moment she enters them.

Some of Burney's prisons become such by apparent accident — a frightening fireworks display in *Evelina* or a practical joke in *Camilla*. However, by the 1790s Burney was able not merely to satirize and rail against social conventions that cripple woman's freedom, but also to marry the then popular accoutrements of the novel of Gothic terror and the political novel with portraits of physical danger. Eugenia is literally held prisoner by Bellamy; she can be liberated only by cold-blooded violence — the gun that shot Bellamy had a second earlier been pointed at his kidnapped wife. And her liberation seems complete only because the narrator emphasizes Bellamy's venal interests: brief telegraphic phrases imply that the marriage remained unconsummated. Tyrold refers to "what had been done at Belfast to Eugenia"

(893–94), and to Camilla's "Is Eugenia greatly affected?" Mrs. Tyrold
cryptically replies, "She is all, every way, and in every respect, . . .
whatever the fondest, or even proudest Mother could wish" (893–94).
That "all . . . every . . . every" asks us to entertain the unlikely possibility that Eugenia has emerged from her failed marriage a virgin.
Force and physical brutality abound in *Camilla,* in the characters' speech,
in the narration itself which claustrophobically weaves a tighter and
tighter net around Camilla until she is suffocated into madness, and
in the incidents themselves. We have looked already at the violence
in Camilla's climactic nightmare: the "sharp, forked" hand of Death
that "struck abruptly upon her breast" and the deep voice that "dreadfully pierced her ear" and the "awful vibration" (874–76). Force in *Camilla* also takes more subtle forms.

The overriding role of force and "forcefulness" in *Camilla* emerges
from Burney's analysis of the social ideology whose blanket assumptions her narrative challenges. Underlying the moments of imprisonment in the novel is the view that there is a particular mode of conduct
available for women and that "misconduct" demands social judgment. When Camilla and Mrs. Mittin evade the public stares of Southampton shopkeepers, they occasion a series of surmises and wagers:

> Such is the prevalent disposition to believe in general depravity, that
> while those who are debased themselves find a consolation in thinking
> others equally worthless, those even, who are of a better sort, nourish
> a secret vanity in supposing few as good as themselves; and fully, with-
> out reflection, the fair candour of their minds, by aiding that insidious
> degeneracy, which robs the community of all confidence in virtue. (611)

While hiding in the bathing room on the quay, the two women hear
footsteps, a "loud and clamorously jovial" unknown voice, and "saw
the door violently flung open, and three persons, dressed like gentlemen, force their way into the small dwelling place" (613). Physical as-
sailants of women in Burney's novels are not usually things or people
of the middle or lower classes; while she may object to the violations
of Tom Branghton, Mr. Smith, Dubster, and shopkeeper Drim, she
does not portray these men as users of criminal physical force.

Significantly, the imposers of force are power-mongers and gentlemen, frequently even titled: Sir Clement Willoughby, Alphonso Bellamy, Lord Valhurst. They insinuate themselves into female space with
the clear and self-satisfied presumption that they will be welcome:

> Boisterously entering, Halder addressed at once to Camilla, such
> unceremonious praise of her beauty, that affrighted and offended, she

hastily seized the arm of Mrs. Mittin, and, in a voice of alarm, though with an air of command that admitted no doubt of her seriousness, and no appeal from her resolution, said, "Let us go home, Mrs. Mitten, immediately." (624)

Fear and offense usually go hand in hand in Burney's works, and frequently resentment cancels out either cowardice or demure shyness. Camilla's "command" causes Halder to back off, struck as he is that she has dared to distance him. While he, "repulsed, stood back," the old lord, "shutting the door, planted himself against it" (614). Even when the third young man, Westwyn, offers to rescue her, Camilla retreats further into the room, looking out the window toward the beach. The bathing room — a "changing" room and thus a location not just for undress but for masquerade and identity transformation — becomes a prison cell from which Camilla must be rescued by the hero. This scene examines a social ideology that privileges male assertions of superiority and control. Women physically retreat in its presence, and can use only speech — the polite speech of self-command — to countermand violation.

Because speech is a woman's only instrument of power, Camilla's repeated silence and stammering mark her as a woman who can be, and is, taken advantage of. Clarendel makes her literally and morally indebted to him when he saves her from wild carriage horses and lends her money; Dubster, Major Cerwood, and Lord Valhurst set her up for Mandlebert's misjudgment because rudeness and social rebuffs are unavailable behaviors for women, who must be polite to all individuals in all situations. More experienced than Evelina but also more schooled in conduct rules, Camilla could never say what Evelina says to Willoughby in anger: "You have no right to make any conditions" (*Evelina,* 357). In *Camilla,* Burney presents a heroine far more threatened than was her first protagonist, despite being Burney's only unorphaned heroine. Evelina, Cecilia, and Juliet must establish and then carve their true identities into their lives, a fearsome task but one imposed from outside. Camilla's difficulty places her in an insoluble bind: she must communicate her loyalty and love for Edgar Mandlebert without ever declaring herself openly. Women cannot take any charge of courtship.

Condemned to remain silent and socially constrained to appear indifferent, Camilla's silence itself imprisons her. No wonder, then, that when she tries to speak her voice cracks, or dies, or she stammers, and that she is unable to meet her interlocutors' eyes. No wonder, either, that when the iron pen is presented to her it offers her only two options: to write words "illuminated with burning sulphur" or to make no mark on the page the pen traverses, to write invisible words (875). Writing, violation, and violence intersect here. The iron pen is an instrument and a weapon of patriarchal social ideology; only when Camilla domesticates it can she use it to give herself a voice.

Three

Fictions of Resistance:
Women and the Marketplace

In *Evelina* and *Camilla,* the heroines are defined by their communication practices: they talk, gesture, and write. Evelina deploys her pen with cunning ease; Camilla finally demilitarizes the iron pen that is offered to her. The metaphor of writing—and of the communication process as a synecdoche for social relations and the political discomfort they embrace—dominates Burney's first and third novels. The thwarting of communication in *Cecilia* and *The Wanderer* comes not from inner turmoil, mistaken or overspontaneous self-expression, or misunderstanding; rather, the heroines of Burney's second and fourth novels submit to impositions of silence from without. Cecilia Beverley and Lady Juliet Granville are controlled, far more than are Evelina and Camilla, by political and legal entanglements imposed on them by systems and chains of law from which they cannot free themselves. Language as political action remains a central issue in all four of the novels, but in *Cecilia* and *The Wanderer* the subversive linguistic fabric of Burney's fiction is rewoven into more overtly material political and legal concerns. All four novels are responses in writing to situations that Burney experienced as oppressive or assaulting, but whereas those situations are social and internalized as private for Evelina and Camilla, Cecilia and Juliet are oppressed by the external exigencies of law, politics, and, most crucially, economics.

This shift from internal to external ideological struggle is best symbolized by the shift in Burney's treatment of one of her central metaphors for the problematic nature of female selfhood and identity, women's names. The problem of a "name" for Evelina becomes a central issue not merely of self but of survival itself for both Cecilia and Juliet. Patrimony and autonomy (themes also in *Evelina* and *Camilla*) take over as paramount in *Cecilia* and *The Wanderer,* novels whose heroines face bankruptcy and must take not only moral and social, but also economic, political, and legal responsibility for themselves and their decision making. Both novels contain blatant critiques of the materialist framework of the female condition—in its relation to money, to family obligations, to marriage, to work, to social sanction, and to the politics of equality—in late eighteenth- and early nineteenth-century Europe.

5

Cecilia: Money
and Anarchy

Cecilia; or, Memoirs of an Heiress was published in 1782 by a far more publicly self-conscious author than had produced the surreptitiously composed *Evelina* in the 1770s. An expectant audience with preconceived notions of what a Burney heroine would be like and familiarity with the mechanisms of ironic narration presented through Burney's comic narrative voice awaited this second work of fiction. Like Evelina "Anville," Cecilia Beverley is bereft of kin and alone in the social world she enters. While Evelina enters a hostile and complicated world that periodically encloses her in a mesh of social ideology metaphorized by Burney as physical or psychological assault, that world remains ringed by a comedic subtlety and its dangers are finally transcendable, though at a cost. *Cecilia*'s world, in contrast, bristles with absolute menace. The plethora of wittily drawn characters and abundance of satirically choreographed social scenes cannot mask in this second novel Burney's stark world view: young women live inside an envelope of continual material threat to their individual selfhood and to their social and economic survival.

Cecilia undergoes a triple orphaning in the first pages of Burney's second novel. Both her parents die, her uncle dies, and she is removed from the home of Mrs. Charlton, her "maternal counsellor." As the novel's title suggests, she is an heiress, receiving ten thousand pounds a year from her father and another three thousand pounds attached to an estate from her uncle. She is to receive this money when she comes of age at twenty-one, a time she is eight months shy of when the story opens, "with no other restriction than that of annexing her name, if she married, to the disposal of her hand and her riches" (1:2). This laconically described restriction will be crucial.

Cecilia's world is far more fraught with danger than is the often uncomfortable but ultimately negotiable world of Evelina. As Clarissa Harlowe's grandfather's will had bound her to a conflict between family responsibility and individual desire, so Cecilia's uncle's will binds her to an impossible choice between public obedience and personal happiness, and between private desire and public wealth. The restriction on Cecilia's name in her uncle's will, presented in a dismissive way as minor when it is first introduced, ultimately controls the novel's plot and the tendentious reading of woman's place in the social world that Burney presents through the economic and legal tribulations of her second and most financially independent heroine. Unlike Evelina and the heroine of *The Wanderer,* who answer to the created nonsense words by which they are called, Cecilia Beverley is tied by law to a family name that has no particular meaning for her but which she cannot shed. That surname — Beverley — becomes the "seal" embedded in Cecilia's given name, and it literally seals her fate.

Witness two key scenes in which Cecilia's problematic name is invoked. In the confrontation between Cecilia's lover, Mortimer Delvile, and his mother concerning his planned marriage to Cecilia, the son argues vigorously that he would not be sinning against any integrity to give up his family name and take on Cecilia's as he takes on her inheritance. "What honour do I injure that is not factitious?" he asks. "In the general commerce of the world, it may be right to yield to its prejudices, but in matters of serious importance, it is weakness to be shackled by scruples so frivolous, and it is cowardly to be governed by the customs we condemn." But when his mother counters that the renunciation of his family name will bring curses on him from his father "when your name becomes a stranger to your ears, and you are first saluted by one so meanly adopted!" (2:215), he blanches. He and Cecilia pledge never to see each other again, at this, the final blow from Augusta Delvile to her son: "Heavens! . . . what in the universe can pay you for that first moment of indignity! Think of it well ere you proceed, and anticipate your sensations, lest the shock should wholly overcome you. How will the blood of your wronged ancestors rise into your guilty cheeks, and how will your heart throb with secret shame and reproach, when wished joy upon your marriage by the name of Mr. *Beverley!*" (2:216). The name itself is not repugnant to the Delviles; the Beverley family is respectable. And certainly the money annexed to that name appeals strongly to the Delviles' depleted and crumbling estates. But Burney's precocious theme — that a woman should retain her maiden name upon her marriage — contains the seeds of revolution for a social order that was entering upon a period of chaotic transition at the end of the eighteenth century. The Delviles represent the tenacious *ancien régime* of the landed gentry's patriarchal family structure, and Cecilia's name challenges familial and marital institutions as well as threatening the sanctity of patrimonial succession.

A second narrative crux involving her name occurs when Cecilia's inheritance is stripped in a scene with the lawyer sent by her uncle's next heir. She has indeed by this time married with the intention of giving up her name, but the wedding was secret, and Cecilia plans to remain in her house until her husband returns from the Continent to "claim" her and to make their union public. Secrets, however, are always dangerous objects in a Burney novel, and, characteristically, they are never well kept. The exchange between Cecilia, now in a nominal limbo but still using the name "Miss Beverley," and Eggleston's lawyer ("an entire stranger: an elderly man, of no pleasant aspect or manners") bears lengthy citation because it underlines the metaphoric functions of naming in a Burney novel:

> She desired to know his business.
> "I presume, madam, you are the lady of this house?"
> She bowed an assent.
> "May I take the liberty, madam, to ask your name?"
> "My name, sir?"
> "You will do me a favour, madam, by telling it me."
> "Is it possible you are come hither without already knowing it?"
> "I know it only by common report, madam."
> "Common report, sir, I believe is seldom wrong in a matter where to be right is so easy."
> "Have you any objection, madam, to telling me your name?"
> "No sir; but your business can hardly be very important, if you are yet to learn whom you are to address. It will be time enough, therefore, for us to meet when you are elsewhere satisfied in this point."
> She would then have left the room.
> "I beg, madam," cried the stranger, "you will have patience; it is necessary, before I can open my business, that I should hear your name from yourself."

"Well, sir," cried she with some hesitation, "you can scarce have come to this house, without knowing that its owner is Cecilia Beverley."

"That, madam, is your maiden name."

"My maiden name?" cried she, starting.

"Are you not married, madam?"

"Married, sir?" she repeated, while her cheeks were the colour of scarlet.

"It is properly, therefore, madam, the name of your husband that I mean to ask."

"And by what authority, sir," cried she, equally astonished and offended, "do you make these extraordinary enquiries?" (2:388–89)

After half a page of further stammering, the attorney, having identified himself and his errand, becomes blunt ("Are you married or are you not?" [2:389]), and Cecilia, while asking for time and being granted a week, is forced into a confession: Eggleston, indeed, now owns the house she is living in, and she owes him money. And it is instructive to remember Mrs. Delvile's threat to Mortimer that he should be "mortified" (his name suggests that susceptibility to this threat) when called Mr. Beverley. It is, instead, Cecilia who must undergo this trial. When Eggleston writes, her disappointment at his news is "embittered by shame and terror, when, upon folding it [the letter] up, she saw it was directed to Mrs. Mortimer Delvile" (2:396). It is Cecilia whose powerfully conceived identity is subsumed into that of her husband, just as Evelina's far more fragile "maiden name" experiences protean shifts from Anville to Belmont to Orville in quick succession.

Naming highlights the issue of class consciousness in Burney's novels. Both Evelina Belmont and Juliet Granville have aristocratic parentage, though they have to struggle for recognition, and both are proud to "own" the lost names they work so hard to regain. Cecilia differs here, and bears more resemblance to Camilla Tyrold, who comes from a respectable, though not wealthy, landed family. But all Burney's heroines have close ties and repeated dealings with the bourgeoisie, and class distinctions — underwritten by the complex of naming rituals — frequently hold center stage in Burney's fiction. Much has been written about the ways Burney uses comedy and dialect to poke fun at these distinctions, something she does in all her novels (witness the hilarious speech of Cecilia's miserly guardian Briggs) and this has particularly been remarked in the Branghton sequences in *Evelina*. But little attention has been paid to the serious critique of class that Burney's novels embody. This critique is especially crucial for *Cecilia*, a novel in which all the characters struggle to get or keep money, by parsimony and niggardliness (Briggs), by marrying their children advantageously (the Delviles, Mrs. Belfield), by marrying themselves advantageously (Monckton, Sir Robert Floyer, Marriot), by fleecing others or gaming (Harrel), or, finally, that rarity, by working for what they earn (the Hills, and, eventually, Belfield). Cecilia, like Clarissa before her and Dorothea Brooke after her, wants money only in order to carry out charity work. *Cecilia* participates in a line of novels about philanthropy by women, of which Sarah Scott's 1762 *Millenium Hall* is perhaps the best known.[1] But not for a minute does anyone, from any class, allow her to forget that she is an heiress, and Burney means to make a social point through the irony of this novel's ending, with its titular heiress penniless. In the novel's final lines, we are told that Cecilia "knew that, at times, the whole family must murmur at her loss of fortune, and at times she murmured herself to be thus portionless, though an HEIRESS" (2:473).

Burney's focus on money as a medium of exchange for her plot and for her materialist social critique is relentless in *Cecilia* and leads to the novel's major achievement: its phantasmagoric metaphor of masquerade develops directly out of the surreal quality Burney gives to money and to financial transactions and their repercussions. Cecilia's economic position is clearly endangered from the outset: the question of where honorably to bestow money (and, behind that question, of how honorably to acquire it) underlies the plot. In the custody of her first guardian, Harrel, Cecilia is inexorably drawn into the household's dissipations, in which the conversation consists of "comparative strictures upon celebrated beauties, hints of impending bankruptcies, and witticisms upon recent divorces" (1:31), all issues that turn on the marketing of class and gender. Her second guardian, Briggs, is a wonderful proto-Dickensian caricature of avarice, practicing penny pinching as a high art and eliding the first person when he speaks, always breathlessly, as though to conserve words as he conserves shillings. He represents the mirror opposite of the spendthrift Harrel. Trapped between these two extremes, Cecilia resolves to forego "the frivolous insipidity of her present life, to make at once a more spirited and more worthy use of the affluence, freedom and power which she possessed" (1:51) through charity and intellectual study. Her efforts, however, fail. She becomes, despite herself, the underwriter of aristocratic pretension and waste through her coerced loans to Harrel, her notes from a moneylender, and her most insidious mentor, Monckton, who reminds us of both Villars and Mandlebert, supposedly benign counselors who, perhaps not so inadvertently, endanger their charges. Burney's tag line for Monckton when we first meet him is to tell the reader aphoristically that "pleasure given in society, like money lent in usury, returns with interest to those who dispense it" (1:5). The financial metaphor pervades the novel.

Harrel bleeds Cecilia of money; Briggs, who controls her cash flow, refuses to advance her any; her third guardian, Compton Delvile, is too proud to interfere in such a vulgar problem. The only expenditure Cecilia makes for herself—bills to a bookseller to provide her with reading that will furnish a mental escape from the implacable materiality surrounding her—draws remonstration. "Words get no cash," Briggs scolds her (1:174), and Delvile exhorts her never to "degrade herself by being put on a level with writers" (1:179). Much more practical than Camilla, who incurs debts through ignorance of marketplace realities as well as through imposition and charity, Cecilia has reason to feel continually frustrated, and Burney may have been using that frustration to convey her own increasingly bitter views on the state of the literary marketplace. Her merciless concern with financial detail—the novel dwells with ledger-book particularity on the elaborate specifications of each exchange of funds and each operation of promissory note collection—marks this as a novel that broke new ground in the eighteenth century. Burney here shines a spotlight on the relations between women and men with a plot that relies on financial complication based on an oddly gynocentric economic foundation.

This foundation supports the novel's reliance on masquerade, carnival, and madness to make its critique of eighteenth-century materialism. The masquerade metaphor in the novel permits Burney to comment on the personal and social toll of shifting class categories that she had begun to analyze comedically with the *ton* and Branghton portraits in *Evelina*. Recent work on the "carnivalesque" as not merely a category of social history and popular culture but of cultural analysis itself derives from Mikhail Bakhtin's seminal study of Rabelais, a work first translated into English in 1968.[2] The literary studies that build most interestingly on Bakhtin also make use of the anthropological work of Edmund Leach and Victor Turner on carnival and liminality.[3] Most recently, Peter Stallybrass and Allon White have at once extended and critiqued Bakhtin's notion of the carnivalesque in their elaboration of a category of what they have called "transgression," a category that focuses on the carnivalesque as an inversion or abrogation of narrative cultural codes leading to "the recoding of high/low relations across the whole social structure."[4] Terry Castle has written importantly on carnival and the masquerade in the eighteenth century, and she offers a detailed reading of *Cecilia* in conjunction with an analysis of masquerade as an organizing metaphor in eighteenth-century fiction.⁵ *Cecilia*'s insistence on inverting economic hierarchies in such a way that the category of "heiress" becomes culturally impossible and its Burneyan reliance on figuring locations of public pleasure as discursive sites for the mapping of social classifications can be read in the light of this recent work on carnival. The carnivalesque in *Cecilia* emerges out of the effects of the ever-present possibility of assault and violence on a protagonist for whom no mask can be fashioned, no disguise can disguise adequately, no niche in the class or gender order can be made safe or appropriate.

Early in the novel, and with the aid of incongruous mixes of classes, Burney establishes the slightly out-of-control atmosphere that pervades *Cecilia*. A character named Morrice figures in many of the carnival scenes, beginning at a breakfast held at Monckton's house in the novel's opening pages. A chameleon and self-appointed lackey, Morrice aims to insinuate himself into society by pleasing, and he shifts roles as quickly as he sees the need to make himself useful to people he wants not to offend. An elastic, silly-putty character, Morrice, not overtly evil, triggers much of the disaster in *Cecilia*. At the breakfast, he usurps Monckton's seat next to Cecilia, and Monckton removes him by suddenly suggesting a game of "move-all"—a sort of hectic musical chairs. Later, in London, a similar scene occurs when Morrice suddenly and loudly leaps over the back of a sofa to sit beside Cecilia, and is again ousted as suddenly and violently by Monckton. Finally, as Cecilia tries to make a quick and clandestine trip to London before her first, aborted wedding, she encounters the ubiquitous Morrice on the road, and he insists not only on accompanying her, but on following her and unearthing her connection with Mortimer Delvile. In the process, he breaks the leg of an already injured pet dog he drops while chasing the disguised Delvile on horseback. Burney is still critiquing manners and social behaviors, but the near-slapstick antics of Morrice go beyond those of a Captain Mirvan or a Lovel and always verge on the chaos of madness, so that when he is present the narrative begins to resemble *Alice in Wonderland*.

The masquerade in book 2, a sequence in which Morrice figures prominently, comprises one of the most extraordinary passages in Burney's fiction, and figures centrally in the atmosphere of baroque carnival permeating this narrative. The question of money—who will pay the workmen? how will the awning over the dessert table for the "masks" be financed?—hovers over everything. No one retrenches expenses in this novel, though significantly it is at the garishly costly Harrel masquerade that Cecilia meets the novel's hero, Mortimer Delvile, her guardian's son. All the characters appear in disguise in this sequence, and the boundaries between characters and their identities, and between social class and acceptable behaviors, are radically broken by the chaotic presence of "masks." Cecilia, in particular, is unable to recognize her companions accurately, at first taking the white domino who protects her to be her friend Belfield and the devil who persecutes her to be her would-be suitor Sir Robert Floyer, though the reader learns that the devil is really Monckton, in a metaphorical revelation of his true self, and the domino turns out to be Mortimer Delvile, the novel's hero. It is a key to the importance of the masquerade in *Cecilia* that the novel's lovers first meet here. Though censorious of the Harrels' extravagance, Cecilia nevertheless looks forward to and relishes the masquerade: "Cecilia herself, however little pleased with the attendant circumstance of wantonly accumulating unnecessary debts, was not the least animated of the party; she was a stranger to every diversion of this sort, and from the novelty of the scene, hoped for uncommon satisfaction" (1:99). As Terry Castle has pointed out, this set scene is a locus simultaneously of social pleasure and of a moral disapproval engendered by its institutionalization of disorder and sexual theater.[6] Cecilia's response to the evening typifies this paradox.

Events at the masquerade demonstrate an observation made by symbolic anthropologists, that body images, clothing, and rules about the control of bodies and their presentation reflect the distribution of social power in a given culture.[7] Cecilia, indeed, becomes the heroine stripped bare as she decides to attend in ordinary dress, a decision that ironically marks her and makes her unwillingly the center of attention: "There were so many masks that Cecilia wished she had herself made one of the number, as she was far more conspicuous in being almost the only female in a common dress, than any masquerade habit could have made her" (1:102). As a consequence, she is literally imprisoned by Monckton in his Don Devil costume. He persecutes her for most of the evening and necessitates that she be rescued—she is metaphorically surrounded by his wand and his insistent silence. The evening literally "breaks up" when Morrice, dressed as a harlequin, pulls down the elaborate awning and colored lights in a failed attempt to impress the company by leaping over the dessert table, a prank that plunges the room into darkness and scatters glass, papier-mâché, lamps, and oil over the screaming crowd.

The Lord of Chaos reigns here: the Harrels' apartments resonate with "the variety of dresses, the medley of characters, the quick succession of figures, and the ludicrous mixture of groups" and with "the conceited efforts at wit, the total thoughtlessness of consistency, and the ridiculous incongruity of the language with the appearance" (1:101) in a cacophony of what Mikhail Bakhtin would call "heteroglossia."[8] In his study of Rabelais, Bakhtin discusses the revolutionary role of carnival and ritual public spectacle, delineating a multiplicity of styles and languages, sensuousness, and an impulse to play as key elements. "Carnival," according to Bakhtin, is neither an art form nor a sphere of life, but inhabits the borderline between life and art: people live inside the carnival, which subsumes all life into it while it lasts. Carnival liberates its participants from social and sexual laws that exist outside it; it breaks down hierarchies of all kinds, obliterating categories of gender, rank, class, age, and profession as it simultaneously frees its actors from norms of etiquette and decency. It represents the mutability of a "world inside out."[9]

A plenitude of unreadable signs takes over at the masquerade in *Cecilia:* "Every room was occupied, and the common crowd of regular masqueraders were dispersed through the various apartments. Dominos of no character, and fancy-dresses of no meaning, made, as is usual at such meetings, the general herd of the company: for the rest, the men were Spaniards, chimney-sweepers, Turks, watchmen, conjurers, and old women; and the ladies shepherdesses, orange girls, Circassians, gipseys, haymakers, and sultanas" (1:102–3). Communication in "local cant" with "*Do you know me? Who are you?* and *I know you;* with the sly pointing of the finger, the arch nod of the head, and the pert squeak of the voice" (1:102) represents a coded fall into Babel in which categories of sex and class intersect, merge, and explode. This Babel fascinates Burney as a polyphonic symbol of the social world her heroines must learn to decode. In the "carnival" sequences of *Cecilia* (and there are less acute, less chaotic parallel sequences in the other three novels as well), forbidden incursions of role reversal and a liberating social blasphemy intrude upon the official rules of social life.[10]

The Babel in *Cecilia* continues in the next important sequence: a duel between Sir Robert Floyer and Belfield occasioned by a dispute over rights to Cecilia's arm at the opera, a dispute in which Cecilia becomes a disembodied anatomy, a metonymic arm. Cecilia fails to recognize the semiotic significance of sexual disputes and their resultant duelling: "All she could find to regret with regard to herself, was wanting the presence of mind to have refused the civilities of both" (1:138). She is misread as Mandlebert had misread Camilla: for Sir Robert, "her silence he only attributed to admiration, her coldness to fear, and her reserve to shame" (1:145). Unlike Elizabeth Bennet, who is only briefly bereft of words when she encounters Darcy at Pemberley, Cecilia seems unable to speak when she must explain appearances that are against her. When she meets Delvile in Belfield's rooms, "notwithstanding the openness and purity of her intentions, [Cecilia] was so much disconcerted by this unexpected meeting, and pointed speech, that she had not the presence of mind to call him back and clear herself" (1:206). And she avoids taking the initiative in communications. Later, at his home, she "chose rather to wait the revival of his own curiosity, than to distress or perplex herself by contriving methods of explanation" (1:232). She also fails to ask Mrs. Delvile if she can remain there rather than return to the Harrels, because "she knew not how to make her proposal; but from the uncommon partiality of Mrs. Delvile, she hoped with a very little encouragement, she would lead to it herself" (1:235). She does not. Like all of Burney's heroines, Cecilia is beset by misunderstanding, missed connections, plots and subterfuge, and economic nightmares. And like Burney's other heroines as well, Cecilia brings some of her troubles on herself through a combination of ignorance, trustingness, and a too-cautious manner of dealing with the world; quite to her harm, "she suffered not her affections to triumph over her principles" and made sure "her passions were under the control of her reason" (1:244). Cecilia's world relies on codes — masks, gestures, games, social regulations, inheritance laws, wills — that control the protagonist's movement.

Moral economy and the economy of morals reign in this coded narrative. Belfield, ashamed of the trade of his father, learns too late that "though discernment teaches us the folly of others, experience singly can teach us our own!" (1:212). Exhorted by Cecilia to fear imminent financial ruin, Mrs. Harrel only "assured her *she did nothing but what everybody else did,* and that it was quite impossible for her to *appear in the world* in any other manner" (1:186). Cecilia herself lives in ignorance of the world's arrangements: "The stations and employments of men she only knew by occasionally hearing that such were their professions, and such their situations in life; but with the means and gradations by which they arose to them she was wholly unacquainted" (1:241). In all the society scenes in *Cecilia,* Burney comments on the idiosyncrasies and superficiality of *ton* life, in which high fashion, demonstrated by the "ennuyé" Meadows, consists of the "happy art in catching the reigning foibles of the times, and carrying them to an extreme yet more absurd than any one had done before him" (1:270).

Fashionable society and fashionable promenade locations always lead back to "carnival" of one sort or another in *Cecilia.* At the Pantheon, for example, Morrice again inserts anarchic potential into the action by overturning a teapot that singes Delvile's shoulder when he bends to protect Cecilia from a burn. A more important "carnival" scene occurs at Vauxhall and leads up to Harrel's suicide. Harrel proposes the Vauxhall expedition "in a hurrying manner" (1:385) and orders a hackney coach. When his wife and Cecilia both become alarmed, Harrel grows violent. On arrival, he "made them take several turns in the midst of the company, and walked so fast, that they could hardly keep pace with him" (1:388). Harrel drinks more and more champagne, and begins to assemble a motley crew of fellow revelers, a crew that resembles the mix-and-match assembly of the Harrel masquerade earlier in the novel. Another of Cecilia's would-be suitors, Marriot, joins them, then Morrice, then Harrel's creditors themselves, Hobson ("a fat, sleek, vulgar-looking man, dressed in a bright purple coat, with a deep red waistcoat, and a wig bulging far from his head with small round curls" [1:390]) and Simkins ("a little mean-looking man, very thin, and almost bent double with perpetual cringing" [1:391]). The *ton* crowd also materializes: Meadows with his disdainful yawning, contrived obliviousness, and complaints; Captain Aresby, with his precious insertion of French phrases into every sentence; and Sir Robert Floyer. At a ball held earlier at the Harrels' after their first near miss with bankruptcy, Meadows' cold but accurate remarks had foreshadowed and prefigured Harrel's later public suicide at Vauxhall when he lamented, "'Tis terrible to be under the same roof with a set of people who would care nothing if they saw one expiring!" (1:327).

Harrel's suicide is one of Burney's most extraordinary fictional achievements. Harrel has on several occasions used threats of suicide to bilk Cecilia of her inheritance in scenes that darken and virtually parallel the Macartney sequence in *Evelina.* And like the later and far more admirable Ferdinando Falkland of William Godwin's 1794 novel *Caleb Williams,* Harrel is periodically beset by "fits of horror" (1:337). While the actual act of suicide, when it finally occurs, takes place just offstage, the narrative does not spare the gory details of Harrel's slow dying. Amid waiters covered with blood and staring spectators, Cecilia herself takes charge of calling for a surgeon and organizing the disposal of the body. Ironically, a scene in which all the difficult work that involves both emotional and physical fortitude is undertaken by a woman (Cecilia soundly lambastes Floyer for allowing his friend to be attended in his dying moments only by servants and strangers) ends with another conflict scene between two men vying to "protect" Cecilia by seeing her home, Floyer and Mortimer Delvile. Delvile wins this time. But they return to find an execution at the Harrels' house, and the chaos of Harrel's uncontrolled life comes to an end as Cecilia and Mrs. Harrel take refuge with the Delviles for the night.

The carnival atmosphere of *Cecilia* touches every facet of the narrative: first and most obviously in the masquerade scene, then in the two actual and several near and averted duels between rivals for the heroine's affections, then at Vauxhall during Harrel's drunken preamble to his suicide, later in the eventually apoplectic screaming confrontation between Delvile and his mother over his marriage, and finally in the scene that precedes Cecilia's madness and imprisonment. Each society scene along the way also adds to this depraved atmosphere: carriage accidents, mindless conversations with idiotic characters such as Captain Aresby and the vapidly chattering Miss Larrolles, maddening interruptions of important meetings by the intrusion of minor characters. Language in these sequences is cacophonous, coded, and meaningless. Meadows and Morrice, each of whom in his way holds all opinions simultaneously, represent the devaluation of communication and the inability of characters trapped in this social system to forge stable identities for themselves. Characters try continually to be what they are not: Monckton, the novel's villain, reveals his true nature only anonymously at the masquerade in which he wears a devil costume; Belfield, ashamed of his family, tries to pass as a gentleman and then as a peasant; Morrice repeats whatever he thinks anyone wants to hear, always on the lookout for the main chance and holding no real opinions of his own; Meadows spouts whatever he thinks will be most disagreeable; and Harrel insists on an appearance of wealth even when he knows his dissipation has ruined not only himself and his wife but his ward as well. In contrast, Briggs and Compton Delvile grasp too assiduously what they are, and so thoroughly exaggerate their characters with arrogance and miserliness that they become almost intentional self-caricatures.

A number of conclusions can be drawn from the carnivalesque qualities of *Cecilia*. When Cecilia participates in the masquerade, albeit without wearing a mask herself, she simultaneously disapproves of the Harrels' way of life and is excited by it. This is a primary quality of the carnival: it represents in ritual fashion the contiguity and simultaneity of pleasure and disapproval in social life—liberation is always balanced by containment, freedom by restraint. It is worth noting here that one criticism of Bakhtin has been his unwillingness to see the central irony in carnival: it is a fundamentally sanctioned social activity, a permissible blurring of categories and norms.[11] This situation produces the intense narrative tension present in *Cecilia*. The tension comes not from suspense—we can anticipate more or less what will happen, if not next, then eventually—but from an ambience of continual threat: "What continual disturbance . . . keeps me thus forever from rest!" laments Cecilia. "No sooner is one wound closed, but another is opened; mortification constantly succeeds distress, and when my heart is spared my pride is attacked, that not a moment of tranquillity may ever be allowed me!" (2:232). The world is forever upside down in *Cecilia,* its hierarchies challenged, its repressed desires erupting when least able to be fulfilled. The scenes play out a perpetual game of gender and class warfare, a theater of masks and crosspurposes.

Cecilia's madness derives directly from these cross-purposes, and from frustration at her own powerlessness in the face of absurd circumstances. In other words, Cecilia goes mad for the same reason Camilla goes mad: there is no sane response to the circumstances she finds herself in. Efforts to enlist others in her aid fail. When, for example, she finally resorts to asking Compton Delvile to intervene for her and disabuse Sir Robert Floyer concerning his presumptions for her hand in marriage, her guardian refuses to debase himself in this way. Cecilia writes to the baronet herself, though not with much effect: "Provoked and wearied, Cecilia resolved no longer to depend upon any body but herself for the management of her own affairs" (1:304). However, taking action herself not only does not extricate her from misunderstanding or financial disaster, it makes things worse, because every action she takes causes the social world around her to impute to her motives which are either false or base or both.

The point Burney makes in all her novels, but preeminently in *Cecilia,* is that a beautiful heiress cannot possibly remain independently single by choice: such an eventuality would not be credited as plausible in polite society. Mr. Hobson puts it well when he notes: "As to a lady, let her be worth never so much, she's a mere nobody, as one may say, till she can get herself a husband, being she knows nothing of business, and is made to pay for everything through the nose" (2:411). As Lady Honoria Pemberton, a cousin of the Delviles, remarks, "Everybody one meets disposes of Miss Beverley to some new person" (1:345). Lady Honoria is a character who performs the same role Camilla's brother Lionel plays in Burney's third novel and the anarchic Morrice plays more brutally in *Cecilia:* she is a disruptive force perpetually amusing herself with practical jokes at the expense of others and of propriety. But Lady Honoria's disruptions are knowing, insightful, and calculated. Her sharp wit refreshingly challenges the staid codes of social behavior in the novel. She recognizes the stakes for women in this society, and she has the novel's last word. When Cecilia chides her on her lack of principles, she responds reasonably, "Not a creature thinks of our principles, till they find them out by our conduct; and nobody can possibly do that till we are married, for they give us no power beforehand. The men know nothing of us in the world while we are single, but how we can dance a minuet, or play a lesson upon the harpsichord" (2:466). Lady Honoria tries to manipulate this slippery female role and to turn slipperiness itself into freedom.

Cecilia is not, however, as calculating as Lady Honoria, because she is not yet as bitter. Cecilia's madness, like Camilla's, is distilled from the frustration of unbearable powerlessness, the frustration of always having to enlist another's authority. Its first symptoms appear when Delvile and Monckton fight a duel, and Monckton is thought fatally wounded. This duel occurs in a parallel place in the narrative to the duel between Sir Robert Floyer and Belfield, and in the intervening pages occur several other averted duels. Indeed, Cecilia becomes adept at managing the rivals for her affections. Disturbed by the duel occasioned after the opera imbroglio, she maneuvers around the simultaneous offers of lemonade from Delvile and Floyer at the Harrels' ball, and makes an ingenious response to their question, "Which is to be the happy man?" "'Each, I hope,' answered Cecilia, with admirable presence of mind, 'since I expect no less than that you will both do me the honour of drinking my health'" (1:322).

At the same time, however, Cecilia begins to be deprived of speech: "All utterance seemed denied her, and she curtseyed without saying a word" (1:339). Her conversations with Mortimer become monosyllabic and halting; in other situations, Cecilia defends herself vociferously and with self-assurance, but with Mortimer Delvile Cecilia is as tongue-tied as is Camilla with Mandlebert. And as Edgar Mandlebert materializes only when least desired, so Cecilia continually meets Delvile unexpectedly and in inopportune and suspicious-looking circumstances (a favorite technique of Burney's for setting up misunderstanding and misreading as well as tension in the reader — sign systems in her novels are always dangerously booby-trapped). An anticipated duel also opens the novel's climactic sequence, when Delvile unexpectedly turns up in London while Cecilia is making plans to join him abroad, and finds her in the company of Belfield in what look like damning circumstances. What follows builds such incredible tension that the reader herself feels lost; Delvile and his wife each order the other around and draw premature conclusions without any evidence.

First, Delvile commands that Cecilia go in her chair to his father's house in St. James-square, but as soon as she leaves, she jumps out of the chair and returns to the Belfields in Portland-street, because it occurs to her that Mortimer will challenge Belfield, and she wants to prevent bloodshed. The men are gone when she returns, but she follows them to a coffeehouse. They have just left. Now she decides to go to the Delvile house, but by then Mortimer has come, inquired for her, found she had not come, and left again, and Compton Delvile, still not crediting her marriage, refuses to admit her. The lovers chase each other around the city in this way for page after page, returning to both Portland-street and the coffeehouse. Cecilia has taken the cringing Simkins with her, who impedes progress, and she finally loses control when the coachman drunkenly demands to be paid and Simkins disputes his bill. The crisis builds: "The inebriety of the coachman became evident; a mob was collecting; Cecilia, breathless with vehemence and terror, was encircled, yet struggled in vain to break away; and the stranger gentleman, protesting, with sundry compliments, he would himself take care of her, very freely seized her hand" (2:428). Encircled and "taken care of," Cecilia is like Evelina at Marylebone Gardens and like herself at the masquerade, a prisoner of men pretending all around her to be gallant and in fact suffocating her with their "protection."

Cecilia is meanwhile convinced that her husband and Belfield have shot each other, and suddenly she screams, "He will be gone! he will be gone! and I must follow him to Nice!" and "with a strength hitherto unknown to her, she forcibly disengaged herself from her persecutors" and runs down the street (2:429). The narrator describes Cecilia's mad rush through London in a prose teeming with palpable tension:

> Meanwhile the frantic Cecilia escaped both pursuit and insult by the velocity of her own motion. She called aloud upon Delvile as she flew to the end of the street. No Delvile was there! — she turned the corner; yet saw nothing of him; she still went on, though unknowing whither, the distraction of her mind every instant growing greater, from the inflammation of fatigue, heat, and disappointment. She was spoken to repeatedly; she was even caught once or twice by her riding habit; but she forced herself along by her own vehement rapidity, not hearing what was said, not heeding what was thought. Delvile, bleeding by the arm of Belfield, was the image before her eyes, and took such full possession of her senses, that still, as she ran on, she fancied it in view. She scarce touched the ground; she scarce felt her own motion; she seemed as if endued with supernatural speed, gliding from place to place, from street to street, with no consciousness of any plan, and following no other direction than that of darting forward wherever there was most room, and turning back when she met with any obstruction; till, quite spent and exhausted, she abruptly ran into a yet open shop,

where, breathless and panting, she sunk upon the floor, and, with a look disconsolate and helpless, sat for some time without speaking. (2:429–30)

The reader is inside the disintegrating mind of the heroine in this passage, following her through the streets of London controlled by a maniacal mental image. The narrator neither judges nor sympathizes. In Burney's most important narrative departure in *Cecilia,* she experiments with a vocally rich and multilayered third-person omniscient narrator. While Burney's post-*Evelina* style has been vilified by critics, some have recognized her contribution to the evolution of a storytelling voice for the novel. Burney experiments in *Cecilia* with pre-Austenian irony, and conveys both comedy, melodrama, and serious social satire in a voice that controls the narrative tone with its overripe sense of vitriolic menace. No one had written like this before Burney.

As Cecilia runs, she retains an image of a bleeding Mortimer Delvile before her eyes. This image echoes the earlier ruptured blood vessel of Augusta Delvile, Mortimer's mother and Burney's most overwhelming mother figure. She collapses in a pawnshop called "Three Blue Balls" where again she is imprisoned, locked into a room while the proprietors place an announcement for her in the *Daily Advertiser.* She has lost her purse to the coachman and Simkins, and the advertisement, entitled MADNESS, mentions the Delviles. For two days, Cecilia remains in the room, refusing food and drink (also a factor in Camilla's madness), and "though naturally and commonly of a silent and quiet disposition, she was now not a moment still, for the irregular starts of a terrified and disordered imagination were changed into the constant ravings of morbid delirium" (2:433). When her friends find her, "her dress was in much disorder, her fine hair was dishevelled, and the feathers of her riding-hat were broken and half falling down, some shading her face, others reaching to her shoulder" (2:434). She resembles Madame Duval thrown into the ditch by Captain Mirvan in *Evelina.*

Chillingly, when Delvile first speaks to Cecilia and is not recognized, he asks, "Is it me or my name you thus disown?" (2:439), making clear the important separate identity of names in Burney's novels. She remains "senseless, speechless, motionless, her features void of all expression, her cheeks without colour, her eyes without meaning" (2:450) until restorative sleep brings her to herself. Among her first gestures when well is to write an accusing letter to Monckton, signed "Cecilia Delvile" (2:460). Camilla went mad when she entered a social limbo as a woman inappropriately alone; Cecilia goes mad effectively for the same reason. Both heroines recover into the arms of men who have learned their lessons from this experience: if you are going to "take care of" and "protect" a woman in the eighteenth century, you had better not leave her side, not for a minute. Danger lurks in every corner, and in the abstract the love of a good man serves no purpose.

It is this omnipresent sense of danger that most distinguishes *Cecilia* from a novel that, thirty years later and using a title from Burney's second novel's ending, addresses the same basic themes: Jane Austen's *Pride and Prejudice*. [12] The elder Bennets and Delviles each present pictures of conjugal mismatch borne for the purpose of social disguise. Burney's clear portrait of marital strife in the Delvile household is groundbreaking for eighteenth-century fiction. Burney and Austen discuss the accommodations these couples have made to their infelicity in strikingly similar fashion. Family pride controls both Mortimer Delvile and Fitzwilliam Darcy, and both first propose to the heroines after prolonged distance and cold behavior, and only when their efforts to give up their feelings have failed. Both offend their chosen women when they make their first declarations, as both focus on their failed attempt to overcome what they see as a damaging and unfortunate prepossession, and Delvile exacerbates this offense with a proposal of secrecy. In both cases, especially in the characters of Compton Delvile and Lady Catherine de Bourgh, immovable pride and prejudice are shown to be duping mechanisms whereby social rules thwart individual desire and the possibility of individual happiness. In both novels, hedonistic people bring ruin on themselves and those close to them: Mr. and Mrs. Harrel; Wickham and Lydia. In both novels, frustrated society women hone their tongues on sarcasm: Lady Honoria Pemberton and the Bingley sisters.

Cecilia is, nevertheless, ultimately a far darker and far more troubling novel than is Austen's *Pride and Prejudice*. The central houses in the two works symbolize this difference. Delvile Castle is surrounded by a moat with its drawbridge drawn up and "no taste was shown in the disposition of the grounds, no openings were contrived through the wood for distant views or beautiful objects" (2:1) — this is a gloomy and entombing place. In Compton Delvile's pompous, self-important, and haughty house, "every thing had an air of state, but of a state so gloomy, that while it inspired awe, it repressed pleasure" (1:93). Delvile Castle is the antithesis of *Pride and Prejudice*'s Pemberley — "dark, heavy, and monastic" (2:1); an austere and decaying object. Pemberley, in bright contrast, stands "on rising ground" and is situated in order to maximize the distance and beauty of its prospects. [13] Delvile

Castle, like Burney's novels, lacks space for "views": it is as claustrophobic as the text which encloses it. Elizabeth Bennet's world is indeed "light and bright and sparkling"; Cecilia Beverley's world is a
dim and narrow passageway.

While no one is as evil as Monckton or as frightening as Briggs
or Compton Delvile in the pages of *Pride and Prejudice,* the entailed
situation of Longbourn and the diminution of Cecilia's inheritance
turn both novels to an underlying emphasis on money and its con-
comitant, class. Collins and Morrice resemble each other as characters whose limbo-like residence in the middle class makes them anxious to curry favor with those above them, and they become absurd
in their efforts to please. The practicality of Charlotte Lucas is similar
to that of Lady Honoria, though the latter is more outspokenly bitter.
Charlotte, at least, gets a "manageable" husband, albeit an insufferable
one. Balls and dances figure prominently as the loci of social hier-
archy and social rule-making in both novels, and both rely almost entirely on dialogue and conversation to forward their plots. Burney's
experimental use of a third-person narrator prefigures Austen's own
ironic narrative voice. The dominant difference between these two
thematically parallel novels concerns the difference in style between
Burney's graphic materiality and Austen's ironic subtlety.

Burney believed the key scene in *Cecilia* to be that in which Mrs.
Delvile responds apoplectically to her son's passion for the heroine.
Samuel Crisp had objected vociferously to this explicitly bloody confrontation, but Burney defended her narrative in a letter dated 15 March
1782:

> The conflict scene for Cecilia, between the mother and son, to which
> you so warmly object, is the very scene for which I wrote the whole
> book, and so entirely does my plan hang upon it, that I must abide
> by its reception in the world, or put the whole behind the fire. . . . I
> meant in Mrs. Delville [*sic*] to show how the greatest virtues and ex-
> cellences may be totally obscured by the indulgence of violent passions
> and the ascendancy of favourite prejudices. (*DL* 1:418)

This was one time that Burney did not allow a "daddy" to censor her,
and it explains her version of the "pride and prejudice" theme and
its treatment in *Cecilia.*

While Cecilia is still ill and incarcerated in the pawnshop, Dr. Lyster
speaks the lines from the novel's last pages that provided Jane Austen
with her well-known title and summarized the plot of Burney's second novel:

The whole of this unfortunate business . . . has been the result of PRIDE and PREJUDICE. Your uncle, the Dean, began it, by his arbitrary will, as if an ordinance of his own could arrest the course of nature! and as if *he* had the power to keep alive, by the loan of a name, a family in the male branch already extinct. Your father, Mr. Mortimer, continued it with the same self-partiality, preferring the wretched gratification of tickling his ear with a favourite sound, to the solid happiness of his son with a rich and deserving wife. Yet this, however, remember; if to PRIDE and PREJUDICE you owe your miseries, so wonderfully is good and evil balanced, that to PRIDE and PREJUDICE you will also owe their termination: for all that I could say to Mr. Delvile, either of reasoning or entreaty,—and I said all I could suggest, and I suggested all a man need wish to hear,—was totally thrown away, till I pointed out to him his *own* disgrace, in having a *daughter-in-law* immured in these mean lodgings. (2:462)

At the end of Jane Austen's novel, both Darcy and his aunt Lady Catherine are effectively chastened: neither will ever again behave with such inhuman arrogance. But Dr. Lyster's treacly moral notwithstanding, only more of the same converts her dreadful father-in-law to Cecilia's side. She and any children she may have (and, we suspect, she had better produce at least one male heir after all this trouble) are to suffer even more greatly in the Delvile pride because now they themselves must participate in it.

In order to achieve the fulfillment of privatized desire, Cecilia gives up a great deal: a name, a fortune, and the ability to act independently. To gain a husband, she loses a self, and it is not at all clear in the novel's denouement that Burney believes this to be a good bargain. The flighty Lady Honoria Pemberton has, perhaps, the last word, given the entrapped helplessness Cecilia has endured until her marriage could be acknowledged: "You can do nothing at all without being married; a single woman is a thousand times more shackled than a wife; for, she is accountable to everybody; and a wife, you know, has nothing to do but just to manage her husband" (2:465). The vision of Cecilia "immured" in Delvile Castle—despite all that propriety and a loving husband can offer—remains a grim vision. Though in the end Burney's lovers begin to take possession of something like happiness, in a Burney novel "happiness" simply means the calm possession of mutual knowledge, the lifting of the veil of secrecy and misunderstanding.

6

The Wanderer:
Money and Entrapment

The Wanderer opens in darkness, as a boatload of distressed English travelers is setting off stealthily from the French coast. The novel announces its themes and tone with its opening sentence: "During the dire reign of the terrific Robespierre, and in the dead of night, braving the cold, the darkness and the damps of December, some English passengers, in a small vessel, were preparing to glide silently from the coast of France, when a voice of distress resounded from the shore, imploring, in the French language, pity and admission" (*Wanderer* I:I). A young woman in rags and blackface begs to be allowed entry, and after Albert Harleigh and a seaman, two of the passengers, quell the less compassionately inclined, she is helped aboard. These passengers will become most of the novel's populace through five volumes. When the boat docks, the young woman discovers that she has lost her purse, and thus is thrown on the mercy of her fellows, one of whom helps her by purchasing a place for her in a coach. She refuses to divulge any information about who she is and travels to Brighthelmstone, where she seeks a letter addressed to "L. S." This letter does not bring her the solace she hopes, but rather tells her she must remain vigilant about her disguise, and steadfastly continue to conceal her name and identity. In volume 3, the reader learns her Christian name—Juliet—but not until volume 4 do we learn her full identity as Lady Juliet Granville.

While in *Evelina* many of the characters learn the heroine's real name and identity only in the novel's denouement, the reader at least has been in on the secret all along. Burney keeps even the reader of *The Wanderer* and virtually all of the characters in the dark, asking us to accept her protagonist on faith as a woman without a history, radically present tense in the story but supported by no narrative framework until very late in the work. The French Revolution with its upheaval of roles and identities serves as a distant but unavoidable and all-pervasive backdrop for the adventures of this ambiguously defined heroine, though nearly all of the novel takes place in England. The hero, Albert Harleigh, and Elinor Joddrel, the novel's compelling antiheroine, debate the collective impact of revolutionary fervor and mores in the novel's opening pages, and the heroine's ultimate fate rests on the defeat of a revolutionary official (who is importantly never identified by name—Juliet is brutally married to this unnamed character who appears only as a dark, maniacal, Gothic figure of terror): throughout, the "new system" is implicitly contrasted with the old.

Least read and most maligned of Burney's novels, *The Wanderer* was not published until 1814, though Burney had been working on it for two decades. Had it been published in the 1790s, when the vogue in novels was to marry elements of Gothicism and polemic in popular fictions such as Charlotte Smith's *Desmond* (1792), William Godwin's *Caleb Williams* (1794), Robert Bage's *Hermsprong* (1796), Mary Hays' *Memoirs of Emma Courtney* (1796), and works by Elizabeth Inchbald, Thomas Holcroft, and, later, Maria Edgeworth, *The Wanderer* might have been read in a more appropriate context and appreciated for its web of politics and the imagination. But Burney's life was in flux during that period, and she lived from 1802 to 1812 in exile with her husband in France (during the end of this period she suffered from the breast disease discussed in chapter 2), remaining isolated from literary life in her own country and unable to smuggle the manuscript to London.

As it was, traveling with the massive work itself became a trial Burney explains in the book's dedication. The early part of the novel, she writes, "has already twice traversed the ocean in manuscript" (1:vii); she had taken the materials with her to France in 1802. At customs, she reports, "upon my given word that the papers contained neither letters, nor political writings; but simply a work of invention and observation; the voluminous manuscript was suffered to pass, without demur, comment, or the smallest examination" (1:viii). Critics have, in fact, faulted Burney for evading politics in *The Wanderer.* But this is a misreading. Politics are indeed subsumed into the personal and familial travails of the heroine, but the absorption of the political into the personal, rather than evading, permits Burney to analyze explicitly the ideological impact of French revolutionary politics on the European social condition.

Evelina "Anville" had been given a surname that was a cipher. An anagram for her Christian name, Anville represented the empty space where a name should go. Cecilia Beverley's surname created for her a social and economic prison. Juliet Granville has even larger name problems. First, concealment demands that she have no name at all. Then, she receives mail addressed to L. S., which becomes Ellis, thus Miss Ellis. Along the way, she is referred to as the Wanderer, the Incognita, the Fair Unknown, and as "a rare hand . . . at hocus pocus work" (5:146) and "an adventurer . . . without even a name" (1:53). She is "Ophelia" (1:241), "a foundling girl" (1:183), a "mysterious charmer" (1:95), "an illegitimate stroller" (1:53), a "toad-eater" (3:336), a "fair Enigma" (3:394), and "Mrs. Thing-a-mi" (3:240). Margaret Anne Doody has pointed out that most of Burney's heroines' names contain the syllable "elle": Evelina, Camilla (whose name was changed from "Ariella" shortly before publication), Ellis, Elgiva, Elinor, et al. In the Wanderer's case, Doody remarks the existential semiology of the name Ellis, "elle is"—a primal Burney statement on the quintessential thereness of the female in society.[1]

But Ellis—as she is known through much of the work's five volumes —is also finally the "Miss Nobody" of Lovel's accusation concerning Evelina and to whom Burney had addressed her adolescent diary. Juliet's radical namelessness makes her the ultimate incarnation of the beautiful mysterious orphan on whose ambiguous identity turns many an eighteenth-century plot.[2] She arrives in England "without name, without fortune, without friends! no parents to receive, no protector to counsel me; unacknowledged by my family,—unknown even to the children of my father!" (5:93). Juliet's stripped-down female status (stateless, placeless, and penniless as well as nameless, married yet not married, of high birth yet not recognized) raises explicitly Burney's political analysis of the position of women. Here the theme is politically timely—the French Revolution and its displacements and realignments—and personally of concern to the author, whose husband was a struggling French émigré uprooted by the Revolution and its aftermath.

The Wanderer's final reference to sinking into nonentity returns us to the ever-present Burneyan problem of naming. Whereas Cecilia was trapped by too tight a marriage, quite literally, to her name — and to the seal in it — Juliet has no full name for most of *The Wanderer*. In volume 4, the history of Juliet's past and its concealments unfolds, but not until the final volume does anyone address her by her proper name (and, as usual in Burney's fictions, once the name problem has been sorted out, a process that catalyzes her novels' plots, the heroine almost immediately exchanges her legal birth name for that of her husband). Juliet's namelessness through most of the narrative — a namelessness far more radically isolating for Juliet than it had been for any of Burney's previous heroines — represents a daring political statement on Burney's part. A woman's name indicates not her identity *tout court*, but her social identity: it tells us, as Evelina puts it, "to whom she most belongs," by referring to her father or husband. To lack a name is to belong to no one, that is, to belong to oneself. The apostrophes in *The Wanderer* point again to this, and to the paradox that "self-dependency" exhilarates even while it denies entry to a social niche. Nobody knows what to do with Juliet; a woman so self-assured, so poised, so able to speak for, defend, and support herself, must have a name. Ellis' literal self-possession comes from a defiance imposed on her by circumstance: "Courage . . . is more frequently than the looker on suspects, the effect of secret reasoning, and cool calculation of consequence, than of fearless temperament, or inborn bravery" (2:83). Making her last heroine nameless was Burney's boldest stroke as a feminist novelist.

Ellis' namelessness permits her to travel across classes, professions, lodgings, and appearances; it serves the role of a "mask" at a masquerade. Being "Miss Nobody" more even than Evelina or the young Burney could pretend to be, "Ellis" shifts clothing, complexion, employment, and behavior at every turn in this narrative, becoming Everywoman at the same time as she is "Nobody" to whom admission is continually denied. As Mrs. Ireton, one of the novel's "three Furies," accuses her:

> You have been bruised and beaten; and dirty and clean; and ragged and whole; and wounded and healed; and a European and a Creole, in less than a week. I suppose, next, you will dwindle into a dwarf; and then, perhaps, find some surprising contrivance to shoot up into a giantess. There is nothing that can be too much to expect from so great an adept in metamorphoses. (1:85)

And at the appropriately fragmented ruins of Stonehenge, the blundering Riley makes Juliet's self-transmogrifying capabilities into a multiform Gothic myth of threatened selfhood:

> "What a rare hand you are, Demoiselle," cried Riley, "at hocus pocus work! Who the deuce, with that Hebe face of yours, could have thought of your being a married woman! Why, even I saw you at that old Bang'em's concert, at Brighthelmstone, I should have taken you for a boarding-school Miss. But you metamorphose yourself about so, one does not know which way to look for you. Ovid was a mere fool to you. His nymphs, turned into trees, and rivers, and flowers, and beasts, and fishes, make such a staring chaos of lies, that one reads them without a ray of reference to truth; like the tales of the Genii, or of old Mother Goose. He makes such a comical hodge podge of animal, vegetable, and mineral choppings and changes, that we should shout over them, as our brats do at a puppet-show, when old Nick teaches punchinello the devil's dance down to hell; or pummels his wife to a mummy; if it were not for the shy rogue's tickling one's ear so cajolingly with the jingle of metre. But Demoiselle, here, scorns all that namby pamby work. . . . I have met with nothing like her . . . all the globe over. Neither juggler nor conjuror is a match for her. She can make herself as ugly as a witch, and as handsome as an angel. She'll answer what one only murmurs in a whisper; and she won't hear a word, when one bawls as loud as a speaking-trumpet. Now she turns herself into a vagrant, not worth sixpence; and now, into a fine player and singer that ravishes all ears, and might make, if it suited her fancy, a thousand pounds at her benefit: and now, again, as you see, you can't tell whether she's a house-maid, or a country girl! Yet a devilish fine creature, faith! as fine a creature as ever I beheld, — when she's in that humour! Look — but what a beautiful head of hair she's displaying to us now! It becomes her mightily. But I won't swear that she does not change it, in a minute or two, for a skull-cap! She's a droll girl, faith! I like her prodigiously!" (5:146–48)

This speech, uttered by an unlikely and minor character, summarizes precisely and insightfully the story of *The Wanderer*. As the masquerade sequence in *Cecilia* defines that novel's carnivalesque atmosphere, so this Stonehenge outburst epitomizes Juliet's fragmented social condition. Juliet has been forced to become a trickster, a Proteus, an Ovidian creature, a punchinello. Her self, like the stylized rocks of Stonehenge that surround the speakers in this scene, is in ruins. Stonehenge represents a literalization of the possibility of "ruin" for an unmarried woman in its stylized, ritualized, monolithic pieces of an unrecapturable whole, and hence serves as a perfect backdrop for Riley's speech.

Burney's novels do not abound in visualization or physical description, but the Stonehenge of *The Wanderer* here becomes a metaphoric geographical center for Juliet's predicament (as it does for Thomas Hardy's *Tess*), and it mediates between the Gothic rusticity of the New Forest sequence where Juliet has undergone a pastoral renewal while hiding and the social portraits of the Brighthelmstone and London scenes. These "vast, irregular, strange" ruins "[excite] sympathy in what seemed lonely and undone" in Juliet and she is "[s]truck with solemn wonder" by "these massy ruins, grand and awful, though terrific rather than attractive" (5:132–33). The sublime, the beautiful, and the picturesque merge here, and Burney describes "this grand, uncouth monument of ancient days" in its unrefined savagery as a place that removes Juliet from her mundane concerns and moves her to "meditation even to madness" (5:134–35):

> She arrived at a stupendous assemblage of enormous stones, of which the magnitude demanded ocular demonstration to be entitled to credibility. Yet, though each of them, taken separately, might seem from its astonishing height and breadth, there, like some rock, to have been placed from "the beginning of things;" and though not even the rudest sculpture denoted any vestige of human art, still the whole was clearly no phenomenon of nature. The form, that might still be traced, of an antique structure, was evidently circular and artificial; and here and there, supported by gigantic posts, or pillars, immense slabs of flat stone were raised horizontally, that could only by manual art and labour have been elevated to such a height. Many were fallen; many, with grim menace, looked nodding; but many, still sustaining their upright direction, were so ponderous that they appeared to have resisted all the wars of the elements, in this high and bleak situation, for ages. (5:132–33)

Juliet's flight and her quest in many ways end here, at the "wild edifice" that puts all elegant sentimentality to shame with stones that speak with their immense silence. The ruins and fragments of a lost vision parallel the fragmentation that Juliet herself has undergone.

Juliet's situation partakes of this peculiar have-and-have-not fragmentation:

> Entitled to an ample fortune, yet pennyless; indebted for her sole preservation from insult and from famine, to pecuniary obligations from accidental acquaintances, and those acquaintances, men! pursued, with documents of legal right, by one whom she shuddered to behold, and to whom she was so irreligiously tied, that she could not, even if she

wished it, regard herself as his lawful wife; though so entangled, that her letters seemed to be linked with duty and honour; unacknowledged, — perhaps disowned by her family; and, though born to a noble and yet untouched fortune, consigned to disguise, to debt, to indigence, and to flight! (5:256–57)

This sense of ambiguity and contradiction run amok is underlined in the novel's last sections when Elinor cites Shakespeare to talk about the body that will "melt, thaw, and resolve itself into a dew" (5:178) and about joy that vanishes "like a baseless fabric of a vision" (5:285). Juliet inhabits a chimerical world, in which external identity and its trappings — name, fortune, estate — can vanish into thin air and she must, like "a female Robinson Crusoe" (5:394) or a female Prospero, depend upon her own abilities to conjure.

Conjuring will not do, however; Juliet must work for a living. Burney's heroine lacks business acumen, and never manages to earn more than will get her from one day to the next. She lives alone through most of the narrative, and struggles to pay for lodgings, food, and clothing. In large measure, *The Wanderer* concerns its protagonist's struggle to tolerate impossible living conditions and repetitive work. Because this struggle departs from Burney's earlier fictional practice, it takes *The Wanderer* well beyond the dangerous social misunderstandings that plague Evelina and Camilla, and, to a lesser extent, Cecilia. Not that Juliet is not, in her turn, continually misread. But she is older and more seasoned than Burney's earlier heroines, bearing a relation to them not unlike the relation of Anne Elliot to Emma Woodhouse. Slanderous misconstructions of her actions beset Juliet, but they never take her by surprise.

Nevertheless, she too resides in an enclosed social world. At key junctures in the novel, when surrounded by rudeness and insult not to be borne, Juliet escapes into the nearest empty and apparently unregarded enclosure; this habit of shutting herself into private spaces creates opportunities for otherwise impossible tête-à-tête meetings. She also gets into serious trouble, ending up accused of burglary, for her presence in one of the novel's misleading "vacant apartments." At the same time, Juliet often finds herself unable to leave rooms because the exit route is blocked. *The Wanderer* is a novel about a woman locked into her identity as though it were a prison and imprisoned by her attendant public namelessness. Like *Camilla*'s, its world is claustrophobic. And the novel's major departure from Burney's earlier drawing-room scenarios is set in motion when the unnamed French husband tracks down his escaping wife: Juliet goes into true hiding, literally running for her life.

Juliet discovers that she, like Cecilia, is sought through a newspaper advertisement. Burney had been outraged when her name appeared in the satirical pamphlet *Warley* after the publication of *Evelina*. Juliet is similarly distressed: "To find herself advertised in a newspaper! — the blood mounted indignantly into her cheeks — Perhaps to be described! — perhaps named! and with a reward for her discovery!" (4: 245). The advertisement indeed designates her as the person "commonly known by the name of Miss Ellis" (4:242), but Juliet has internalized that name; "elle is." At the climactic moment when the plot begins to resolve itself — Harleigh and the French commissary converge on Juliet's hiding place in a roadside inn — nine months have elapsed since the novel's opening. When the elderly Sir Jaspar Herrington calls Juliet "Miss Granville" for the first time in the book, she is born into her true name. Like a newborn and like Mary Shelley's monster in *Frankenstein* when he acquires language, Juliet is enthralled by the new kinship and identity terms she can claim: "I am going now to be happy! — How big a word! — how new to my feelings! — A sister! — a brother! — Have I, indeed, such relations?" (5:105). She resembles Victor Frankenstein's unnamed monster when he discovers the concept of family and hears "of brother, sister, and all the various relationships which bind one human being to another in mutual bonds."[3]

Class consciousness and class analysis hold center stage in *The Wanderer*. Juliet's arrival and circumstances in England provide a virtual blueprint for Elinor Joddrel's political agenda by placing the heroine into relentlessly unconventional and therefore socially untenable circumstances. The loss of her money immediately makes her dependent on the goodwill of others, as Cecilia's inherited wealth had inevitably made her public prey. As in *Cecilia*, Burney's subject is the economics of eighteenth-century womanhood. Juliet's initial transformation from blackface, patches, and rags to beauty foreshadows a series of shifting identities and professions. Juliet's nameless and stateless situation permits her to belong to no class and to all classes simultaneously and to pass easily from one to another. In fact, her most uncomfortable predicaments emerge early, when she is living in the house of the imperious Mrs. Maple, because there she has no defined role, and when she works as a music instructor, because she is then expected to behave in as genteel a fashion as her pupils and to make her status differentiation from them as invisible as possible. She is bored in the millinery shop and finds needlework drudgery, but she identifies herself nevertheless with the working-class women who share her labors even when she feels intellectually superior to others of her condition, as in the case of Flora Pierson, whom Juliet intervenes to "save" from being used as a sexual object by the novel's libertine Sir Lyell Sycamore, a direct descendant of Sir Clement Willoughby, Lovel, and Sir Sedley Clarendel.

Juliet exploits the talents and crafts she has been taught by an aristocratic education to pass from one class to another in downward mobility, exchanging her lodgings for ever smaller rooms and her clothing for ever coarser fabrics and fewer ornaments as she goes. Juliet's drawing-room accomplishments provide her with all she needs to earn a subsistence living, as she turns her entertainment abilities and elegant crafts into cash. That may be *The Wanderer*'s central irony and one of Burney's most biting statements on femininity and its trappings of passive ornament. Juliet plays the harp like an angel, sings like a nightingale, draws with the deft strokes of a Leonardo, sews accurately, quickly, and beautifully, performs on the stage with the poise of a Sarah Siddons (whom Burney knew), and copies in a clear, elegant, and correct hand. Her abilities prove a past that embraces a gentlewoman's cultivated upbringing in the array of taught "useful and appropriate female accomplishments" (1:163) they bring to light. Not incidentally, her artistry also provides Burney with an opportunity to rail against the inevitably low social position of those who attempt to live by their creative talents. These cultivated aptitudes permit Juliet to earn a living as a music teacher, needle worker, and paid companion, but of course they were not meant to be thus put to employment for pay. Indeed, these talents are to be displayed precisely for nothing, for the privilege of charming, as a down payment and mortgage on a future husband.

Women perform their feminine crafts in private only. Therefore, the sequence that begins with a scheme to market "Ellis" in a subscription-concert (Burney surely had her prepublication marketing of *Camilla* in mind here) and ends with Elinor's attempted suicide just as Juliet descends to the stage (in a scene that echoes Harrel's public suicide in *Cecilia*) comprises most of an entire volume and is played out with prolonged narrative anxiety. Female accomplishments turn into shameful self-display when presented publicly and for money. Harleigh persecutes Juliet with this view when he asks how she can "enter into a career of public life, subversive — perhaps — to me, of even any eventual amelioration?" (2:350). He wields the term "propriety" like a sword over her, writing a letter in which he invokes "the received notion of the world, the hitherto unacknowledged boundaries of elegant life!" (2:364) to rebuke her, and crushes her with "the high responsibility of all actions that are voluntary" that will haunt her "for deviating, alone and unsupported as you appear, from the long-beaten track of female timidity" (2:365), which she translates as "delicacy" (2:366). For a woman to be a public artist and to receive payment for her artistry is to fall permanently from grace, to degrade the state of womanhood. This is *The Wanderer*'s critique throughout: "What is woman, — with the most upright designs, the most rigid circumspection, — what is woman unprotected? She is pronounced upon only from outward semblance: and, indeed, what other criterion has the world? Can it read the heart?" (2:367). By definition required to be radically private, to dwell in the enclosed space of the heart, woman is judged as though her exterior purely mirrors her privacy, so that privacy is invaded even as its inviolability is socially extolled.

Burney must have been thinking about her own ill-paying profession when she dedicated so much of *The Wanderer* to an analysis of woman's alienated, paradoxical, and, for aristocratic women, forbidden relation to work in the chapters leading up to the melodramatic stabbing that drops the curtain on Ellis' public career before it has a chance to begin. Juliet worries about Harleigh's imputations of indelicacy in public performance, but her anxiety and repugnance come not so much from that indulgent concern as from "the dread of public disapprobation." Alone or in a small group, she plays and sings beautifully, but as soon as the audience expands to staring strangers, she becomes nervous, hoarse, mute. She deplores the social conditions of artistry in a pampered society and remarks on "the hardship of those professions which cast their votaries upon the mercy of superficial judges; who, without investigation, discernment, or candour, make their decisions from common public prejudice; or current, but unexamined opinions" (2:307). That is one of Burney's harsher indictments of the function of criticism in her time.

Juliet also learns to appreciate the public masquerade involved in performance (and publication): "Alas! she cried, how little do we know either of the labours, or the privations, of those whose business it is to administer pleasure to the public! We receive it so lightly, that we imagine it to be lightly given!" (2:309). A discussion about the social aspects of art among the novel's meaner-spirited characters occasions the argument that there should be no relation between creating amusement and earning bread and meat, and that such "light" professions as artists follow should not command the same fees as are due for more useful services, since sonatas, minuets, and paintings are luxuries. One of Ellis' more inept, but nevertheless well-meaning, supporters, launches into a dissertation and defense of the artist's social role:

Luxury! What is it you all of you mean by luxury? Is it your own going to hear singing and playing? and to see dancing and capering? and to loll at your ease, while a painter makes you look pretty, if you are ever so plain? If it be, do those things no more, and there will soon be an end to them! but don't excite people to such feats, and then starve them for their pains. Luxury? do you suppose, because such sights, and such sounds, and such flattery, are luxuries to you, they are luxuries to those who produce them? Because you are in extacies to behold yourself grow younger and more blooming every moment, do you conclude that he who mixes your colours, and covers your defects, shares your transports? No; he is sick to death of you; and longing to set his pencil at liberty. And because you, at idle hours and from mere love of dissipation, lounge in your box at operas and concerts, to hear a tune, or to look at a jump, do you imagine he who sings, or who dances, must be a voluptuary? No! all he does is pain and toil to himself; learnt with labour, and exhibited with difficulty. The better he performs, the harder he has worked. All the ease, and all the luxury are yours, Mrs. Maple, yours, Miss Bydel, and yours, ladies all, that are the lookers on! for he does not pipe or skip at his own hours, but at yours; he does not adorn himself for his own warmth, or convenience, but to please your tastes and fancies; he does not execute what is easiest, and what he likes best, but what is hardest, and has most chance to force your applause. He sings, perhaps, when he may be ready to cry; he plays upon those harps and fiddles, when he is half dying with hunger; and he skips those gavots, and fandangos, when he would rather go to bed! And all this, to gain himself a hard and fatiguing maintenance, in amusing your dainty idleness, and insufficiency to yourselves. (2:319-21)

This impassioned speech could be applied to novelists and playwrights as well as to musicians, painters, and other performers, and it implicates women artists particularly since "all public appeals," Juliet proclaims, "are injurious to female fame" (1:323).

Work, despite Juliet's laments and Burney's social commentary, also energizes the heroine. When she has a full schedule of music students, she is able to shake the self-pitying lethargy that at times weighs on her and to galvanize herself into action: "Her spirits, from the fullness of her occupations, revived; and she soon grew a stranger to the depression of that ruminating leisure, which is wasted in regret, in repining, or in watering meditation" (2:111). As well as possibly explaining Burney's own reliance on keeping busy with her pen, this passage places Juliet's current wage-earning status in relief against the status to which she will be entitled when eventually she gains recognition in her full legal name as Lady Juliet Granville. Along with all her heroines, Burney feared the melancholy of idleness. The social and economic limbo Juliet inhabits illustrates a halfway point between the degrading work available to lower- and middle-class women and the enforced leisure of upper-class women.

The novel's final paragraphs, in which Juliet as the Wanderer is described as "a being who had been cast upon herself; a female Robinson Crusoe . . . reduced either to sink through inanition, to nonentity, or to be rescued from famine and death by such resources as she could find, independently in herself" (5:394–95), underline the heroine's relationship to productive, respectable, paying work. The advice she receives from her friend Gabriella's mother, her original protector, corroborates Juliet's desire to create a compromise between good breeding and civility on the one hand, and brute survival on the other:

> That where occasion calls for female exertion, mental strength must combat bodily weakness; and intellectual vigour must supply the inherent deficiencies of personal courage; and that those, only, are fitted for the vicissitudes of human fortune, who, whether female or male, learn to suffice to themselves. Be this the motto of your story. (2:62)

Indeed, this is the motto of Burney's last work of fiction, a daring motto for a novel written by a woman at the turn of the nineteenth century.

The themes of metamorphosis and fragmentation foregrounded so powerfully in the climactic Stonehenge sequence (a sequence that parallels the "madness" scenes that occur just before the denouements of *Cecilia* and *Camilla*) may also be seen in the use Burney makes of the revolutionary character of Elinor Joddrel. Elinor is Juliet's mirror image and alter-ego. In the Elinor/Harleigh unrequited love plot, Elinor resorts to the most transparently manipulative gestures of the swooning eighteenth-century damsel Jane Austen had lampooned in *Love and Freindship,* but in every other respect she represents the powerful liberating potential of unconventionality. She is a female slave to passion whose very enslavement turns her into an agent for the novel's radical assault on the barricades of gender. Even in her pleading desperation with Harleigh, she epitomizes the oppressed degradation of the woman who cannot act on her own without a man's sanction. At the same time, she challenges that degradation by throwing aside all the behavioral injunctions and social expectations of courtship. This is not a woman who will wait to be asked. Elinor has no patience with Juliet when she pleads the circumscription of her lot as an unprotected woman: "Debility and folly! Put aside your prejudices, and forget that you are a dawdling woman," she tells her, "to remember that you are an active human being and your FEMALE DIFFICULTIES will vanish into the vapour of which they are formed" (4:36). Elinor leaves her mark on the novel by serving as a countermand to all the narrative's ostensibly received notions: she champions the French Revolution and challenges male hegemony. Though both central female characters are conscious of the social, economic, and political muting of their selfhood, Elinor represents as well a divisive, unsettling textual effect in *The Wanderer;* she resists simple assimilation into the novel. The key to her character belongs, however, to her use of disguises. Like Ellis/Juliet, Elinor is a self-activating chameleon.

Elinor's central metamorphic appearance occurs at the subscription-concert, where she appears dressed as a man, "a strange figure, with something foreign in his appearance" (2:396). This cross-dressed figure disconcerts Juliet; "he" speaks in a whisper, purports to be deaf and mute, wears a slouched hat, and behaves with brusque arrogance. Elinor periodically lives on her own, an unmarried woman functioning as is Juliet, autonomously. She defies all rules of genteel conduct when she proposes to Harleigh, writes him letters, and wields a dagger. Elinor is androgynous and, tellingly, she is also bodiless, never physically described, and treated by Burney throughout as a disembodied intellect. Her other metamorphic appearance occurs at the Brighthelmstone churchyard. Juliet first spies her as "a female, with arms uplifted" (4:31) and as "some shadowy motion" (4:40) that catches her eye. Elinor presents herself to Juliet and Harleigh, both of whom she has lured to this dawn meeting, "half hidden behind a monument, a form in white; whose dress appeared to be made in the shape, and of the materials, used for our last mortal covering, a shroud" and wearing "[a] veil of the same stuff" over her face (4:40). A servant describes her as wearing "a white trimmed stuff dress over her cloaths, that made her look as if she were buried alive, and just the same as a ghost" (4:50). Her face is covered, whether by a slouched hat or a veil, in these appearances, and her body is at once supersexualized and desexualized by its enclosure in drapery.

Elinor is Burney's most passionate and most sexually repressed character, and she herself is aware of the contradictions and explosions she contains. "You must never mind what I say nor what I do," Elinor tells Juliet, "for I sport all sort of things, and in all sort of manners" (1:148). Given this androgynous, ambiguously draped, smolderingly repressed sexuality, Elinor serves as Burney's most subversive character, because in the novel's narrative economy it is possible for Burney to situate Elinor's politics underground as a subterranean lode of political heresy and feminist revolutionary fervor. Elinor reproves Ellis, for example, when she primly announces the impropriety of a woman who "exhibits herself a willing candidate for public applause" when she is forced to perform: "Oh woman! poor, subdued woman! thou art as dependent, mentally, upon the arbitrary customs of man, as man is, corporally, upon the established laws of his country!" (3:40). And Elinor offers a Wollstonecraftian analysis of woman's condition:

> By the oppressions of their [men's] own statutes and institutions, they render us insignificant; and then speak of us as if we were so born! But what have we tried, in which we have been foiled? They dare not trust us with their own education, and their own opportunities for distinction: — I except the article for fighting; against that, there may, perhaps be some obstacles: but to be condemned, as weaker vessels in intellect, because, inferior in bodily strength and stature, we cannot cope with them as boxers and wrestlers! They appreciate not the understandings of one another by such manual and muscular criterions. They assert not that one man has more brains than another, because he is taller; that he is endowed with more illustrious virtues, because he is stouter. They judge him not to be less ably formed for haranguing in the senate; for administering justice in the courts of law; for teaching science at the universities, because he could ill resist a bully, or conquer a foot pad! No! — woman is left out in the scales of human merit, only because they dare not weigh her! (3:41–42)

By pushing Elinor's defiance of normative behavior between the sexes to extremes, Burney makes her seem potentially dismissible as the novel's intellectual force. The dagger, the shroud, the gravestone: Elinor plays out the trappings of female Gothic. However, in so doing she lampoons the very conventions she defies by overplaying them. She thereby becomes the intellectual center of the novel, Juliet's revolutionary and outspoken counterpart. Juliet lives a necessarily defiant role in her namelessness, remaining ambiguous in nationality, marital status, and class as well as name. But while Juliet must maintain silence, Elinor, safely identified, can be read as speaking for her and expressing her resentments.[4]

The "masculine" and outspoken Mrs. Selwyn and cheeky Madame Duval in *Evelina,* the imperious and sharp-witted Mrs. Delvile in *Cecilia,* and the independent Mrs. Arlbery in *Camilla* had prepared Burney's characterization of Elinor Joddrel, but Elinor differs from her matrilineal predecessors in two crucial respects. First, as they are middle-aged and have been married, she is young and single. Second, the feminism of the matrons in the first three novels extends primarily to the social and domestic spheres, with only occasional, uncommitted tilts at contemporary affairs. Elinor, by contrast, is Burney's most political figure, defying not only the rules of courtship, but also championing the French Revolution against all the novel's other characters and, in so doing, taking a stand for women's political opinions. "I dare speak and act, as well as think and feel for myself!" (1:349) Elinor announces to Juliet, and she views the Revolution across the Channel as "that noble flame that nearly consumed the old world, to raise a new one, pheonix like, from its ashes" (1:345). Elinor discourses on this renewal and on the "Rights of Man" virtually from the outset of the novel, when during the crossing she disagrees with Harleigh about the Terror. Elinor believes in the leveling rightness of revolutionary upheaval, a leveling demonstrated by Juliet's plight and oddly lamented by Gabriella, who does not seem sure of her own voice:

> The French Revolution has opened our eyes to a species of equality more rational, because more feasible, than that of lands or of ranks; an equality not alone of mental sufferings, but of manual exertions. No state of life, however low, or however hard, has been left untried, either by the highest, or by the most delicate, in the various dispersions and desolation of the ancient French nobility. And to see, — as I, alas! have seen, — the willing efforts, the even glad toil, of the remnants of the first families of Europe, to procure, — not luxuries, not elegancies, not even comforts, — but maintenance! mean, laborious maintenance! — to preserve, — not state, not fortune, not rank, — but life itself! but simple existence. (4:188–89)

No doubt thinking of her husband's emigrant trials and wartime displacements in her analysis of the Revolution's impact on individual and family lives, Burney depicts Juliet's story and Elinor's political opinions as angles of vision from which to view a particularly turbulent period of European history.

"It was not Fanny Burney's policy to write about politics — a sphere allotted to men by the plan of creation and the advice of the courtesy-book," writes Joyce Hemlow in *The History of Fanny Burney*.[5] But *The Wanderer* strongly belies that view in its complex portrait of lives realigned and tempest-tossed by the political storms in France. Burney herself held the conservative views proposed by her friend Edmund Burke in his 1790 *Reflections on the Revolution in France* and of her husband, a nobleman and soldier loyal to the French monarchy and later to Napoleon Bonaparte. The characterization of the Bishop in *The Wanderer*, a character present in the narrative's machinery but who appears directly only at its resolution, reminds us that in 1793 Burney had published a pamphlet titled *Brief Reflections relative to the Emigrant French Clergy earnestly submitted to the humane consideration of The Ladies of Great Britain* and intended to plead the cause of hundreds of banished and destitute clergymen living in England. The pamphlet, a plea to affluent women to give money to this cause, was praised by the *British Critic* (December 1793), the *Monthly Review* (December 1793), and the *Critical Review* (March 1794). But Burney's anti-Jacobinism is not as vehement as that of Burke (or of her father). In a 1792 letter to her sister Susanna and the Lockes, she cites an evening with Burke:

> The French Revolution, he said, which began by authorising and legalising injustice, and which by rapid steps had proceeded to every species of Despotism except owning a Despot, was now menacing all the Universe, and all Mankind with the most violent concussion of principle and order.
>
> My Father heartily joined, and I tacitly assented to his doctrines, though I feared not with his fears. (*JL* 1:196)

Burney's own view of the Terror was ecumenical and virtually apolitical: to Susanna she wrote, "as to France—it weighs upon all our spirits—there is no driving it from our minds—all parties, all conditions must join in bewailing such barbarism" (1:224). To her father, she was more orthodoxly Burkean on the subject of the Duke of Brunswick's military endeavors:

> The depression, or encouragement, it must give to political adventurers, who, at all times, can stimulate the Rabble to what they please, will sure spread far, deep, and wide, according to the event of French experiment upon the minds, manners, and powers of men, and the feasibility of expunging all past experience, for the purpose of treating the World as if it were created yesterday, and every man, woman, and child, were let loose to act from their immediate suggestion, without reference to what is past, or sympathy in any thing that is present, or precaution for whatever is to come. (1:230)

"ANY Government is better than MOB-Government," she wrote to Mrs. Waddington (1:254), and "God keep us from any struggle beyond verbal discussion!" (1:261). Burney talked an anti-Jacobin, staunchly royalist party line to her father, and a more moderate pacifist dismay at French events to others. "[W]hat of misery can equal the misery of such a Revolution!—I am daily more & more in charity with all fixed Governments. *Let every one mend one,* as Will Chip [the "author" of Hannah More's 1793 *Village Politics*] says, and then, states, as well as families, may be safely reformed" (2:6). Another light on her view of the Revolution emerges in *The Wanderer*, where the deposed and now nomadic aristocratic characters receive individual sympathy for their victimization by an ideology turned demogogic, but equal sympathy goes to Elinor Joddrel, who courageously envisions the utopian possibilities embodied in a politics of equality and renewal.

The project Burney set out to complete in *The Wanderer* required a major deviation from the paths she had already trod: to engage a group of characters defined in large measure by their differing responses to the political, historical, economic, and social upheavals represented by the French Revolution. *The Wanderer* is both a historical and a philosophical novel, though it has not been much recognized or read as such. Burney here does what no writer had dared before her. She traces and analyzes the lot of women in every class of life, from pampered aristocrat to comfortable bourgeoise to respectable working woman to starving shopgirl to farmer's wife to rural cottager.

The Revolution also forcefully underlies one of Burney's central concerns in her life and in her writing: dual national identity. Burney's maternal grandmother was descended from the Huguenots; her great-grandfather (Dubois) left France when the Edict of Nantes was revoked. So Burney herself had French blood (and echoed the names of her ancestors in the appellations Duval and Du Bois used in *Evelina*, where she toys with an Anglo-French identity). Evelina's mother has been seduced by Belmont in France, and a trip to Paris hangs over Evelina herself as a threat to repeat her mother's destiny. Juliet is born and raised in France. Actual French blood runs in the veins neither of Evelina nor of Juliet as it in fact ran in the veins of their creator. But Juliet's exile in particular in many ways echoes and reverses the exile of General Alexandre d'Arblay in England, and Burney's own ten-year stint in France. Burney's characters are always searching for a home and for safety, the domestic bliss and security she and d'Arblay briefly found at Camilla Cottage. The possibility of exile, of forced emigration, menaces them, sometimes literally as with Evelina and Juliet, sometimes metaphorically, as a self-division from name, family, or sanity in the cases of Cecilia and Camilla. Other eighteenth-century writers had explored this territory by setting their protagonists into the world as unprotected orphans. Burney uses the conventional orphan plot but takes it one step further by unsettling all aspects of her heroines' identities.

Four

Critical Afterlife

I have argued that Burney's writings house multivalent conceptions of the woman artist's lot at the end of the eighteenth century. Decorous yet angry, submissive yet defiant, silenced yet bursting with speech, Burney's work, like her life, embraces the tensions that came from living with, and within, a contradictory world in which what was expected of her as sister, daughter, and wife clashed with her literary ambitions as well as with her financial needs. Echoes of these contradictions can be located by examining two centuries of shifting tides in Burney's treatment at the hands of reviewers and literary critics. Like all writers who continue to be read beyond their publishers' initial publicity announcements, Burney has enjoyed a critical afterlife. I have been arguing that my reading of the covert hostility in her work as a particular manifestation of the politics of women's writing in the late eighteenth century is a new reading. Only recently have feminist and materialist critics begun to uncover Burney's insistent, and insistently low-key, cries of rage, of ambitious pride, and of occasional triumph. Why did earlier readers not see these elements in her work? Why are they becoming visible to critics now? How do fluctuations in critical practice and cultural expectation illuminate the politicized relationship between a writer and the meanings ascribed to her? These are general questions that can be answered only particularly, and I offer in this chapter a case study of one writer's popular and academic critical reception in order to situate my own interpretation within a self-conscious context of the social and ideological functions and constraints of literary critical practice. The preceding chapters have analyzed the tensions that drove Burney to grasp and domesticate the iron pen; public response to her writings constitutes the ground on which this ambivalence is figured.

Burney suffered early from misreadings, and she worried about her audience, her critics, and her social role as a writer from the beginning of her career. I have examined several moments that reveal this authorial anxiety. The conflagration she constructed of her juvenile manuscripts, she explained in *The Wanderer's* dedication, was inspired by "ideas that fastened degradation to this class of composition" (i:xx). When *Evelina's* publication brought acclaim, Burney expressed concern that the only direction from a pinnacle of success is downhill, and the presence of her name in a satirical pamphlet shortly thereafter prompted her to remark to Crisp that she "had always dreaded as a real evil" her name's appearance in print (*DL* i:101). She prophesied accurately the downhill path her popular career would take. A look at the fortunes of Burney's literary reputation with the critics and her place in literary history from 1778 to the present reveals an intense ideological overlay in criticism itself, as well as in moral and political change. As Burney's work over time became less anxiously indirect in its representations of social contradiction in the marginalization of women, as her reproduction and demystification of women's voices became ever testier and she began to use radical metamorphosis and fragmentation as metaphors for the female condition, her interpreters moved from comic appreciation to patronizing tolerance to condescending contempt to outright dismissal. Burney's fictions, I have argued, are subversively feminist ideological productions. Likewise, interpretations of them have participated in the social and aesthetic ideologies of hegemonic criticism.

7

"A very woman"
and Her Readers

In 1778, the *Critical Review* opened its unsigned article on *Evelina* with "This performance deserves no common praise, whether we consider it in a moral or literary light. It would have disgraced neither the head nor the heart of Richardson." This reviewer, like most who extolled the merits of Burney's first published novel, inverted his praise into negative clauses, suggesting surprise, as did Samuel Johnson's famous line about women preaching—not that it is done well, but that it is done at all. The *Critical Review*'s only reservation was one it administered equally to other novels of this period: there are too many lords and ladies, while novel readers themselves come predominantly from "the middle ranks of life." The comparisons to Richardson were both positive (*Evelina* was declared "amusing and instructive") and negative ("the gold is in some places beat out considerably too fine").[1] The *Gentleman's Magazine* called Burney's first novel "a pleasing, innocent amusement"[2] and the *Monthly Review,* chiding Burney for Captain Mirvan's rough manners, pronounced it "one of the most sprightly, entertaining, and agreeable productions of this land."[3] While universally applauded, *Evelina* was also infantilized, as was its author (who was popularly thought to be seventeen rather than twenty-five).

Posthumous editions of *Evelina* elicited more "historical" reviews, and the book came to be read primarily as a cultural phenomenon. J. M. Dent's 1893 reissue edited by R. Brimley Johnson prompted the *Dial*'s reviewer, who judged Burney's portraits of the vulgar bourgeoisie to "excel" those of Thackeray, to find in the book a mixture of "gusto" and "delicacy" and to remark that "'Evelina' is truly feminine in touch, and sometimes weakly so in an inclination toward crude sentimentalism and toward overdrawing characters and overdoing situations."[4] The *Spectator* also doled out praise, offering that "Miss Burney stands absolutely first in order of time on the list of female novelists" in one of the few later hierarchies that did not subordinate Burney to Jane Austen, not to mention Maria Edgeworth, the Brontës, and George Eliot, on the list of women novelists. An intriguing botanical metaphor surfaced in the *Spectator*'s review:

> We hear much talk about "annuals" and "perennials" nowadays. The interest taken in old-fashioned flowering plants and shrubs is a very marked feature of present-day gardening. Every one starts a herbaceous border, and every one exults over half-forgotten flowers — peonies, lupins, and sweet bergamot — transplanted from cottage-gardens. In like manner, the works of authors are either annual, springing up like the grass of the field one day, dead and forgotten the next, or perennial, starting up in unexpected places, returning in new editions to delight successive generations of readers. Among these evergreens is a new edition of Evelina.[5]

Evelina pleased by the very terms that we have seen carrying multivalent meanings for Burney — its "femininity" and propriety, its freshness and youth. While already cunning and politically aware in *Evelina,* as I have argued, in 1778 Burney did not yet write with the cynical and far more hostile voice of her later fiction. Critical commentary reflected this. William Dean Howells called Burney's first heroine "a bewitching goose," but "though a goose, . . . perhaps the sweetest and the dearest goose in all fiction."[6] This heroine did not threaten her readers. R. Brimley Johnson, writing in 1919, also suggested that Burney's essential quality is "femininity"; she teaches us, Johnson wrote, "what women actually thought and felt. . . . She was, always, and everywhere, the mouthpiece of her sex."[7] Muriel Masefield also saw Burney as immured in time, place, and gender, writing in 1934 that "it is as a photographic character-monger, a show-woman of a period and class, that Fanny Burney excels."[8] Christopher Lloyd, in a 1936

biography of Burney, marveled at *Evelina*'s "abiding popularity" and
parenthetically quipped that "at this moment there are plenty of retired
ladies reading it to each other to pass a quiet evening."[9] A critic writing in 1949 accused Evelina of being "timid and easily flustered" and
Burney of creating "female difficulties" that "seem often to have been
trumped up."[10]

More recent critical views continue this tradition of reading *Evelina*
as an old-fashioned, genteel diversion. Its plot has been viewed as
"highly conventional and hoary with age: a king or lord falls in love
with a beautiful maiden of unknown parentage and without worldly
goods; he marries her for herself alone and she proves to be a king's
daughter or the like, her father's only heir," with Burney freighting
the conventionality with "motherly elaboration."[11] It has been called
"the first novel of manners" and traditionally interpreted as the light-
hearted production of a female Hogarth, containing "sprightly humor"
and "feminine playfulness."[12] As recently as 1983, a review of the Oxford World's Classics edition of *Evelina* read the novel as a Cinderella
myth in a contradictory "society whose forms of civility conceal yet
license frequent incivility," and called the novel "the archetypal best-
selling novel — racy, sententious, wish-fulfilling, compulsively readable"
and "ideally suited to television serialisation" in an essay that makes
Burney sound like an eighteenth-century Jacqueline Susann or Judith Krantz.[13] Indeed, until the very recent revaluations by feminist
critics, the predominant critical response to *Evelina* has been to focus
on its stereotypical "feminine" traits of amusement and light entertainment while not taking seriously the novel's claims to literary achievement in its own right.

A German critic has argued that *Evelina* inaugurated the flowering
of women writers at the end of the eighteenth century and was the
first of the "women's" novels.[14] Susan Staves and Judith Newton have
noted that Evelina's central experience is of assault, danger, and violence.[15] Lillian D. Bloom and Edward A. Bloom see *Evelina* as an effort at autobiographical revision on Burney's part, an attempt to "meet
a challenge of identity" by creating "a fairy tale,"[16] while Mary Poovey
reads it as an analysis of the crucial displacement a woman's allegiance
and dependence undergo in the shift from father to lover.[17] Katharine
Rogers understands Burney's heroines to be, allegedly like their author, conventionally sentimental, timid, flat, unassertive, embarrassed
by public recognition, and conscious of their superiority but fearful
of making use of it.[18]

Until recently, *Evelina* has been appreciated largely for its wit, its
social satire in critiquing licentious manners and morals and punc-

turing behavioral facades, and its archetypal characterization of the innocent female and her social education.[19] But even most recent feminist assessments, insightful and useful as they are in getting us to reread Burney's most successful work, have failed to challenge Evelina's childlike innocence or to examine her position with respect to moral, emotional, social, and economic authority.[20] Feminist critics have begun to read beneath the novel's surface achievements to its underlying ethos, its critique not only of the eighteenth century's polished surfaces but of the period's deeply anxious sexual ideologies as well. In the course of the novel, Catherine Parke argues, Evelina becomes "aware of herself, aware of her presence in the world, aware of the social function of her being that is marked by a name" and she constructs "a history, of and for herself."[21] Susan Staves privileges Evelina's pain and anxiety over the comic descriptions Burney provides, suggesting that Burney "could not finally deny the self-abnegation society required of ladies."[22] The novel teaches us, Judith Newton asserts, "that only good and ruling-class male control is effective against bad, that women's power in particular is not effectual, that female abdication of autonomy is therefore justified, and that in a world demonstrably full of bad male energies the only lasting protection is to marry."[23] *Evelina* has been judged by Eva Figes to contain "a satiric conservatism which is highly ambiguous and allows the author to keep her private opinions to herself."[24] According to Mary Poovey, *Evelina* explores the ideological nature of propriety. Poovey writes that "just as a woman's modest demeanor actually disguises her essential sexuality, so a woman's situation, her reputation, or her countenance could dramatically *mis*represent her character," and claims that Evelina's predicament is a perfect example of a phenomenon that Mary Wollstonecraft explores: that "a woman's situation, far from being either an accurate index of her heart or even simply a misrepresentation of her actual position, can actually help constitute the responses it seems to represent."[25]

As these excerpts demonstrate, the element that all *Evelina*'s reviews have in common, from 1778 to the present, is a reading that holds it of fundamental importance that the novel's author should have been a woman. The value placed on that gender designation has shifted according to the ideological status of femaleness in given periods, but authorial gender has always been foregrounded in readings of Burney's works. Recently, the results of that emphasis have changed to generate new approaches to *Evelina* from feminist critical perspectives and from contextual perspectives that attempt to account for *Evelina*'s place in the social and cultural history of women and of fiction writing in the last decades of the eighteenth century. In many ways, *Evelina; or,*

A Young Lady's Entrance into the World has been called upon to stand as the archetypal woman's novel. It might well, therefore, have been subtitled *A Woman Novelist's Entrance into the World.*

Cecilia is a far more complex novel than its predecessor, and contemporary reviewers tried to read around its complexities in order to compare it with the "sprightly" *Evelina. Cecilia,* the *Gentleman's Magazine* reviewer proclaimed, "holds up a mirror to the gay and dissipated of both sexes, in which they may see themselves and their deformities at full length, and exhibits more knowledge of the world, or the *ton,* than could be expected from the years of the fair authoress."[26] Burney was thirty-one in 1782 when *Cecilia* appeared; at what age did this reviewer expect her to have achieved "knowledge of the world"? The *Monthly Review* found some small faults — excessive length, occasional dullness, some characters too extreme — but generally praised the book, allotting it "the dignity and pathos of Richardson," "the acuteness and ingenuity of Fielding," and "a style peculiarly nervous and perspicuous, . . . formed on the best model of Dr. Johnson's." Not only did the *Monthly Review* not single out Burney's femaleness, but in a digressive paragraph it defended an earlier negative comparison to Burney's work of a novel by Elizabeth Blower called *George Bateman* by remarking that "the Author of Cecilia asks no undue lenity; she doth not plead any privilege of her sex: she stands on firmer ground; and with a spirit superior to solicitation or fear, may meet the decision of impartial criticism."[27] These first reviews, dependent on author recognition and reader preconception, did not go much beyond general praise.

Annie Raine Ellis, a nineteenth-century Burney editor, was responsible for a centennial reissuing of *Cecilia* in a Bohn's Novelist's Library edition published by George Bell and Sons in 1882. By this time, readers had become more familiar with Burney's diaries and letters than with her novels. A writer in the *Saturday Review,* citing Gibbon, Burke, and Johnson as the author's admirers during her lifetime, asked, "Yet who reads Fanny Burney now?" This reviewer believed Burney's chief merit to lie in her humorous portraits of social vulgarity, and compared her favorably on that count to everyone "from Richardson to George Eliot." But this review refused to read political subject matter in *Cecilia,* despite its heroine's predicament:

> Miss Burney, though the whole course of her life was changed by the French Revolution, yet in her writings almost entirely belonged to the authors who preceded it. There are few traces indeed to be seen in her novels of the coming storm and of the swell on which so many minds were already beginning to toss.[28]

This reviewer had apparently not read *The Wanderer,* whose manuscript was nearly confiscated, and forgotten that *Cecilia* appeared in 1782, before the English obsession with revolutionary activities across the Channel was quite universal. In a review of the same 1882 edition in the *Spectator, Cecilia* was compared unfavorably to *Evelina,* praise of which, the reviewer alleged, had "spoilt her for literature," in an argument that Burney's style grew worse and worse under "the influence of the Great Cham of letters." After some rather abusive assertions (for example, that while "more moral in purpose" than many other female novelists, Burney nonetheless seems more knowledgeable about vice than is consistent with Macaulay's ascription to her of "virgin delicacy"), the reviewer praised *Cecilia*'s humor and variety and concluded that it "has a place, though not a very high place, in literature."[29]

Critical readings of *Cecilia,* after the laudatory initial reviews it received, do not abound. Burney's first two novels achieved popular success, and the received critical view holds that the intervening fourteen years between *Cecilia* and *Camilla,* years that included the dreadful period of Burney's incarceration at court, created both a shift in reader expectations of novels and a forced artificiality in Burney's style that signaled a downturn in her reception and in her ability itself. But while most readers ignore the fiction after *Evelina,* those who read *Cecilia* concede that it has merits even while generally seeing in it the beginnings of the end of Burney's talents as a novelist. Only the recent studies by Kristina Straub and Margaret Anne Doody contain complete and systematic analyses of the novel; earlier commentary on it tends to be embedded in larger discussions of Burney's fiction.[30] Edward W. Copeland, for example, gives *Cecilia* a sympathetic reading in an essay titled "Money in the Novels of Fanny Burney." Copeland argues that *Cecilia*'s love plot is intricately tied to its "plot of hard cash" in that the real crisis for Cecilia and Mortimer Delvile is what to do, first with, and then without, Cecilia's money. Copeland believes that Cecilia's money problems parallel Burney's own: *Cecilia*'s publication brought its author only two hundred pounds, barely enough to pay for one of the Harrels' parties, let alone permit a writer her independence, and Burney's disastrous stint at court was unavoidable largely because the author, like her heroines, was "an unprovided, unprotected woman."[31] Rose Marie Cutting, analyzing the increasingly feminist politics of Burney's novels, singles out Mrs. Delvile and her cousin Lady Honoria Pemberton in *Cecilia* as rebellious female characters who, each differently, defy the world around them. Not so openly "political" as Mrs. Selwyn, Mrs. Arlbery, or the later Elinor Joddrel, the Delvile women nevertheless rely on themselves and refuse to conform to acceptable patterns of social behavior.[32] In their psychoanalytic reading of Burney's regressive development as a writer, the Blooms call *Cecilia,* as they call *Evelina,* a "psychodrama." They read auto-biographical details in *Cecilia* — Burney's growing disillusion with "this continual round of visiting, and these eternal new acquaintances" — and see the book as more somber and pessimistic than its predecessor, though they interpret its heroine to be untouched by "what is sordid about her," a fairy-tale Cinderella character. Cecilia's descent into madness, the Blooms argue, is Burney's "vicarious escape" from inhibition.[33]

Margaret Anne Doody has insightfully dubbed *Cecilia* Burney's "anti-daddy novel"; she points out that while Evelina seeks a father and Joyce in Burney's play *The Woman-Hater* tries to shed one, Cecilia has only inappropriate daddies who complicate life for her at every turn.[34] Patricia Meyer Spacks views Burney's novels in general as commentaries on woman's circumscribed lot in the late eighteenth century, and she reads Cecilia Beverley as a heroine "who suffers from the failings of others but from no flaw more serious than inexperience in herself. As a woman, though, she is necessarily at the mercy of other people."[35] *Cecilia,* Spacks argues, "acknowledges more openly [than had *Evelina*] the high psychic cost of female compliance."[36] *Cecilia* has, indeed, been read in the light of courtesy books for women and Wollstonecraft's *Vindication.*[37] Burney herself should be granted the last word on interpretations of her second novel, perhaps best expressed in her response to Edmund Burke's complaint about *Cecilia*'s ending. "He wished the conclusion either more happy or more miserable; 'for in a work of imagination,' said he, 'there is no medium.'" Wrote Burney, "I was not easy enough to answer him, or I have much, though perhaps not good for much, to say in defence of following life and nature as much in the conclusion as in the progress of a tale; and when is life and nature completely happy or miserable?" (*DL* 1:473). *Cecilia* ends, indeed, with no guarantee of happiness for its protagonists, who face financial difficulties (albeit minor ones), internal family turmoil and discontent, and social awkwardness if not ostracism at the conclusion of the narrative.

Cecilia had appeared relatively quickly after *Evelina.* In four years, years of unexciting publication activity for fiction, Burney's name had remained in the public's mind, and of course the second production of a famous and successful first novelist is always awaited with an eager anticipation of pleasure that is frequently disappointed. *Cecilia* had not disappointed, though it was read more critically than *Evelina* had been. But fourteen years then passed before another Burney novel appeared in print, years in which the author suffered the stifling, imprisoning oppression of court life, married, and bore a child, and years that witnessed a shift in fictive conventions away from the experimental realism of Richardson, Fielding, Smollett, and the early Burney to the political Gothicism of Charlotte Smith, Elizabeth Inchbald, Ann Radcliffe, William Godwin, Thomas Holcroft, and Robert Bage. Burney too had changed with the times. She had buried the dark underside of sexual and power relations in *Evelina* under an apparently decorous comedy—the small incursions of violence and the larger ones of social critique subordinated themselves to the text's dominant drive to a happy domestic ending. In *Cecilia,* the socioeconomic critique threatens to take over the text and succeeds in key scenes, though ultimately a flawed compromise denouement masks Burney's revolutionary project. The truth is, though, that *Evelina* was the aberrant text for her: derivative in plot outline despite its subversive power.

Cecilia already anticipates the shifts of the 1790s with its themes of pursuit, persecution, and danger. Monckton could as well have been Montoni. And *Camilla* continues Burney's development along these lines. However, rather than being correctly read as a work that participated in the new concerns, structures, and discourses of shifts in fictional practice, *Camilla* was read in 1796 as an anachronistic work, the unfortunate throwback production of a writer locked into the outmoded expectations of her original public, a view not far removed from the psychological interpretation of Burney promulgated by Madame de Staël when she complained that Burney seemed to be perennially fourteen years old. The early public understanding of Burney's work saw her as ringing witty changes on the morally uplifting story of an innocent heroine struggling to find and finally achieving financially comfortable true love and social acceptance. In this vein, the *Critical Review*'s writer, after citing as excellent long excerpts from *Camilla* (including the whole of Mr. Tyrold's sermon) and arguing that the book instructs as well as entertains, complained that Burney's "female characters [in *Evelina* as well as *Camilla*] are *too young* to act the part which she assigns them. The errors of Camilla are not errors in one who is almost a child,—and the wisdom, knowledge, and prudence of Eugenia at fifteen, are preposterous."[38]

Not only did critics not read Burney's third novel as belonging to its period, but the conservative reviewer for the *British Critic* opposed *Camilla,* albeit in terms meant to approve, to the novels of the 1790s: "To astonish by the marvellous, and appal by the terrific, have lately been the favourite designs of many writers of novels; who, in pursuit of those effects, have frequently appeared to desert, and sometimes have really transgressed the bounds of nature and possibility. We cannot approve these extravagances." This review, not surprisingly, was largely positive, though it condemned the novel for its "immoderate length." The *British Critic* especially liked Burney's characterizations. Camilla herself, however, received unwarrantedly almost the same criticism from this reviewer as she had suffered from Mandlebert: "Preserving the most perfect innocence of character, with all this natural liveliness of disposition, she is often hurried by precipitance, into steps that produce an effect directly contrary to her intention, and forms conclusions very little warranted by the premises from which she draws them."[39] This represents the kindest of the reviews *Camilla* received, as most other reviewers read it merely for nuggets of a dying aristocratic moral sense and condemned it for length and solecism.

The *Monthly Review* also condemned the new Gothic vogue and praised *Camilla* (wrongly) for avoiding "the infection of that taste for the marvellous and the terrible, which, since the appearance of her former productions, has, with some writers, become the fashion of the day." The "Gothic," itself a vexed term, can be defined in its relation to women as emphasizing power relations and entanglements, and developing themes of veiling and entrapment. On this definition, Burney deserves an important place among Gothic novelists. Burney had, of course, undergone her own private Gothic harrowing at the hands of her court nemesis Mrs. Schwellenberg in the years between *Cecilia* and *Camilla,* and it shows in her third work of fiction. The *Monthly*'s reviewers (probably William Enfield and Ralph Griffiths) wrote that "it may be difficult to find any novels, except those of Fielding, in which characters are more accurately drawn than in those of this very ingenious lady" and recommended the novel "as a guide for the conduct of young females in the most important circumstances and situations of life."[40]

The *Monthly*'s ties with Charles Burney make its review suspect as honest criticism. Charles Burney's close relationship to the *Monthly Review,* to which he contributed regularly for seventeen years and for which Burney's brother Charles, a classical scholar, also wrote, deserves some notice in any attempt to summarize the reviews her work received during her lifetime. The case of *Camilla* is particularly interesting. Dr. Burney thought *Camilla* his daughter's greatest novel and in a letter dated 3 August 1796 urged his son Charles to review it:

It w^d be a worthy action that you will long think of with pleasure, to preserve & augment the fame of such a Sister, & such a work. Griff. if you give him a hint before it is put into other hands, will I dare say

gladly accept your offer. — *I* w^d not recommend to you such a task if
not stimulated by the peculiar intrinsic merit of the work.[41]

The *Monthly Review*'s editor, Ralph Griffiths, did occasionally permit
books he particularly admired to be reviewed by writers he knew to
be friends of their authors; he had, indeed, let Dr. Burney correct proofs
for Thomas Twining's piece on the third and fourth volumes of his
History of Music, though Griffiths remarked that he found the arrangement a "delicate matter."[42] In the case of *Camilla,* Griffiths apparently
thought better of keeping the review in the Burney family. The *Critical Review,* where the elder Burney also had some influence, equally
disliked the book. George Robinson, under whose direction the *Critical Review* was published, was also a bookseller concerned with *Camilla* (and Charles Burney's publisher), and he had been refused any
share in the novel's copyright. In August 1796, Robinson told Dr. Burney "that his reviewers disliked the novel and that they were openly
saying 'that the book w^d be praised in the M. Review by Dr. Charles
B. [son] — & that's all the praise it w^d get.'"[43]

   The *Analytical Review* labored under no such familial constraints to
praise *Camilla.* Its review, signed "M." and probably written by Mary
Wollstonecraft, judged *Camilla* "inferiour to the first-fruits of her talents,
though we boldly assert, that Camilla contains parts superiour to anything she has yet produced." Again, past reputation came into play:
"The celebrity which Miss Burney has so deservedly acquired by her
two former novels, naturally roused the expectation of the public for
the promised production of madame d'Arblay."[44] "Miss Burney"'s late
metamorphosis into "Madame d'Arblay" — a transformation that has
been reenacted and reclaimed by references to the writer as Frances
Burney and that Burney's heroines' various nominal crises renders
significant — frequently figured in reviews. As a 1972 *Times Literary Supplement* headline sardonically put it in a review of the first two volumes
of *The Journals and Letters of Fanny Burney (Madame D'Arblay),* "the butterfly becomes a moth."[45] Burney was beginning the downhill slide
in popular opinion she had predicted for herself when *Evelina* appeared.

   An American review, filled with misinformation, appeared in *The
Philadelphia Minerva* in 1796. After an utterly wrong biographical sketch
(it claims, for example, that Burney served as reader to the queen and
lost her position when she married), this review went on to offer sappy
praise of *Camilla:*

   As the sun after a long concealment behind the darkening cloud, breaks
   forth with redoubled lustre, to the joy and exhilaration of mankind —

so does this amiable writer appear to the votaries of taste and literature, holding in her hand the interesting history of Camilla — depicted
in the most striking and variegated colours the feelings and propen-
sities of the youthful mind, whether actuated by the celestial principles
inspired by heaven, or stimulated by the bias of evil examples or vi-
cious inclinations. Nor does she here omit the opportunity of display-
ing virtue in the most fascinating garb, while vice is depicted in the
most forbidding and hateful dress. The sentiments she here inculcates,
are of the most noble, refined and exalted nature — such as if generally
diffused, would contribute to instill in the heart of man, the divine
attributes of his maker, and render him as happy as would be consistent with the frailty of his probationary state. In fine, we may pronounce
Camilla a *chef d'oeuvre*, worthy the perusal of all who are desirous of
rational entertainment, or anxious to have the feelings of the heart
awakened to impressions of the most delightful and charming nature.[46]

This review, cloying enough in itself, gives no sign that the reviewer
had read the book.

Camilla had a difficult publication history, even after the d'Arblays
sold its copyright to Thomas Payne for one thousand pounds. Criticized as overlong, it was cut drastically by Burney for an 1802 edition,
then augmented again in 1836. When the Oxford University Press
published a new edition in 1972 (based on the 1796 edition), it was the
book's first reissue since 1840. Reviewing the 1972 edition, Françoise
Moreux suggested that Burney tried to shape her fiction to fit the temper
of the times: "*Camilla* marks an intriguing moment in the development of the author's personality, if only in her desire more or less proclaimed to adapt herself once more to the changing inclinations of
her public and their repercussions on the framing of the story."[47]
Reissued in paperback in 1983, *Camilla* received a promising 1984 notice
in the *Voice Literary Supplement*.[48] But on the whole it has fared badly.
As John Thorpe mumbles in Jane Austen's *Northanger Abbey, Camilla*
is "that other stupid book, written by that woman they make such a
fuss about; she who married the French emigrant."[49]

Unquestionably, *The Wanderer* received the worst treatment at the
hands of Burney's critics until we arrive at the execration hurled at
her *Memoirs of Doctor Burney* in 1832. That Burney's reputation preceded
her became a liability by the time *The Wanderer*, in part composed much
earlier, was finally published in 1814. The *British Critic*'s review began,
"We can scarcely remember an instance, where the public expectation was excited in so high a degree, as by the promise of a new novel
from the pen of their old favourite, Madame D'Arblay." This reviewer
liked the plot, but criticized its long-winded and repetitive unravel-

ing, and especially condemned the Frenchification of Burney's prose style. He called Elinor Joddrel a *"philosophe"* and remarked of her that "[t]he revolutionary spirit, which displays itself in the sentiments and actions of Miss Elinor Joddrel, is, fortunately for a bleeding world, now no longer in existence; few of our female readers can remember the *égalité* mania, which once infested the bosoms of their sex."[50] *Evelina's* refreshing wit during a period of drought for fiction had created popular expectations that Burney was never again fully able to satisfy. While *Cecilia* was also relatively well reviewed, *Camilla* and especially *The Wanderer* were treated as maimed children, deformed and disabled by the atrophy of their mother's literary muscles. "None of our female novelists (not even Miss Edgeworth)," explained John Wilson Croker's *Quarterly Review* article on *The Wanderer,* "ever attained so early and so high a reputation as Miss Burney, or as we must now call her, Madame D'Arblay." Her change in name and marital status, to Croker, signaled a blunting of edges, and the reviewer went on to portray the novelist's aging as comparable to that of "an old coquette who endeavours, by the wild tawdriness and laborious gaiety of her attire, to compensate for the loss of the natural charms of freshness, novelty, and youth."[51] If the author of *Evelina* was fresh and modest and childlike, the author of *The Wanderer* is overpainted, overaggressive, and decaying.

In the *Monthly Review,* William Taylor expostulated in 1815 about what he called *The Wanderer's* failure: "Since the modest entrance of Evelina into the world, the sparkling triumphs of Cecilia, and the delicate embarrassments of Camilla, many years have elapsed, fertile not only in political but in moral revolutions. A new generation has grown up in the saloons of Great Britain; fresh *pinks of fashion* are selected for the exemplary scollop; and an alteration insensibly progressive has effected considerable change in our idea of the gentleman and the lady."[52] Taylor focused his analysis on the outmodedness of *The Wanderer* and its yielding to the new "pinks of fashion," and thereby not only condescended to Burney but ridiculed her as well. Having announced the shift since Burney's previous works in concepts of behavior, Taylor went on to remark, "Whether a corresponding modification of the canon of propriety, or internal rule of excellence, has taken place in the mind of Madame D'Arblay, during her long residence in France, may perhaps be liable to question: but we are glad to see depicted again such society as our matrons remember; and to escape occasionally from the smooth insipidity of modern polish, by reverting to the more various singularities and broader humour of an age of social tolerance and comparative indiscipline." Still, the reviewer wondered whether perhaps the "vulgar personages" appear too much "for fastidious readers."[53]

Whereas the *Monthly Review,* because of its connections with Burney's father, was diplomatically and subtly negative, Croker's *Quarterly Review* article overtly condemned Burney's final work of fiction. "[W]e regret to say that *The Wanderer,*" Croker wrote, with no apparent regret, "which might be expected to finish and crown her literary labours, is not only inferior to its sister works, but cannot, in our judgment, claim any very decided superiority over the thousand-and-one-volumes with which the Minerva Press [roughly the period's equivalent to the twentieth century's Harlequin Romances in North America or to Mills & Boon in Great Britain] inundates the shelves of circulating libraries, and increases, instead of diverting the ennui of the loungers at watering places."[54] As Croker accused Burney herself of using the tired ploys of an aging harlot, so he accused the book of exploiting an aging Evelina, "Evelina grown old; the vivacity, the bloom, the elegance, 'the purple light of love' are vanished; the eyes are there, but they are dim; the cheek, but it is furrowed; the lips, but they are withered."[55] The metaphor of a woman of pleasure gone to seed carries throughout this review, in its references to the novel under discussion as well as to the person of its author.

Croker also accused Burney, scathingly, of pandering to Napoleon in *The Wanderer* by "debas[ing] herself to the little annotatory flatteries of the scourge of the human race," and even suggested that since Bonapartism had been overthrown, Burney would print a revised second edition because "Madame D'Arblay is not likely to continue to flatter, when her flattery can no longer conduce to her personal convenience"[56] (that of course never came about). Mistakenly accepting the myth that Burney was seventeen when she wrote *Evelina* and confusing the creator with her heroine, Croker announced that her first work "was a most extraordinary instance of early talent, and excited an expectation of excellence which her Cecilia almost fulfilled, and which her Camilla did not altogether disappoint." *The Wanderer,* however, he read as a mannerist imitation of Burney's own younger style and alleged that the new work contained a "total want of vigour, vivacity, and originality" in its "dull mediocrity." Not only is Burney a mannerist, Croker held, but she is "a mannerist who is *épuisée,* whose last manner is the worst."[57] The reviewer wrote that "we conceived ourselves duty bound to attend the lifeless remains of our old and dear friends Evelina and Cecilia to their last abode."[58]

In a response to Burney's 1832 publication of the *Memoirs of Doctor Burney,* Leigh Hunt offered a more positive account of Burney's literary accomplishments, but, like Croker, Hunt could not bring himself to separate the writer from her work. Speaking of Burney's reputed timidity when young, Hunt speculates that "perhaps she was not so handsome as her sisters, and had been kept comparatively in the background, and not petted so much." He refers to the "excess of reserve and diffidence" with which she guarded her authorship of *Evelina* and, with justification, questions her suspiciously intense insistence on this reserve. "Thus bashful and hanging back, with a secret stock of fun and glee, and the sharpest powers of looking out of her corner and studying others," Hunt writes, "Fanny Burney must herself have been a character as fit for a novel as almost any she drew." "Her stubbornness, seems never to have left her," he continues, "At least, she could exercise it *manfully* when she chose" (my italics). Hunt sees the paradoxes here, the clash of insistence on decorous reserve with the simple fact of insistence itself. He, too, sees a decline of style in her later works as they reflected a Johnsonian influence, lamenting "that Fanny Burney was not left to her corner, to be sly, and laughing, and natural forever" and concludes her to be "a comic genius." A curious editorial caveat glosses Hunt's remarks on Burney's later "spoilt . . . style." The editor comments in a footnote: "Style spoilt, — God wot, is that all! The whole of the book [*Memoirs*], save only the letters written before Madame d'Arblay's marriage, may perhaps be taken as a specimen of the worst English composition that the age has produced."[59]

By far the most famous review of any of her works published during Burney's lifetime was the article attributed to William Hazlitt that appeared in the February 1815 issue of the *Edinburgh Review*. Significantly, this article occupied fifteen pages to delineate the literary history of the novel form in a discussion of Cervantes, Lesage, Fielding, Richardson, Smollett, and Sterne before it began, in its final three pages, to attend to the subject at hand, Burney's *Wanderer,* and then gave the book itself only the final page. Hazlitt's preliminary, pontificating exposition related the novel form to moral philosophy. More than any other reviewer, Hazlitt directly related Burney's writing to her sex: no screen metaphors of tawdry prostitution here. Hazlitt contrasted Burney with the new school of romance writers (Inchbald, Radcliffe, Edgeworth), though he did not rank her with the masters he set up as models. When he connected Burney with "the old school," he meant that she was "a mere common observer of manners." But he moved immediately away from any general assessment of Burney's achievement. Along with observing manners, Burney, Hazlitt wrote, was "also a very woman" and "[i]t is this last circumstance which forms the peculiarity of her writings, and distinguishes them from those masterpieces which we have before mentioned."

Hazlitt accused Burney of a trait he understood to be negative, a "consciousness of her sex," and explained his analysis of sex coding in literature in a well-known passage that merits full citation:

> Women, in general, have a quicker perception of any oddity or singularity of character than men, and are more alive to every absurdity which arises from a violation of the rules of society, or a deviation from established custom. This partly arises from the restraints on their own behaviour, which turn their attention constantly on the subject, and partly from other causes. The surface of their minds, like that of their bodies, seems of a finer texture than ours; more soft, and susceptible of immediate impression. They have less muscular power, — less power of continued voluntary attention, — of reason — passion and imagination. But they are more easily impressed with whatever appeals to their senses or habitual prejudices. The intuitive perception of their minds is less disturbed by any general reasonings on causes or consequences. They learn the idiom of character and manner, as they acquire that of language, by rote merely, without troubling themselves about the principles. Their observation is not the less accurate on that account, as far as it goes; for it has been well said, that "there is nothing so true as habit."

Interestingly, Hazlitt's use of gender as a crucial category for literary understanding is similar (theoretically at least) to twentieth-century discussions of gender as socially and culturally constructed. In a skewed way, the beginning of this passage rather astutely describes Burney's obsessions, despite its odd gender analysis: the rules of society tightly circumscribe women. Deviations from those rules seduce and endanger the women thus circumscribed. Women in Burney's fictional worlds therefore must be passionately rule-conscious in order to survive. But from there Hazlitt moves on to the equation of female minds with female bodies, in a biological passage Virginia Woolf might have used in her coyly witty critique of men's writing at the opening of *A Room of One's Own*. Soft bodies, soft minds; muscular bodies, muscular minds. A woman's mind, like clay, molds to the stimulation it receives; a man's mind is thrusting and seminal. Critiques of these sexually explicit metaphors and their patriarchal provenance are by now legion. But the conclusions are always newly antagonistic: the positive feminine virtues of nurturing softness and emotional intuition mean a lack of reason, imagination, and principle.

Hence Hazlitt's reading of *The Wanderer*, when he finally gets to it:

The difficulties in which she involves her heroines are, indeed, "Female Difficulties"; — they are difficulties created out of nothing. . . . The whole artifice of her fable consists in coming to no conclusion. Her ladies stand so upon the order of their going, that they do not go at all. They will not abate an ace of their punctilio, in any circumstances, or on any emergency. They would consider it as quite indecorous to run down stairs though the house were in flames, or to move off the pavement though a scaffolding was falling.

Hazlitt was actually quite correct here, though what irritated him is precisely Burney's point: women have no choice but to gag on "punctilio," the eighteenth-century term for rigid etiquette. A glance back at her court-directions letter demonstrates that Burney took exception to this rigidity, yet recognized its power. Elinor Joddrel, after all, also argues that the Wanderer's "female difficulties" are constructed of "vapour," but with the important condition that these difficulties can only "vanish into the vapour of which they are formed" if their bearer forgets that she is "a dawdling woman" and behaves as "an active human being" (*Wanderer* 4:36). It is precisely her coerced inability to act that galls Burney's protagonist as each of her attempts at action is either blocked or reproved. Femaleness is a void, a blank, that place where resides the empty (for Hazlitt) and therefore ideologically depleted and nonthreatening Other. This five-volume, two-thousand page novel contains nothing: it is the same blank page that faced Camilla when her iron pen left no mark in the Records of Eternity.

The rules that obsess women in Hazlitt's original allegation become something more than rules in his review — mindless, debilitating, and ultimately sinister "punctilio" (a term Mrs. Arlbery accurately uses to describe Mandlebert in *Camilla*) endangers women's lives in burning houses and traps them under falling construction materials. Because Burney always observes "with a consciousness of her sex," Hazlitt argues, "[w]e thus get a kind of supplement and gloss to our original text, which we could not otherwise have obtained." This is precisely what I have argued: there *is* a supplemental gloss, an indirect subtext, that informs Burney's writings. Her *"forte,"* according to Hazlitt, is the delineation of external behavior, and her people, thereby, "are such characters as people might be expected to assume for a night at a masquerade." While Hazlitt's gender-laden reading of Burney's fictional worlds was undeniably pejorative, it also inadvertently opened the way for a differently ideologized analysis of gender categories fueled by Burney herself. Hazlitt apparently forgot that in *Cecilia* Burney had created one of the finest masquerades of the age in a deliberate metaphorization of human slipperiness and untrustworthiness. Burney herself experiments with categories, boundary crossing, and exchange. "The whole," Hazlitt suggested, not inappropriately, "is a question of form, whether that form is adhered to, or violated." For Burney, indeed, form entraps women and cripples them. It is this power of form that Hazlitt dismissed as negligible when he wrote that "Madame D'Arblay has woven a web of difficulties for her heroine, something like the green silken threads in which the shepherdesses entangled the steed of Cervantes' hero, who swore, in his fine enthusiastic way, that he would sooner cut his passage to another world than disturb the least of those beautiful meshes."[60]

The Wanderer has received less attention than Burney's other three novels, and has been the least available of the fictional works, never reprinted in English after its publication year of 1814 until 1988.[61] A French critic attempted a "rehabilitation" in 1962, but even in that essay appear apologies for the novel's lack of brisk satire, variety, and new ideas among the claims for its interest for a twentieth-century reader.[62] Several other critics mention *The Wanderer* in passing, but most frequently these critics use Burney's last novel to buoy up particular theses, and dismiss it as a novel on its own merits, attacking its style and denying that it offers any aesthetic pleasure.[63] One of its characters—Elinor Joddrel—has been usefully analyzed as the "most defiant and most 'liberated' of Fanny Burney's female characters" in a discussion that also examines Juliet's portrayal and insightfully concludes that *The Wanderer* is "a powerful study of the paranoia induced in women by the constant suspicion directed against them" (Burney deals with this theme in all four novels, but especially prepares for its emergence in *The Wanderer* with Edgar's vigilant watch over Camilla).[64] Margaret Anne Doody offers a reading of *The Wanderer* as a historical novel with a political point, a "bold experiment" in asking readers to accept a heroine about whom we know no background, not even a name, and as one of the first novels to explore Marx's notion of "alienation" in its depiction of work and workers. Doody concludes that *The Wanderer* was too disturbing in 1814, given Burney's accepted role "as a cheerful late Augustan didactic moralist," and that, in fact, it is a much better novel than *Evelina.*[65] But finally, most critics have been misled by John Wilson Croker's haranguing attack in the *Quarterly Review* when the work appeared,[66] and by Thomas Babington Macaulay's mean-spirited pronouncement: "In 1814 she published her last novel, *The Wanderer,* a book which no judicious friend to her memory will attempt to draw from the oblivion into which it has justly fallen."[67]

Complaints about *The Wanderer* — many of them raise questions about whether the complainer has actually read the novel — focus on its style and on the repletion of incident that makes up its heroine's "female difficulties." These same complaints, slightly less dismissive and in altered biographical context, were leveled as well at *Camilla*. Burney's last two novels were written in what she herself labeled "the prose Epic style" (*JL* 3:129). Rather than being "self-imitative," as the Blooms have alleged,[68] *Camilla* and *The Wanderer* marked formal and stylistic departures from *Evelina* and *Cecilia*. Whereas *Evelina* could be fairly easily assimilated into a sentimental romance tradition and *Cecilia* could be shoehorned into this tradition despite the deviations of its gender and class analysis, the last two fictions merge elements from more naturalistic, more political, and darker versions of the novel. Burney's language — called pedantic and precious and accused of an overboard imitation of Johnson's philosophical prose style — has taken the most abuse. Macaulay argues (using linguistic snobbism and racist insults) that Burney's novelistic powers failed because she turned her prose into "a sort of broken Johnsonese, a barbarous *patois*, bearing the same relation to the language of *Rasselas*, which the jibberish of the Negroes of Jamaica bears to the English of the House of Lords."[69] After the mild shock registered by some to the lower-class vulgarisms and dialects that had achieved comic effect in *Evelina*, it has been said, Burney grew too conscious of straining after elegance. Hester Thrale remarked as early as February 1779 of "our Miss Burney" that "her conversation would be more pleasing if She thought less of herself; but her early Reputation embarrasses her Talk, & clouds her Mind with scruples about Elegancies which either come uncalled for or will not come at all."[70]

Periodical reviews in the late eighteenth century flourished because they served as important instruments of cultural ideology. They participated in creating and developing a bourgeois understanding of the place of literary production and consumption in social and economic life, and they reflected that understanding. The new capitalist classes altered conditions in the literary marketplace with their new sensibility and with their takeover of a literary economy that had earlier been founded on patronage. And as the rules of the literary marketplace changed in response to changing social and economic conditions, the public's demand for reading material of a different sort came to occupy a larger and larger role in dictating the operations of a growing publishing industry. Ian Watt's standard history of the rise of the novel claims the genre's crucial defining characteristic to be its service to this new class of readers through an invention he called "formal realism."[71] Michael McKeon offers an important challenge to Watt's view in his larger and more ambitious treatment of the early novel as a genre that derived from cultural instability and was flexible enough to contain ideological conflict.[72]

Novels became commodities as well as, or even perhaps in consequence of, their function as repositories of cultural ideology. It is necessary to view the popularity of terror literature and the Gothic, in particular, in light of the commodification of literature and the new role of periodicals in its marketing. It was this commodification that permitted women to begin to produce fiction — *Cecilia* was published in an unprecedentedly large run of two thousand copies in its first edition — and women's literary productivity for its part produced a conservative backlash against sentimental and Gothic writing that embodied a progressive turn to individualism and to questions of personal and social identity.[73] The contemporary criticism of Burney's published writings — covering as it does the years 1778 to 1832 — charts these shifts. As her writing came more strongly to challenge social organization and the subordination of women, critics came more strongly to condemn her for moral relativism. Echoes of the concerns that emerge from this contemporary response can be heard as well in the reception accorded Burney's sister novelists.

In 1799, for example, the *Critical Review* published an article on Mary Hays's *Victim of Prejudice*. Hays's protagonist is the daughter of a murderer father and prostitute mother, and her lover, enraged by the fact that he cannot marry her because of her improper connections, rapes her. The story relates her failed efforts to fight the double stigmata of unchastity and bloodline transgression, and rages intensely both against men and against English law. The *Critical Review*'s reviewer concluded:

> "The Victim of Prejudice" is a tale of considerable interest; it has many passages which, for warmth and vigour of pathos and composition, are scarcely inferiour to the effusions of Rousseau; but it also exhibits that splenetic irritability which, by distorting decorum into prejudice, and custom into tyranny, tends to excite and to nourish the contagious and consuming fever of perverted sensibility.[74]

This reviewer here rehearses the attack Hazlitt was to make in 1814 on Burney's *Wanderer:* form, he suggests, is paramount, and he alleges that Hays exaggerated the violations of form to insist that such violations created real problems for women. Hays's "victim," then, was no such thing. The response to Mary Hays, a radical novelist whose best-known work, *The Memoirs of Emma Courtney* (1796), depicts a young woman who openly declares her love for and unsuccessfully courts a man (à la Elinor Joddrel), represented an extreme. Hays was a disciple of William Godwin, and though she claimed in the preface of *Emma Courtney* that her protagonist was to be taken as a warning rather than a model, Emma is sympathetically portrayed. Hays was a novelist whose books strongly advocated reform; not until Burney's *Wanderer* would another female novelist so overtly argue for social revolution.

In fact, novels that offered direct critiques of the social order fared rather poorly overall in the review sweepstakes during this period. As early as 1783, James Beattie wrote in his *Dissertations Moral and Critical:*

> Romances are a dangerous recreation. . . . A few, no doubt, of the best may be friendly to good taste and good morals; but far the greater part are unskilfully written, and tend to corrupt the heart, and stimulate the passions. A habit of reading them breeds a dislike to history, and all the substantial parts of knowledge; withdraws the attention from nature, and truth; and fills the mind with extravagant thoughts and too often with criminal propensities.[75]

Beattie clearly aimed this volley at "impressionable" young female readers.

Hannah More, a key conservative, also felt that novels combined "the taste of the Goths with the morals of Bagshot,"[76] and the *Gentleman's Magazine* proposed a tax on them. In a parody of these views, Jane West concocted a comic recipe for modern novel writing in her 1810 work *The Refusal:*

> To one grain of Johnson add a pound of Sterne, melt them in a crucible till they perfectly amalgamate; this is the only difficult part of the process, for the particles are extremely heterogeneous. You must pour in a little tincture of religion, which you may produce either from "Economy of human life," the "Essay on Man" or any German treatise on divinity. Sweeten it with a great quantity of Voltaire's liberality, beat it to a froth, then swallow it while in a state of effervescence, and begin to write immediately.[77]

Jane West's satiric recipe focused on the moral and ignored the political elements of recent radical fiction. She upheld the school of thought that produced Mary Russell Mitford's remarks on Burney written in an 1819 letter to Sir William Elford: "Madame d'Arblay has much talent but no taste. She degrades her heroines in every possible way, bodily and mental."[78]

In many ways, things got worse for women in the period after Burney ceased to write fiction. An early biography of Charles Lamb cites, for example, its subject's remarks on women writers:

> Lamb delivered himself of some very free utterances concerning authoresses. Spoke of Mrs. Inchbald as the only endurable clever woman he had ever known; called them impudent, forward, unfeminine, and unhealthy in their minds. Instanced amongst many others, Mrs. Barbauld, who was a torment and curse to her husband. "Yet," said Lamb, "Letitia was only just tinted; she was not what the she-dogs now call an intellectual woman."[79]

Frequently, praise was uttered in reviews of the works of women with the qualifying phrase "for a woman"; the highest praise, in reviews of the works of Lady Mary Wortley Montagu, Germaine de Staël, and Maria Edgeworth, came in the attribution to these authors of a prized "manly understanding." An interesting disquietude of tone emerges in these reviews: it may be unfeminine to publish, but it is also decidedly ungentlemanly to attack a woman publicly, so a curious diplomatic hedging occurs. This phenomenon produced left-handed praise like that accorded to Mrs. Opie in the July 1806 *Edinburgh Review:*

> There is something delightfully feminine in all Mrs. Opie's writings; an apparent artlessness in the composition of her narrative, and something which looks like want of skill or of practice in writing for the public, that gives a powerful effect to the occasional beauties and successes of her genius. . . . She does not reason well; but she has, like most accomplished women, the talent of perceiving truth, without the process of reasoning.[80]

Reviews of fiction during the productive years of Burney's novel writing generally evinced a concern for the novel's ability to depict moral nature. Even Mary Wollstonecraft, reviewing Charlotte Smith's first novel, *Emmeline, the Orphan of the Castle* (1788), for the *Analytical Review,* succumbed to the protective rhetoric of contemporary fiction reviewing:

> The false expectations these wild scenes excite, tend to debauch the mind, and throw an insipid kind of uniformity over the moderate and rational prospects of life, consequently *adventures* are sought for and

created, when duties are neglected, and content despised. We will ven-
ture to ask any young girl if Lady Adelina's theatrical contrition did
not catch her attention, while Mrs. Strafford's rational resignation escaped her notice?[81]

It might be argued that Wollstonecraft's true agenda here was to warn
young women against the seductive helplessness of overwrought emotion, a kind of protection to which male reviewers did not subscribe.
Nevertheless she harbored the same concern that novels can corrupt,
and that their corrosive properties can work especially to blight female virtue.

Charlotte Smith, Mary Wollstonecraft's subject, suffered in one respect a similar fate to that of Burney. She was also treated as a meteoric
phenomenon, the thing Burney had feared most when she addressed
her diary after the overwhelming popular success of *Evelina*. Smith's
early works were realistic romances such as *Emmeline;* later, in novels
such as *Desmond* (1792), her most polemical work, and *The Banished
Man* (1794), in which she reversed the radical view promulgated in *Desmond* and attacked the French Revolution, she focused on the politi-
cization of social life. With her interest in political issues came a con-
comitant loss of interest in her work by the reviewing press. By the
time her last work, *The Letters of a Solitary Wanderer,* was published in
1801, reviewers were virtually writing her literary obituary, as they
would for Burney in 1814, and applying the same awkward organic
theory of style and reputation:

> Genius has its dawn, its maturity and decline. While we admit that
> Mrs. Smith has possessed this quality in a considerable degree, we must
> also confess that it now only sparkles in occasional corruscations, and
> that she often borrows from "meaner spirits of the muses' train," and
> not unfrequently from herself. . . . Yet, though the discharge of our
> duty to the public has led us to a somewhat scrutinous criticism on
> these volumes, we must remember, with kindness and gratitude, the
> author who has so often interested and entertained us, who has, for
> a time, checked the tear, or induced a temporary oblivion of the
> wounded spirit.[82]

Women novelists of the last decades of the eighteenth century and
the first decades of the nineteenth produced an imaginative literature
of resistance and refusal along both class and gender lines. The period's reviews can tell us much about the production and reception
of this fiction in the late eighteenth century. Identified with women
both as writers and as readers, the novel was expected first and fore-

most to provide moral instruction. "To a refined and sensible people, — says Mr. Rousseau, —" begins the preface to Robert Bage's *Man as He Is,* "instruction can only be offered in form of a novel."[83] But most novels were found sorely lacking, so much so that reviewer William Enfield asked the *Monthly Review's* editor Ralph Griffiths to send him as few specimens of the genre as possible. Reviews in important periodicals such as the *Monthly Review,* the *Quarterly Review,* the *Edinburgh Review,* and *Blackwood's Magazine,* all of which were flourishing at the beginning of the nineteenth century, offered the first sustained public theoretical discussion of the function of novels to uphold traditional moral standards and to replicate social conventions.[84]

To this end, critics saved their greatest praise for realistic depictions of contemporary society, and the novel of manners took its impetus from this. No theory of literary taste, however, backed up these conduct-manual prescriptions for fiction. Aesthetic categories were fuzzy enough during this period in the realms of painting, architecture, and landscape design; standards of taste and rules of beauty did not exist at all for novels outside the moral realm. And the critical vocabulary of the period lagged behind its literary production. The periodicals were unable to read resistance in the domestic novel or in the psychic upheaval traced in Gothic fiction. For a novelist such as Burney, the moral overlay of fiction criticism locked her into saying what she wanted to say only if she could arrange outwardly to play by the rules. So in many ways Burney's fear of condemnation as "a very woman" was precisely what taught her the subversive tactic of deliberately writing as "a very woman." She did not invent her indirect narrative strategies merely as a formal experiment; these strategies came into being because Burney needed them to undermine the very moral order she seemed to be upholding.

The case of novel reviews and their place in the period's social and cultural ideology illuminates the various Burneyan tactics I have been trying to uncover. Here is an extreme example, taken from a 1795 number of the *Sylph:*

> Women of every age, of every condition, contract and retain a taste for novels. . . . The depravity is universal. My sight is everywhere offended by these foolish, yet dangerous books. I find them in the toilette of fashion, and in the work-bag of the sempstress; in the hands of the *lady,* who lounges on the sofa, and of the *lady,* who sits at the counter. From the *mistresses* of nobles they descend to the *mistresses* of snuff-shops — from the belles who *read* them in town, to the chits who *spell* them in the country. I have actually seen mothers, in miserable garrets, *crying for the imaginary distress of an heroine,* while their children were

crying for bread: and the mistress of a family losing hours over a novel
in the parlour, while her maids, in emulation of the example, were
similarly employed in the kitchen. I have seen a scullion-wench with
a dishclout in one hand, and a novel in the other, sobbing o'er the sorrows of a *Julia,* or a *Jemima.*[85]

This writer's annoyance stemmed from the universality of the "deprav-
ity" he claimed to uncover; in particular, he was bothered by the crossing
of class lines in women's fiction. He was threatened indeed precisely
by what he did not name: women turned to imaginative outlets in
order to inhabit, however briefly, other worlds, worlds in which heroines escaped from social conscription and achieved adventure, romance,
and economic security. That is what Burney offered her female readers: a chance to condemn their invisible prison, in order then to feel
its bars spring open.

Periodical reviews, of course, depended on their public, and they
were in the late eighteenth and early nineteenth centuries, and have
remained, largely a middle-class phenomenon. They catered to that
segment of the bourgeois public that believed its taste to be sophisticated and intellectual. The periodicals had been nurtured in the gap
left by the demise of political patronage for writers, which occurred
roughly around 1714, the year that saw Queen Anne's death and the
beginnings of Robert Walpole's rise to power. While the periodicals
continued to foster important political affiliations, and the more conservative among them seemed to share the political agenda of the
landed gentry, they also set themselves up as final arbiters of a universal and definitive standard of judgment for the new middle classes,
and they tended at bottom to agree with one another on literary critical matters.

A specifically English criticism, it must be remembered, was a
relatively new invention in this period if we accept Samuel Johnson's
argument that "Dryden may be properly considered as the father of
English criticism, as the writer who first taught us to determine upon
principles the merit of composition."[86] This criticism was fundamentally opposed to change. As Alvin B. Kernan has pointed out, the crisis
in the eighteenth-century world of letters that stemmed from new class
developments "was the exact reverse of the 'literacy crisis' of our own
time." New classes of people who could read and write—women and
the working poor and mercantile classes—"endangered the established
order in polite letters" and marked a radical and permanent slippage
of power in literary relations.[87] No more could a writer speak, as Milton had, of a "fit audience . . . though few." Burney's treatment at the

hands of critics responding to these marketplace changes, and critics' conservative assessments of the morally restricted social functions of the novel, reflect, then, not just an earlier period's readings of her works against which we might juxtapose our own readings. The periodicals provide a framework within which to situate the cultural and ideological constraints Burney and her sister novelists were writing against in their production of a fiction of resistance.[88]

When Frances Burney died, her papers went to her niece Charlotte Barrett and, in 1842, two years after their author's death, the first volumes of Burney's diaries and letters appeared in print. Burney had already ceased to be a literary personage who mattered to the world of letters. While *Evelina* and *Cecilia* remained in print through the nineteenth century, after Burney's death *Camilla* did not see the light again until 1972, and *The Wanderer* was not reissued until 1988. But the diaries went through several important editions in the decades following Burney's death, and were widely reviewed. Through them, Burney returned to the public literary mind, this time retrospectively as a promising novelist whose talent had been exhausted early but who had produced brilliant diaries that rival those of Samuel Pepys. She came to be seen as the consummate gossip, and began to be read as a reservoir of witty anecdotes, sparkling repartee, and clever observations about famous people and famous events from an innocent world now lost in the industrial shuffle. And as she was lionized for her ability to give the inside view, so she was again celebrated as "a very woman."

Colburn's *New Monthly Magazine* fawned over Burney: "The gentlest, the softest, the most pure-minded, the most simple-thoughted, the most home-loving, the most retiring of her sex" wrote with an "exquisite sense of the ridiculous, kept in awe by her almost prudishly fastidious notions of female delicacy and propriety."[89] The *Monthly Review* ran a series of reviews from February 1842 to January 1843 as the volumes of diaries came out. As did John Wilson Croker in the *Quarterly Review* and the reviewer for *Blackwood's Edinburgh Magazine,* the *Monthly* reviewer found Burney's self-absorption cloying, but nonetheless declared the diaries to be an "entertaining work, so full of portraits, of anecdotes, of chroniclings, and of self-complacency" that it "will, in spite of its egotism, affected sensibilities, and wiredrawn conversations, present something almost in every page, that is an antidote to dulness."[90] John Wilson Croker was, again, especially harsh, blasting the diaries as "the boldest, the most *horse-leech* egotism that literature or Bedlam has yet exhibited."[91]

The historian and essayist Thomas Babington Macaulay wrote the best-known early review-essay on the diaries for the *Edinburgh Review* in 1842. Like Samuel Johnson, he exuded paternalism — he too called his subject "little Burney" — and he spoke of her primarily as a "character-monger," but Macaulay was one of the first to recognize Burney's place in the development of the English novel·

> Miss Burney did for the English novel what Jeremy Collier did for the English drama; and she did it in a better way. She first showed that a tale might be written in which both the fashionable and the vulgar life of London might be exhibited with great force, and with broad comic humour, and which yet should not contain a single line inconsistent with rigid morality, or even with virgin delicacy. She took away the reproach which lay on a most useful and delightful species of composition. She vindicated the right of her sex to an equal share in a fair and noble province of letters. Several accomplished women have followed in her track. At present, the novels which we owe to English ladies form no small part of the literary glory of our country. No class of works is more honourably distinguished by fine observation, by grace, by delicate wit, by pure moral feeling. Several among the successors of Madame D'Arblay have equalled her; two, we think, have surpassed her [Austen and Edgeworth]. But the fact that she has been surpassed gives her an additional claim to our respect and gratitude; for, in truth, we owe to her not only Evelina, Cecilia, and Camilla, but also Mansfield Park and the Absentee.[92]

Other mid-Victorian reviewers were less able to see the broad picture. William Makepeace Thackeray, for example, applauded the quaint authenticity of Burney's diaries and letters in the *Morning Chronicle,* but also referred to their author with such phrases as "poor Fanny" and "that indomitable virgin Fanny Burney."[93] The original response to Burney's private papers, then, converted her from a minor novelist to a priggish but racy diarist, and posthumously altered her literary reputation and her public image. From 1842 on, Burney's works never received comment without a bow to the idiosyncrasies of her biography and the society she depicted in her private writings.

Later editions of the diaries and letters elicited similar responses, though as time passed and Burney faded into historical oblivion, she became more and more of a curiosity. An 1880 American edition of the diary prompted Joseph Kirkland to write in the *Dial* that "all the bright young woman's best freshness, her innocent gaiety and her keen powers of observation, she threw into her daily jottings, and these never overbloomed and went to seed as did her style of writing for the press

when she grew older."[94] Burney's afterlife as a diarist began to eclipse
her reputation as a novelist. In 1890, the *Nation* referred to her *Early
Diary* as "the portrait of a woman endowed with rare genius; it is the
graphic picture of a society," and argued that "the diaries of Madame
d'Arblay are fully as good reading as her novels."[95] In 1903, the *Atlantic
Monthly* pronounced the diaries "the real classic" of Burney's writings
and compared these volumes to Pepys' as "inadvertent" literature.[96]
In this process of revaluating Burney essentially as a diarist, her private
papers took on the literary stature of novels. "Madame D'Arblay's Diary
is her masterpiece," declared a reviewer of the Austin Dobson edition
of the *Diaries and Letters,* writing in the *Nation* in 1905, "and it is no
exaggeration to say that it is as good as a novel."[97] Later that year,
the *Nation* called the diaries "certainly Fanny Burney's most important
and most permanent contribution to literature," and J. H. Lobham,
in the *Bookman,* referred to Burney as "a born diarist" and to these
volumes as "Fanny Burney's greatest work."[98]

"Was there ever any one who, in her books and in her life, began,
continued, and ended more narrowly a woman than she?" asked J. C.
Bailey in a 1906 *Quarterly Review* article. Bailey continued: "A shyness
that is almost morbid, a shrinking from notice that is almost ridiculous, a timidity in speech and action that is almost contemptible—
such is her character as it is laid bare in her Journal; and, beautiful
as people with a certain feminine ideal may hold it, what could seem
more certain to be ineffectual? And yet it was this woman, the frightened schoolgirl of society, the unresisting victim of Madame Schwellenberg, who wrote 'Evelina,' 'Cecilia,' and this incomparable Journal.
Did anything so exquisitely, exclusively, ridiculously feminine, ever
rise so high?"[99] This review reflects the general assessment Burney's
posthumous reputation settled for her. She was read as a consummately demure creature whose specifically feminine traits would have
appeared to preclude literary ambition: shyness, embarrassment, passivity. She was painted, indeed, as the watchful wallflower at the ball.
Peter Quennell summed up this view—this tortuous taking into account of the author's femaleness—in a 1940 article that judged the diary
to be "without any doubt Miss Burney's masterpiece." "That native
modesty was perhaps her greatest asset," Quennell wrote. "Her *Diary*
is the record of an exceedingly limited mind—of a spirit circumscribed
by upbringing and taste and temperament."[100]

The trajectory of Burney's critical afterlife as it is embodied in these
reviews moves her from an acclaimed best-selling novelist to a patheti-
cally imitative old lady of letters in her lifetime, and transforms her
into a lively gossip-monger and a prudishly repressed neurotic after

her death. A further change began in this trajectory with the publication of the twelve-volume *The Journals and Letters of Fanny Burney
(Madame d'Arblay)*, an ambitious project begun in 1972 and completed
in 1984, and covering the years from 1791 to 1840. Reviewers of these
volumes still tend to lean heavily on the undigested notion that Burney's character was organized around the various social and cultural
disabilities of femaleness. This notion has inspired the concoction of
some curious headlines for recent reviews: "The Soft-Voiced Miss Burney"; "The Butterfly Becomes a Moth"; "The Prudent Heart"; "Stranded
in France"; "Travels of a Housewife"; "Acts of Enclosure"; "True Romantic"; "Miss Slyboots in Mayfair."[101] But recent reviewers have also
begun to see that femaleness and the conduct-book platitudes that
attended women in the eighteenth century played a role in Burney's
public self-presentation and at the same time offered her a subversive
literary strategy. Patricia Meyer Spacks, for example, notes that the
journals "reveal unexpected hard-headedness and equally surprising
emotional depths in a woman whose self-created image of extreme
propriety has long encouraged readers to underestimate her," and points
out that "we can now appreciate Fanny Burney in her full complexity:
the decorous woman she has always been thought, but also a writer
using her decorum for private purposes."[102]

Feminist reviewers in particular have detected the layers of complexity in Burney's writing. While Anita Brookner quips that "Fanny
preferred her friends to be ladies, either very old or very young, benevolent and sweet-tempered and with no discernible organs below
the heart," she also remarks that "Fanny Burney was a woman liberated far beyond the expectations of even the chummier sections of the
Sunday newspaper."[103] Louise Bernikow asserts, on the basis of the
diaries, that "*Evelina* was a landmark in its time and is not to be over-
looked in all our current scurrying after thoughts about 'The Woman
Writer' or 'The Female Aesthetic.'"[104] And Margaret Drabble points
out the ambiguities that mark Burney's readers as they marked the
author herself. "How hard it is to make up one's mind about Miss
Burney," Drabble writes. "She is so pretty, so trivial, so timid, so ambiguous about fame and society, so bourgeois, so lacking in moral
independence, even, occasionally, so vulgar, and yet just as one has
decided that she represents all that must be most deadening for Victorian womanhood, she will reveal herself as courageous, strong,
daring."[105] Drabble succeeds in that sentence in characterizing the
competing selves that speak in Burney's prose and the ambiguity, indirection, disjunction, and tension with which these selves — these dic-
tated constructions of eighteenth-century social ideology — confront

Burney's readers. I have tried to reread the letters and the novels from within the vise of this tension and thereby to read the tension itself as an enabling, even empowering, force in Burney's "writing mania."

Burney, I have argued, wrote out of pain and anger, and out of a need to protect herself by exposing the social codes she pretended to live by. Her social criticism, at first wittily spry and later darkly brooding and occasionally savage, masks a hidden political agenda: to locate female suppression precisely within those behavioral conventions most lauded as protective of women. Burney's heroines (and she herself) not only were not "safe" within the confines of these imprisoning conventions, but they were indeed made available for persecution and exploitation by social convention itself. It is no longer possible to dismiss the dark politicized side of Burney's work either as concocted out of nothing (Hazlitt on "female difficulties") or as a sign of her declining imaginative powers. It is no longer necessary to argue against Hazlitt and his ilk in order to prove that the social and cultural situation of eighteenth-century women was "difficult." I have also tried to argue that Burney's later writings come to terms with these "female difficulties" in sophisticatedly imagined ways, in strategic narratives that dissect the economic and social binds of early modern woman and cogently, albeit often indirectly, make a case for social change.

Critics have frequently tried to read Burney's life into her works, and recently scholars have begun to unearth the complex psychosocial registers of the Burney household in examining Burney's need to write and the themes and forms she chose to meet that need. That examination still leads some critics to analyses of Burney as repressed, childlike, clinging to her father for approval, constructing fantasies in order to assuage her own guilt at crossing the borders of acceptable behavior by bringing her name in front of the public. Edward A. and Lillian D. Bloom and Patricia Meyer Spacks, for example, while affording Burney new attention as an important literary figure, have seen her in this light, as a self-effacing woman struggling to project any sense of self at all onto a world she feared almost pathologically.[106] These views paradoxically explain Burney's imaginative power in her fiction and drama by arguing that that power derived from a peculiar inversion of her powerlessness in real life, a powerlessness she was unable to confront or defy. Other recent critical studies have begun to explore the subversive possibilities in Burney's writing, to look beyond her unyielding bows in the direction of eighteenth-century notions of propriety and decorum in order to locate a discourse of protest and challenge. Susan Staves, Judith Newton, Kristina Straub, and Catherine Parke have proposed readings of *Evelina* that posit Burney as a covert freedom fighter for a woman's right to emotional, physical, and economic autonomy.[107] Burney's first heroine, in these readings, seeks a unified self to project onto the world and, having located that self, secures it with the bric-à-brac of respectability: a husband, a name, a family. Yet these important feminist readings still offer no adequate account for the intense violence in Burney's works or the bitterness that produced the court-torture letter or the terrorized resentment that appears in the nightmare of Camilla's iron pen and its sulfuric residue.

The nature of literary criticism as a professional endeavor provides some explanations for the critical shifting I have traced here. The critical profession represents a relatively new vocational invention: it came into being as a specialized (and specialist) discourse only in relation to social organs that could disseminate it. These have been of two sorts. First, the periodical press born in the late seventeenth century came of age in the eighteenth, and spawned journals substantially devoted to book reviewing—among them those surveyed in this chapter—by the end of the century. These were popular periodicals addressed to intellectual audiences, and spanned the readership that today would subscribe to newspapers and magazines such as the *New York Review of Books* and the *Times Literary Supplement* and to more academically oriented but still general literary publications such as *Salmagundi* and the *Hudson Review*.[108] Second, universities invented and institutionalized a discipline called "English" in the mid-nineteenth century. This discipline grew out of philology, and codified as well as canonized the study of English prose, drama, and poetry as a national literature.[109] It is not, of course, that Aristotle and Dante and Sidney and Boileau did not write about literature, but they did so more as literary generalists and theorists, and as technicians (in the Greek sense of "art" as "technē"), than as critical practitioners in the way I mean here.

Whereas literary practice in the West has been politicized since Plato's *Republic* and Horace's "Epistle to Augustus," literary criticism does not really exist as a social and political force except in relation to the cultural institutions that promote it, the press (both popular and academic) and the university. The function of this criticism, and the identity of its practitioners, varies somewhat from period to period and place to place, but critics are nonetheless always situated in relation to the operative social and cultural ideologies that prevail at the moment (this has largely meant that critics have been male and of the dominant

race and class). Critics belong to, are employed and financially underwritten by, social institutions. In my introduction, I defined ideology
as those systems of social relations and values and representations that
dominate in a given period, place, and situation by being taken for
granted as inalterable givens, thereby masking social contradictions
by apparently fostering a univocal world view. Another way of stating
this is to say simply that ideology represents those ideas that contribute to maintaining the power of the dominant group. [110] Ideology, however, does not seem to me to be a set of things that can be talked about
as a monolith. There are always plural "ideologies" and they frequently
compete with one another. It is more useful, I think, to consider social ideology to refer to something like what Samuel Johnson meant
when he appealed to the concept of "universal reason" to support his
opinions: those ideas that a given segment of a society would hold
up as "obvious" or "commonsensical." If we apply this notion to criticism by arguing as I am doing here that criticism participates in and
is shaped by social institutions and their ideologies, then we accept
that criticism always rests, virtually by definition, on shifting sands.

There are, it has been said, as many interpretations of *Hamlet* as
there are readers of *Hamlet*. A more historical version of that old cliché
has been put forward by Hans Robert Jauss, the German critical theorist
who coined the term "aesthetics of reception" ("Rezeptionsästhetik"),
when he wrote that every generation reads a different *Madame Bovary*. [111]
The interpretations that take hold at a particular moment, in this view,
position themselves in relation to social ideologies and to the way
criticism functions as a social discipline. When Hazlitt calls Burney
"a very woman," in other words, he is bowing to the same set of gender relations that Burney wanted to resist in producing her fictions
to begin with. For Hazlitt, "female difficulties" are "created out of
nothing" because he speaks as a mouthpiece for a dominant patriarchy
that does not recognize its own social ideologies as anything but the
"obvious" and inevitable way the world is organized. Hazlitt illustrates
in this way the maxim coined by Berger and Luckmann about doing
fieldwork in your own society: it is difficult "to push a bus in which
you are riding."[112] Ironically, Hazlitt demonstrates that criticism bears
no necessary relation to literature; criticism, instead, creates its own
literature to "explain."

As a consequence of this yoking of literary critical practice to the
institutions that foster it and the ideologies embodied in those institutions, criticism is as subject to fads and fashions as are clothing styles.
The 1970s and early 1980s, for example, a period of political retrench-
ment and growing conservatism, nurtured deconstruction as one of

the predominant critical practices: the reading of all works as texts that are always about a slippery and untrustworthy language that can never be purely referential and that thereby twists back upon itself in an endless spiral of becoming. Deconstruction, of course, has since been "rehabilitated" as a mode of critical discourse not inherently apolitical.[113] If criticism is always already imbricated in competing ideologies, it also always struggles to achieve hegemony for itself as a leading participant in the dominant discourse.

The case I have presented of the historical trajectory of critical readings accorded to Burney illustrates the point I am making about criticism as a social institution that serves hegemonic interests. Burney's stylistic indirection and ambivalent authorial presence made it virtually impossible for eighteenth- and early nineteenth-century readers to see her social satire as anything other or more than benignly humorous. That satire was read, in addition, as exempting the landed classes. Later nineteenth-century readers of the diaries and letters, hampered by Burney's niece's and her own copious use of scissors and paste, read her as a quaint "character-monger" of a former age, sweetly and sometimes irritatingly old-fashioned. *Evelina* survived these views as a historical artifact of moderate interest for the evolution of the novel of manners, then as an early example of women's fiction. I am arguing that these critical readings never emerge from a vacuum and cannot be separated from the sociopolitical context of criticism at any given historical moment.

Criticism as a discipline has alleged itself to be neutral, objective, and scientific in various of its incarnations — from philological to poststructuralist. But critics have recently not been able to agree even on their own central enterprise: is it to seek in literature not merely referential meaning but substance, values, truth? to convert works of literature into rigorously analyzable systems? to plumb literary depths for the linguistic wreckage of unreliable worlds? to search for moments of repressed sexuality beneath metaphor? to locate covert analyses of class, gender, and race oppression? We have lost the Enlightenment's ability to believe in the existence of philosophic or aesthetic truths and to hold out for a coherent univocal voice of cultural judgment. Our critical readings, therefore, necessarily entail a circular process: we move (and must try to move consciously) back and forth between our own historical moment and social ideologies, and the historical moment and social ideologies whose imperatives are inscribed in the texts we are interpreting. In order not only to "read" Burney's writings, but to understand the historical shifts in responses to them, we have to disengage the material available for study from this process

of its appropriation into critical systems. Only through this inevitably
incomplete process of disengagement does it become possible to see
the ways in which literary texts are embedded in and perverted by
the ideological constructions of criticism.

My survey of Burney's critical fortunes suggests that she can serve
well as a test case for shifts in the popular image of women who write.
Notions of what it means to be a female author have changed from
the eighteenth century to the present, a change now receiving ample
scholarly attention. These notions have been embraced by critical practice as well. We have come not only to read gender as a crucial textual
marker, as Hazlitt and other reactionaries also did before us; we have
recognized in addition that that marker requires a sociohistorical context and a consciousness of the politics of critical discourse to make
sense as a factor in literary interpretation. Critics have always incorporated Burney into their particular gender systems and ideologies.
That Burney can now be made to serve a feminist political agenda
is no exception to this, and in itself deserves some interrogation as
a cultural phenomenon.

The 1984 completion of the twelve-volume publication of Burney's
later journals and letters and the inauguration of a multi-volume publication of the earlier journals and letters, the 1983 reissue of *Camilla*
and 1986 reprinting and new 1988 edition of *Cecilia,* the 1985 first publication of Burney's play *A Busy Day* all coincide with the third wave
of feminist social and political activity that began to emerge in the
early 1970s, and with the coming of age of feminist critical theory and
practice no longer merely as a challenge to the dominant discourse
of the academy but as itself a burgeoning (and pluralistic) alternative
dominant discourse. It is a characteristic of the practice of literary
criticism—and of the broader process of interpretation itself—that it
situates readings under the canopy of a given generation's set of critical questions. This occurs whether the critic acknowledges it or not,
but part of the process of validating an interpretation must come
from the self-consciousness with which the interpreter recognizes her
own ideological positions.

My reading of Burney's work, then, is a sign of a certain kind of
reading that is possible within the context of late twentieth-century
understandings of literary meaning. I have established my own interpretive practice as occurring at the end (for the moment) of a historical trajectory of other interpretations and within a critical understanding of literature as produced by cultural ideologies. I do not want to
suggest that my reading is only of passing value because it participates in yet another self-renewing fashion of interpretive approaches

that await, inevitably, their own obsolescence and supersession. Rather, I want to validate my reading at least in part because it self-consciously takes into account and analyzes the history and sociology of previous readings of Burney's body of work and her literary career. There can be no such thing as an ahistorical or a positivist-universal criticism. We have been forced by default to turn to a plurality of ideological critical discourses in order to interpret writers who, like Burney, embody constant tension and contradiction in their work. I too am arguing that Burney wrote as "a very woman," as how, after all, could she write otherwise? But as that phrase for Hazlitt designated fearfulness and reluctance, timidity and "punctilio," for me it designates Burney's tense yet intensely committed use of her literary voice to represent social violence in writing, to encode her rage in imaginative narrative, to invent, finally, a discourse of empowerment for women. If I consider the ways my critical practice is imbued with the cultural trends that currently affect academic institutions in North America, and take seriously Jim Merod's injunction to interrogate how critical work is positioned and put to use in the culture—how critics are cultural pawns[114]—then I need to embrace that use as a participant in a discourse that wants to renegotiate institutionalized and domesticated power relations.

What critical apparatus may we bring to the work of a complicated woman who compulsively clung to her family until, in one grand gesture, she defied her father by marrying, when she was forty, a renegade and penniless French émigré? who wrote obsessively but claimed not to want her name in print? If my interpretation is useful, then how can we revalue Burney's place in the history of the novel and the history of women writers in accordance with it? Does an overlay of feminist critical theory onto Burney's literary practice reflect an anachronistic patching job? a bandaging of eighteenth-century conventions and mores with the gauze of twentieth-century ideological hindsight?

    Beginning with my readings of Burney's ordeal by water in the cave at Ilfracombe, her account of Alexandre d'Arblay's slow dying, and her mastectomy letter, I have attempted to analyze not merely the physicality and violence that emerge in the relationship Burney traces between her body and her text—her textualization of the female body—but to trace as well the detours she took to be able to present eighteenth-century gender politics without offending or even bending much the rules she had come to believe must be adhered to. It is precisely her apparent lack of overt feminism that enriches a reading of her work for what it can tell us about daily life and emotional compromise in a period of social transition and political upheaval. Burney had her hands full just surviving — keeping her paternal family's various sorrows at bay, supporting herself and her husband and child, grieving for dear relatives and friends dead in their prime, fleeing with d'Arblay from the ravages of war in France, living in exile in a post-revolutionary country not natively her own.

Writing polemics more fiery than her 1793 *Brief Reflections relative to the Emigrant French Clergy* would have been both out of character and illogical given Burney's circumstances. We might complain, with justification, that notwithstanding her father's insistence (which has been mistaken for her own), she treated her friends Hester Thrale Piozzi and Germaine de Staël shabbily, but it would make no sense to ask her to have written *A Vindication of the Rights of Woman* or even *Persuasion*. What she wrote instead were biting commentaries on the absurdity of outmoded etiquette, handbooks protesting against women's economic dependence not only on men but on male rules. She produced manifestos on the rights of women not only to speak their minds but to be heard clearly and without prior trivializing assumptions about female speech. Burney's novels analyze the social good that woman's autonomy could promise to a changing society.

Burney did not merely divert middle-class readers during the several bleak decades for fiction between Smollett's death in 1771 and Austen's first publication in 1811. She participated in a rich literary movement of the 1790s that produced and examined the links between tales of terror and of political reform. She made possible the achievements of Jane Austen, and of the Brontës and George Eliot after her, by fixing and dissecting the complicated rules of gender politics, from how to negotiate with a potential dance partner to how to manage an inheritance, from how to earn a living from "feminine" accomplishments to how to flee from a brutalizing, state-empowered husband. Burney's heroines had broken rules thrust upon them — made-up surnames; unavailable or entailed inheritances; misread communications; secret marriage, imprisonment, and exile. They salvaged their autonomy from the shards of these broken rules. Burney wrote the book Evelina wanted, "a book, of the laws and customs *à-la-mode*" (*Evelina*, 83), and she glossed its margins with a supplemental critique of the very "laws and customs" her book inscribed.

NOTES
SELECTED BIBLIOGRAPHY
INDEX

Notes

Introduction

1 The slang usage of "fanny" to refer to the buttocks of a female has been attributed to John Cleland's 1748–49 *Memoirs of a Woman of Pleasure (Fanny Hill)*, but there is no real evidence for this, and this vulgar meaning may actually not have originated until after the eighteenth century.

2 Staves, "*Evelina*; or, Female Difficulties," *Modern Philology* 73 (1976): 368–81; Newton, "Evelina; or, The History of a Young Lady's Entrance into the Marriage Market," *Modern Language Studies* 6 (1976): 48–56, and an expanded version in "*Evelina*," in *Women, Power, and Subversion: Social Strategies in British Fiction, 1778–1860* (Athens, Ga.: University of Georgia Press, 1981; New York and London: Methuen, 1985), chap. 1, 23–54; Poovey, "Fathers and Daughters: The Trauma of Growing Up Female," in *Men and Women*, ed. Janet Todd, *Women & Literature*, n.s., 2 (1981): 39–58; Parke, "Vision and Revision: A Model for Reading the Eighteenth-Century Novel of Education," *Eighteenth-Century Studies* 16 (1982–83): 162–74; Scheuermann, "*Evelina*/Fanny Burney," in *Social Protest in the Eighteenth-Century Novel* (Columbus: Ohio State University Press, 1985), 69–88; Straub, "Fanny Burney's *Evelina* and the 'Gulphs, Pits, and Precipices' of Eighteenth-Century Female Life," *The Eighteenth Century: Theory and Interpretation* 27 (1986): 230–46.

3 Spacks, "Dynamics of Fear: Fanny Burney," in her *Imagining a Self: Autobiography and Novel in Eighteenth-Century England* (Cambridge, Mass.: Harvard University Press, 1976), 158–92; Rogers, "The Private Self and the Published Self," *International Journal of Women's Studies* 7 (1984): 110–17, and *Feminism in Eighteenth-Century England* (Urbana: University of Illinois Press, 1985); Simons, *Fanny Burney* (Totowa, N.J.: Barnes & Noble Books, 1987).

4 Doody, *Frances Burney: The Life in the Works* (New Brunswick, N.J.: Rutgers University Press; Cambridge: Cambridge University Press, 1988); Straub, *Divided Fictions: Fanny Burney and Feminine Strategy* (Lexington: University Press of Kentucky, 1987).

5 Martha G. Brown, "Fanny Burney's 'Feminism': Gender or Genre?" in *Fetter'd or Free: British Women Novelists, 1670–1815*, ed. Mary Anne Schofield and Cecilia Macheski (Athens, Ohio: Ohio University Press, 1986): 29–39.

6 Cutting discusses all four novels in "Defiant Women: The Growth of Feminism in Fanny Burney's Novels," *Studies in English Literature, 1500–1900* 17 (1977): 519–30; Castle, in *Masquerade and Civilization: The Carnivalesque in Eighteenth-Century English Culture and Fiction* (Stanford: Stanford University Press, 1986), focuses on *Cecilia* in an important analysis of Burney's relation to eighteenth-century popular culture.

7   Hemlow has overseen the publication of *The Journals and Letters of Fanny Burney (Madame d'Arblay),* from 1791–1840 in twelve volumes (Oxford: Clarendon Press, 1972–84); a second long-term editorial project covering the early years is anticipated to produce twelve volumes, the first of which appeared as this book was going to press: *The Early Journals and Letters of Fanny Burney,* vol. 1, ed. Lars E. Troide (Kingston and Montreal: McGill-Queen's University Press, 1988). Edward A. Bloom has edited *Evelina* (London: Oxford University Press, 1970) and Edward A. Bloom and Lillian D. Bloom have edited *Camilla* (London: Oxford University Press, 1972). Lillian D. Bloom has written an important article, "Fanny Burney's *Camilla:* The Author as Editor," *Bulletin of Research in the Humanities* 82 (1979): 367–93. Margaret Anne Doody and Peter Sabor have prepared editions of *Cecilia* (1988) and *The Wanderer* (due in 1989 or 1990) for the Oxford World's Classics series of Oxford University Press.

8   Hobsbawm, *Industry and Empire: From 1750 to the Present Day,* vol. 3 of *The Pelican Economic History of England* (Harmondsworth: Penguin Books, 1968), 82. For an important discussion of how "the notion of class entails the notion of historical relationship," see E. P. Thompson, *The Making of the English Working Class* (New York: Vintage Books, 1966).

9   See Eve Kosofsky Sedgwick, *The Coherence of Gothic Conventions* (London: Methuen, 1986). By this definition, the genre of "female Gothic" may embrace not just the work of Ann Radcliffe, Charlotte Smith, and the later Burney; novels such as *Wuthering Heights, Jane Eyre,* Djuna Barnes's *Nightwood,* Jean Rhys's *Wide Sargasso Sea,* and Toni Morrison's *The Bluest Eye* may also be read as "containing" powerfully Gothic elements.

10   For a sophisticated analysis of household management and class formation in relation to women, see Leonore Davidoff and Catherine Hall, *Family Fortunes: Men and Women of the English Middle Class, 1780–1850* (Chicago: University of Chicago Press, 1987).

11   See chap. 1, "The Proper Lady," in Poovey, *The Proper Lady and the Woman Writer: Ideology as Style in the Works of Mary Wollstonecraft, Mary Shelley, and Jane Austen* (Chicago: University of Chicago Press, 1984), 3–47. Ellen Pollak traces this path for the earlier part of the century in "The Eighteenth-Century Myth of Passive Womanhood," in her work *The Poetics of Sexual Myth: Gender and Ideology in the Verse of Swift and Pope* (Chicago: University of Chicago Press, 1985), chap. 2, 22–76. See also the introduction, "Power and the Ideology of 'Woman's Sphere,'" in Newton, *Women, Power, and Subversion,* 1–22.

12   See *Desire and Domestic Fiction: A Political History of the Novel* (Oxford: Oxford University Press, 1987), especially chapter 2, "The Rise of the Domestic Woman," pp. 59–95.

13   See Pollak, *Poetics of Sexual Myth,* 25, and Stone, *The Family, Sex and Marriage in England, 1500–1800* (New York: Harper & Row, 1977).

14 Poovey and Pollak (see n. 10 above) both comment on this phenomenon. For the early period Pollak discusses, see also Ruth Perry, *Women, Letters, and the Novel* (New York: AMS Press, Inc., 1980). Newton, in *Women, Power, and Subversion,* and Sandra M. Gilbert and Susan Gubar, *The Madwoman in the Attic: The Woman Writer and the Nineteenth-Century Literary Imagination* (New Haven: Yale University Press, 1979), discuss a period that extends into the nineteenth century, as does Poovey. Janet Todd, in *Women's Friendship in Literature* (New York: Columbia University Press, 1980), and Nancy K. Miller, in *The Heroine's Text: Readings in the French and English Novel, 1722–1782* (New York: Columbia University Press, 1980), look at this situation with regard to women as they are portrayed in novels by men in the eighteenth century.

15 Armstrong, *Desire and Domestic Fiction: A Political History of the Novel,* 14, 21, 37. Armstrong offers an original and important new view of the relations between female subjectivity and the development of the novel by examining the modern invention of domesticity and the power arrangements and authority structures that invention embodies.

16 I am indebted here to commentary by Lynn Hunt at the Penn Mid-Atlantic Seminar for the Study of Women in Society, University of Pennsylvania, 3 December 1987. Terry Lovell discusses the commodification of the novel in *Consuming Fiction* (London: Verso, 1987).

17 For a recent discussion of the complexities involved in attempts to define feminist criticism, see Elizabeth A. Meese, *Crossing the Double-Cross: The Practice of Feminist Criticism* (Chapel Hill, N.C.: University of North Carolina Press, 1986). Meese sees feminist criticism as a political project whose "motive . . . must be resistance in the interest of social transformation through interpretation" (14).

18 For useful discussions and definitions, see Pierre Macherey, *A Theory of Literary Production,* trans. Geoffrey Wall (Boston: Routledge & Kegan Paul, 1978); Terry Eagleton, *Criticism and Ideology: A Study in Marxist Literary Theory* (London: Verso, 1978); and Louis Althusser, *Lenin and Philosophy,* trans. Ben Brewster (London: New Left Books, 1971). Joseph Allen Boone offers a helpful discussion of ideology in relation to marriage in the novel in "Wedlock as Deadlock and Beyond: An Introduction," in his *Tradition Counter Tradition: Love and the Form of Fiction* (Chicago: University of Chicago Press, 1987), especially 5–8.

19 Eagleton, *Criticism and Ideology,* 17; Eagleton, *The Function of Criticism: From The Spectator to Post-Structuralism* (London: Verso, 1984), 39.

20 Merod, *The Political Responsibility of the Critic* (Ithaca: Cornell University Press, 1987), 19, 80.

Part One: Private Voices

1 Margaret Anne Doody presents an especially important analysis of Burney's relation to her father, Charles Burney, in her *Frances Burney: The Life in the Works* (New Brunswick, N.J.: Rutgers University Press; Cambridge: Cambridge University Press, 1988).

1   Compulsive Writing

1   The edition used here is *Camilla; or, A Picture of Youth,* ed. Edward A. Bloom and Lillian D. Bloom (London: Oxford University Press, 1972). All citations in the text and notes are to this edition, with page numbers given parenthetically in the text.

2   Susan Gubar provocatively discusses the implications for women writers of the blank page in her "'The Blank Page' and the Issues of Female Creativity," *Critical Inquiry* 8 (1981): 243–63. Barbara Johnson analyzes the figuration of women's writing in a discussion of feminism and psychoanalysis that works from readings of Nathaniel Hawthorne's "The Birthmark," Charlotte Perkins Gilman's *The Yellow Wallpaper,* and Freud's case history of Dora, in "Is Female to Male as Ground Is to Figure?" delivered at a conference on Feminism and Psychoanalysis at Normal, Illinois, in June 1986 and to the Seminar on Interpretation at Bryn Mawr College on 6 November 1987.

3   For another interpretation of Camilla's vision, see Margaret Anne Doody, "Deserts, Ruins and Troubled Waters: Female Dreams in Fiction and the Development of the Gothic Novel," *Genre* 10 (1977): 529–72, especially 546–51.

4   All references to Blake are from *The Complete Poetry and Prose of William Blake,* rev. ed., ed. David V. Erdman with commentary by Harold Bloom (Berkeley: University of California Press, 1982). Page numbers are given parenthetically in the text.

5   The King James version of Jeremiah 17 opens with this verse: "The sin of Judah *is* written with a pen of iron, *and* with the point of a diamond: *it* is graven upon the table of their heart, and upon the horns of your altars." Judah's sin is indelibly engraved on the hardened heart of the nation, and the pen of iron is necessary for writing on hard, stony surfaces. I am indebted to Deborah Roberts for this reference.

The iron pen that Job calls for in 19:23–24 is even more apt for Camilla's desperate, abandoned situation from which inscription in the Records of Eternity is both a temptation and a possibility for release. At the end of a long lament in response to Bildad the Shuhite, Job cries, "Oh that my words were now written! Oh that they were printed in a book! / That they were graven with an iron pen and lead in the rock for ever!" Job longs for a written record of his innocence and his suffering, a commitment to and in writing. He wants his words to be etched into the rock where they may stand indelible for all time. Engraved with iron, the words would then be touched by dark lead to make them legible. Clarissa Harlowe also cited this verse, and it is possible that Burney had these verses in mind when she composed Camilla's dream. The connections here explain my epigraph.

6   See editorial notes to Exod. 10:22, Jer. 6:28, and Ezek. 22:17–22 on Old Testament metallurgical semiology in *The Soncino Chumash: The Five Books of Moses with Haphtaroth,* ed. A. Cohen (London: Soncino Press, 1947), 464.

The editor refers these ideas to the commentaries of Rashi, Nachmanides, and Abraham Ibn Ezra. The Bible contains a whole symbology of metals. For example, the pointer used by the reader to follow the lines of the Torah in a synagogue, shaped like a hand and called the "Yad," must be made of silver because silver cannot be used for weapons. I am indebted to Sima N. Godfrey for help with Hebrew liturgical semiology.

7   *Memoirs of Doctor Burney,* 3 vols. (London: Edward Moxon, 1832). This work is hereafter referred to as *Memoirs,* with volume and page numbers given parenthetically in the text.

8   See Kathryn Kris, "A 70-Year Follow-up of a Childhood Learning Disability: The Case of Fanny Burney," *Psychoanalytic Study of the Child* 38 (1983): 637–52. Kris attributes " a lifelong propensity for shame and cognitive disorganization" and a "tendency to regression," views of Burney with which I would take strong issue, to what she calls her childhood learning disability. I am indebted to conversations with Margaret Doody for some of the critique of this diagnosis.

9   In a review of the *Memoirs of Doctor Burney* published in the *New Monthly Magazine* in 1833, Leigh Hunt commented that "it is remarkable, that while all her sisters were regularly educated, she had no instruction whatsoever, not even from her father. She was literally self-taught." See Hunt's essay, "Men and Books," reprinted in *Leigh Hunt's Literary Criticism,* ed. Lawrence Huston Houtchens and Carolyn Washburn Houtchens (New York: Columbia University Press, 1956), 416. For a useful discussion of women's education in the eighteenth century which mentions Burney, see Beth Kowaleski-Wallace, "Milton's Daughters: The Education of Eighteenth-Century Women Writers," *Feminist Studies* 12 (1986): 275–93.

10   The grim circumstances that surrounded Burney's preliminary work on *Camilla* provide more possible evidence for the view that the image of the iron pen derives from Job's lamentations.

11   Burney's complicated embarrassment about revealing herself as the author of *Evelina* appears throughout her private papers of 1778 and 1779. The quotation is from the *Diary and Letters of Madame d'Arblay,* ed. Charlotte Barrett (Burney's niece), 4 vols. (London: George Bell and Sons, 1891), 1:19 and passim. This edition is hereafter designated as *DL* in the text, with volume and page numbers given parenthetically.

12   For a discussion of the problematics of female authority and authorship, see Nancy Armstrong, "The Rise of Feminine Authority in the Novel," *Novel* 15 (1982): 127–45.

13   In an unpublished letter cited by Joyce M. Horner, *The English Women Novelists and their Connection with the Feminist Movement, 1688–1797* (Northampton, Mass.: Smith College Studies in Modern Languages, 1930), 11:59.

14   *Cecilia; or, Memoirs of an Heiress* (London: George Bell and Sons 1882).

15   Quotations in the text are from *The Wanderer; or, Female Difficulties,* 5 vols. (London: Longman et al., 1814). Volume and page numbers are given parenthetically in the text.

16   Spacks, *Imagining a Self: Autobiography and Novel in Eighteenth-Century*

England (Cambridge, Mass.: Harvard University Press, 1976), 170, 176. Spacks tellingly titles her chapter on Burney "Dynamics of Fear: Fanny Burney."

17   Bloom and Bloom, "Fanny Burney's Novels: The Retreat from Wonder," *Novel* 12 (1979): 220, 222.

18   Glassman, "Acts of Enclosure," *Hudson Review* 30 (1977): 142, 143.

19   Lustig, "The Prudent Heart: Fanny Burney's Journals Restored," *Studies in Burke and His Time* 15 (1974): 291, 292.

20   *The Early Diary of Frances Burney, 1768–1778,* ed. Annie Raine Ellis, 2 vols. (London: George Bell and Sons, 1889), 1:14. This edition is hereafter referred to in the text as *ED,* with volume and page numbers given parenthetically.

21   For a discussion of space and protection in the letter, see Christina Marsden Gillis, "Private Room and Public Space: the Paradox of Form in *Clarissa,*" *Studies on Voltaire and the Eighteenth Century* 176 (1979): 153–68, and *The Paradox of Privacy: Epistolary Form in "Clarissa"* (Gainesville: University of Florida Press, 1983).

22   Chesterfield's well-known letter to his son warning against "audible" laughter is dated 9 March 1748: see *The Letters of Philip Dormer Stanhope, 4th Earl of Chesterfield,* ed. Bonamy Dobrée (London: Eyre and Spottiswoode [The King's Printers Edition], 1932), 3:1114–18. Burney's passage may also be compared with Swift's parody of "Court Style" in book 3 of *Gulliver's Travels* (New York: W. W. Norton, 1970), in which the narrator receives permission to "lick the Dust before [the King's] footstool" (175).

23   *The Journals and Letters of Fanny Burney (Madame D'Arblay),* ed. Joyce Hemlow et al., 12 vols. (Oxford: Clarendon Press, 1972–84). This edition is hereafter cited in the text and notes as *JL.* Volume and page numbers are given parenthetically in the text.

24   The entire passage reads:

> But see the angry Victor hath recall'd
> His Ministers of vengeance and pursuit
> Back to the Gates of Heav'n: the Sulphurous Hail
> Shot after us in storm, o'erblown hath laid
> The fiery Surge, that from the Precipice
> Of Heav'n receiv'd us falling, and the Thunder,
> Wing'd with red Lightning and impetuous rage,
> Perhaps hath spent his shafts, and ceases now
> To bellow through the vast and boundless Deep.
>   (*Paradise Lost,* bk. 1, lines 169–77)

John Milton, *Complete Poems and Major Prose,* ed. Merritt Y. Hughes (Indianapolis: Odyssey Press, 1957), 215–16.

25   For a meticulous and useful discussion of Burney's editorial relationship to her third novel, see Lillian D. Bloom, "Fanny Burney's *Camilla:* The Author as Editor," *Bulletin of Research in the Humanities* 82 (1979): 367–93.

26   This view is most forcefully stated in Bloom and Bloom, "Fanny Burney's Novels," 215–35.

27   An anonymous reviewer of the first two volumes of *JL* ("The Butterfly Becomes a Moth," *Times Literary Supplement,* 15 December 1972, 1531–32) sees

Burney's editorial zeal as schizophrenic caution, her second personality as "the ponderous literary lady" Madame d'Arblay censoring and bowdlerizing the "witty girl" Fanny Burney in a "self-remaking."

28   For a discussion of letters and periodical prose in the eighteenth century, see Kathryn Ann Shevelow, "'Fair-Sexing It': Richard Steele's *Tatler* and the Evolution of a Feminized Prose in English Periodical Literature" (Ph.D. diss., University of California, San Diego, 1981), especially chapter 2.

29   The best discussion of this development remains Sister Mary Humiliata, "Standards of Taste Advocated for Feminine Letter Writing, 1640–1797," *Huntington Library Quarterly* 13 (1950): 261–77.

30   Virginia Woolf, *A Room of One's Own* (New York: Harcourt, Brace, and Jovanovich, 1929), 65. For a discussion, see Genie S. Lerch-Davis, "Rebellion Against Public Prose: The Letters of Dorothy Osborne to William Temple (1652–54)," *Texas Studies in Literature and Language* 20 (1978): 386–415.

31   Josephine Donovan discusses the entry of women into the world of legitimate literature via the letter in her essay "The Silence Is Broken," in *Women and Language in Literature and Society,* ed. Sally McConnell-Ginet, Ruth Borker, and Nelly Furman (New York: Praeger Scientific Press, 1980): 205–18.

32   The date of this letter is 3 January 1801. See *Jane Austen's Letters to her Sister Cassandra and Others,* 2d ed., ed. R. W. Chapman (London: Oxford University Press, 1952), 102.

33   Johnson, *Life of Pope,* vol. II of *The Works of Samuel Johnson* (London: F. C. and J. Rivington et al., 1823), 157.

34   Cited by Janet Gurkin Altman in *Epistolarity: Approaches to a Form* (Columbus: Ohio State University Press, 1982), 2. Altman's work provides an important theoretical discussion of the formal operations of the letter.

35   *The Correspondence of Samuel Richardson,* ed. Anna Laetitia Barbauld, 6 vols. (London: Richard Phillips, 1804), 3:248. See also Bruce Redford, who takes his title from Richardson's epistolary theory as it is outlined in the letters to Sophia Westcomb, *The Converse of the Pen: Acts of Intimacy in the Eighteenth-Century Familiar Letter* (Chicago: University of Chicago Press, 1986). I carry this analysis further in another context in my "Fanny's Fanny: Epistolarity, Eroticism and the Transsexual Text," in *Writing The Female Voice: Essays on Epistolary Literature,* ed. Elizabeth C. Goldsmith (Boston: Northeastern University Press, 1989): 135–53.

36   Ronald C. Rosbottom, "Motifs in Epistolary Fiction: Analysis of a Narrative Sub-genre," *L'Esprit Créateur* 17 (1977): 297.

37   Miller, "Narrative and History," *ELH* 41 (1974): 456.

38   Pope was the first writer to oversee the publication of his own letters, though he denied any role in his correspondence's appearance in print. For studies of the literary properties and possibilities of the letter-text in the eighteenth century, see Redford, *The Converse of the Pen;* Altman, *Epistolarity: Approaches to a Form;* Homer Obed Brown, "The Errant Letter and the Whispering Gallery," *Genre* 10 (1977): 573–99; and Keith Stewart, "Towards Defining an Aesthetic for the Familiar Letter in Eighteenth-Century England," *Prose Studies* 5 (1982): 179–92. Patricia Meyer Spacks discusses the social functions of familiar letters in "Borderlands," chap. 4 of her *Gossip* (New York:

Knopf, 1985), 65–91. Spacks focuses on the letters of Lady Mary Wortley Montagu and Horace Walpole.

2   Writing the Unspeakable

1   Les Confessions, ed. Jacques Voisine (Paris: Garnier Frères, 1980), 87, 90–91. The English translation is from the Everyman edition, ed. R. Niklaus, 2 vols. (New York: Dutton, 1931), 1:71, 74.

2   The two manuscripts of Burney's mastectomy letter are housed in the Henry W. and Albert A. Berg Collection of the New York Public Library, and the letter is printed in *JL* 6:596–616. Volumes 11 and 12 contain full accounts of Burney's editorial work on her manuscripts in the years 1819–35. Esther Burney died in 1832, and in the normal course of events, the 1812 letter would not have been returned until after its recipient's death, so revision on this letter may have been especially late. The symbols ✠ and ❋ are, according to Hemlow, infallible signs of late revision. See Joyce Hemlow, "Letters and Journals of Fanny Burney: Establishing the Text," in *Editing Eighteenth-Century Texts,* ed. D. I. B. Smith (Toronto: University of Toronto Press, 1968), 25–43.

3   Cited in *JL* 7:20, n. 4. This remark is inaccurate on two counts: first, it was the right breast that was affected; second, the diagnosis was already of cancer.

4   See Owen H. Wangensteen and Sarah D. Wangensteen, *The Rise of Surgery: From Empiric Craft to Scientific Discipline* (Minneapolis: University of Minnesota Press, 1978), 456.

5   Ibid.

6   The letter from Larrey survives and is sewn to the cover of the fair copy in the Berg Collection.

7   Cited by William C. Wigglesworth, "Surgery in Massachusetts, 1620–1800," in *Medicine in Colonial Massachusetts, 1620–1820,* ed. Philip Cash, Eric H. Christianson, and J. Worth Estes (Boston: Publications of the Colonial Society of Massachusetts, vol. 57, 1980; Charlottesville: University Press of Virginia, 1980), 224–25.

8   Hemlow, *The History of Fanny Burney* (Oxford: Clarendon Press, 1958), 322.

9   A mastectomy procedure lasts much longer today. In preanesthetic surgery speed, of course, was of the essence.

10   Cited by Edward A. Bloom and Lillian D. Bloom in a note to *Camilla; or, A Picture of Youth* (London: Oxford University Press, 1972), 937.

11   Pepys underwent a lithotomy on 26 March 1658, and he always kept that date as an anniversary "festival." See *The Diary of Samuel Pepys,* ed. Robert Latham and William Matthews, 11 vols. (Berkeley: University of California Press, 1970–83), 1:97; for a discussion of Pepys's medical writing, see Francis Barker, "The Tremulous Private Body," in *1642: Literature and Power in the Seventeenth Century,* ed. Francis Barker et al. (Colchester: University of

Essex, 1981), 1–10; Norman Cousins, *Anatomy of an Illness as Perceived by the Patient: Reflections on Healing and Regeneration* (New York: Norton, 1979); Audre Lorde, *The Cancer Journals* (Argyle, N.Y.: Spinsters Ink, 1980).

12 Michel de Montaigne, *Essais,* 5 vols. (Paris: Imprimerie Nationale, 1963), 5:303. The English version comes from *The Complete Works of Montaigne,* trans. Donald M. Frame (Stanford: Stanford University Press, 1958), 837–38. John O'Neill cites this passage in "Essaying Illness," in *The Humanity of the Ill: Phenomenological Perspectives,* ed. Victor Kestenbaum (Knoxville: University of Tennessee Press, 1982), 132.

13 For a discussion of Burney's procedure by a practicing surgeon, see Anthony R. Moore, "Preanesthetic Mastectomy: A Patient's Experience," *Surgery* 83 (February 1978): 200–205.

14 Henry E. Sigerist outlines "the history of the patient in society" in "The Social History of Medicine," *The Western Journal of Surgery, Obstetrics, and Gynecology* 48 (1940): 715–22.

15 See Norman Jewison, "The Disappearance of the Sick Man from Medical Cosmology, 1770–1870," *Sociology* 10 (1976): 225–44. On the "historicity" of the patient as writer, see G. S. Rousseau, "Literature and Medicine: The State of the Field," *Isis* 72 (1981): 418. A call to broaden the scope of medical history appears in Roy Porter, "The Patient's View: Doing Medical History from Below," *Theory and Society* 14 (1985): 175–98. See also *Patients and Practitioners: Lay Perceptions of Medicine in Preindustrial Society,* ed. Roy Porter (Cambridge: Cambridge University Press, 1985).

16 Geoffrey Hartman uses this term in his essay "Words and Wounds," in *Medicine and Literature,* ed. Enid Rhodes Peschel (New York: Neale Watson Academic Publications, 1980), 179.

17 Elmer L. DeGowin and Richard L. DeGowin, *Bedside Diagnostic Examination,* 3d ed. (New York: Macmillan, 1976), 12. E. H. Ackerknecht, in *Medicine at the Paris Hospital, 1794–1848* (Baltimore: Johns Hopkins University Press, 1967) discusses the history of clinical record keeping. For other discussions of the patient history, see George Blumer, "History Taking," *Connecticut State Medical Journal* 13 (1949): 449–53; W. Riese, "The Structure of the Clinical History," *Bulletin of the History of Medicine* 16 (1944): 437–49; and Wolf Stewart et al., "Instruction in Medical History Taking," *Journal of Medical Education* 27 (1952): 244–52. I am indebted to M. Elizabeth Sandel, M.D., for information concerning current clinical practice in history taking.

18 T. R. Harrison, *Harrison's Principles of Internal Medicine,* 8th ed., ed. George W. Thorn et al. (New York: McGraw-Hill, 1977), xxix. *Harrison's* is the standard textbook of internal medicine.

19 See Roy Schafer, "Narration in the Psychoanalytic Dialogue," *Critical Inquiry* 7 (1980): 29–53.

20 White, "The Question of Narrative in Contemporary Historical Theory," *History and Theory* 23 (1984): 1. See also Hayden White, "The Value of Narrativity in the Representation of Reality," *Critical Inquiry* 7 (1980): 5–27; idem, *The Content of the Form: Narrative Discourse and Historical Representation* (Baltimore: Johns Hopkins University Press, 1987). White suggests that perhaps a "narrativized" world is necessary in order to establish moral authority.

21   Mink, "The Autonomy of Historical Understanding," in *Philosophical Analysis and History,* ed. William H. Dray (1968; reprint, Westport, Conn.: Greenwood Press, 1978), 180–81; cited by Roger G. Seamon, "Narrative Practice and the Theoretical Distinction between History and Fiction," *Genre* 16 (1983): 203.

22   For a historian's approach to this theoretical question, see David Carr, "Narrative and the Real World: An Argument for Continuity," *History and Theory* 25 (1986): 117–31. See also Mink, "Narrative Form as a Cognitive Instrument," in *The Writing of History: Literary Form and Historical Understanding,* ed. Robert H. Canary and Henry Kozicki (Madison: University of Wisconsin Press, 1978), 129–49.

23   Warren, *Affecting Scenes: Being Passages from the Diary of a Physician,* new and complete ed., 2 vols. (New York: J. and J. Harper, 1831), 1:49–50.

24   Cited by Sir D'Arcy Power, "The History of the Amputation of the Breast to 1904," *Liverpool Medico-Chirurgical Journal* 42 (1934): 35.

25   John Brown, M.D., "Rab and His Friends," in *Horae Subsecivae,* 3 vols., new ed., 2d ser. (London: A. and C. Black, 1897), 2:378.

26   *Belinda,* vol. 3 of Maria Edgeworth's *Tales and Novels* (London: Routledge, 1893), 58. Elizabeth Blackwell, the first woman to be granted an M.D. degree by an American medical school, was said to have been persuaded to go into medicine by a friend afflicted with "a painful disease of a female organ" who explained to Blackwell that her worst sufferings could have been alleviated had she been able to be treated by a female physician. See John R. Blake, "Women and Medicine in Ante-Bellum America," *Bulletin of the History of Medicine* 39 (1965): 102.

27   Ballard, *Memoirs of British Ladies, Who Have Been Celebrated for their Writings or Skill in the Learned Languages, Arts and Sciences,* 2d ed. (London: T. Evans, 1774), 316.

28   See L. J. Jordanova, "Natural Facts: A Historical Perspective on Science and Sexuality," in *Nature, Culture and Gender,* ed. Carol P. MacCormack and Marilyn Strathern (Cambridge: Cambridge University Press, 1980), 42–69. Jordanova especially cites William Cadogan's *Essay upon Nursing and the Management of Children from their Birth to Three Years of Age* (1748) and Pierre Roussel's *Système physique et moral de la femme* (1775).

29   See Stephen Heath, *The Sexual Fix* (New York: Schocken Books, 1983), and L. J. Jordanova, "Guarding the Body Politic: Voleny's Catechism of 1793," in *1789: Reading Writing Revolution,* Proceedings of the Essex Conference on the Sociology of Literature, July 1981, ed. Francis Barker et al. (Essex: University of Essex, 1982), 12–21.

30   Eugène Bouchut, *Practical Treatise on the Diseases of Children and Infants at the Breast,* trans. Peter Huickes Bird (London, 1844). Excerpted in *Victorian Women: A Documentary Account of Women's Lives in Nineteenth-Century England, France, and the United States,* ed. Erna Olafson Hellerstein, Leslie Parker Hume, and Karen M. Offen (Stanford: Stanford University Press, 1981), 228.

31 For a survey of physiological, medical, and metaphysical views of women in the eighteenth century, see Paul Hoffmann, *La Femme dans la pensée des lumières* (Paris: Editions Ophrys, 1977). See also Maurice Bloch and Jean H. Bloch, "Women and the Dialectics of Nature in Eighteenth-Century French Thought," in MacCormack and Strathern, *Nature, Culture and Gender*, 25–41.

32 Edward Tilt, *The Change of Life in Health and Disease: A Practical Treatise on the Nervous and Other Affections Incidental to Women at the Decline of Life*, 2d ed. (London: J. Churchill, 1857), cited in Hellerstein, Hume, and Offen, *Victorian Women*, 464.

33 Breast amputation has been inflicted as a punishment for wayward or nonconforming women, and its punishment history dates to the Paleolithic age. The Assyrian library of cuneiform tablets from Nineveh, which has been dated to around 2250 B.C.E. and preserved in the Louvre, is the earliest written record of this practice. In the *Code of Hammurabi*, the King of Babylon orders that, for a wet nurse's crimes, "they shall cut off her breasts," thereby denying the punished woman her means of earning a living. A number of female saints—Barbara, Foya, Apollina, Christina, and Agatha—were also tortured in this way. Saint Agatha, the best known, has become the patron saint of diseases of the breast, and through her, breast amputation has come to symbolize a particularly female martyrdom. The iconography of Saint Agatha reveals much about early surgical instruments used for mastectomy, and surgical historians have studied the history of her depictions in painting (especially in portraits by Van Dyck, Giovenone, and Tiepolo), as painters used instruments from Scultetus' *Armamentarium chirurgicum* (1655) as models for their instruments of torture. This nonmedical history of mastectomy is important for the chronicle it exposes of the breast as a symbol not only of femaleness, but also of female autonomy and power. For discussions, see Richard Hardaway Meade, *An Introduction to the History of General Surgery* (Philadelphia: Saunders, 1968), 151; David Charles Schechter and Henry Swan, "Of Saints, Surgical Instruments, and Breast Amputation," *Surgery* 52 (October 1962): 693–98; and Edward F. Lewison, "Saint Agatha, the Patron Saint of Diseases of the Breast, in Legend and Art," *Bulletin of the History of Medicine* 24 (1950): 409–20.

34 Fontanis, *The Womans Doctour; or, an exact and distinct Explanation of all such Disease as are peculiar to that Sex with Choise and Experimental Remedies against the same* (London, 1652), 1. Cited by Hilda Smith, "Gynecology and Ideology in Seventeenth-Century England," in *Liberating Women's History: Theoretical and Critical Essays,* ed. Berenice A. Carroll (Urbana: University of Illinois Press, 1976), 107.

35 Alan D. Steinfeld, "A Historical Report of a Mastectomy for Carcinoma of the Breast," *Surgery, Gynecology, & Obstetrics* 141 (October 1975): 616–17. Boylston was the physician who introduced smallpox inoculation to the colonies, against strong protest, in 1721. For a discussion of one aspect of the popular response to surgical cures and surgical professionalization, see Toby Gelfand, "Demystification and Surgical Power in the French Enlightenment," *Bulletin of the History of Medicine* 57 (1983): 203–17.

36   For histories of cancer theories and therapies, see L. J. Rather, *The Genesis of Cancer: A Study in the History of Ideas* (Baltimore: Johns Hopkins University Press, 1978) and F. H. Garrison, "The History of Cancer," *The New York Academy of Medicine* 2, no. 4 (April 1926): 179–85. The classic article on the history of mastectomy in Sir D'Arcy Power, "The History of the Amputation of the Breast to 1904," *Liverpool Medico-Chirurgical Journal* 42 (1934): 29–56. Other useful surveys include G. Keynes, "Carcinoma of the Breast: A Brief Historical Survey of the Treatment," *St. Bartholomew's Hospital Journal* 56 (August 1952): 462–66; E. F. Lewison, "The Surgical Treatment of Breast Cancer. An Historical and Collective Review," *Surgery* 34 (November 1953): 904–53; and D. de Moulin, "Historical Notes on Breast Cancer, with Emphasis on The Netherlands. I. Pathological and Therapeutic concepts in the Seventeenth Century," *The Netherlands Journal of Surgery* 32–34 (1980): 129–34. See also Daniel de Moulin, *A Short History of Breast Cancer* (The Hague: Martinus Nijhoff, 1983).

37   Foucault, *The Birth of the Clinic: An Archaelogy of Medical Perception*, trans. A. M. Sheridan Smith (New York: Vintage Books, 1975), 195, 137. Foucault's reference here concerns the invention of the stethoscope. Foucault's views have been widely disputed, but not his assertion that this period was revolutionary for the history of medicine.

38   For an account of these developments, see Stanley Joel Reiser, *Medicine and the Reign of Technology* (Cambridge: Cambridge University Press, 1978).

39   For a discussion of the relations between pen and scalpel and paintbrush and wounds in a visual context, see Michael Fried's "Realism, Writing, and Disfiguration in Thomas Eakins's *Gross Clinic*," *Representations* 9 (1985), especially 70–75. Eakins's *Agnew Clinic* (1889), of course, depicts a mastectomy. Two recent books discuss related ideas about the narratives and functions of violence: Leo Bersani and Ulysse Dutoit, *The Forms of Violence: Narrative in Assyrian Art and Modern Culture* (New York: Schocken Books, 1985), and Elaine Scarry, *The Body in Pain: The Making and Unmaking of the World* (New York: Oxford University Press, 1985).

40   Montaigne, *Essais*, 5:299–300. The English version is from Frame, *Complete Works of Montaigne*, 835–36. Cited in English by Jean Starobinski in "The Body's Moment," *Yale French Studies* 64 (1983): 293. Starobinski here discusses the protest against medico-mechanical theories of the body by the authority of personal experience.

Part Two: Fictions of Violation: Women and Social Ideology

1   Citations in the text and notes are from *Evelina; or, the History of a Young Lady's Entrance into the World*, ed. Edward A. Bloom (London: Oxford University Press, 1970). Page numbers are given parenthetically in the text.

2   See Susan Staves, "*Evelina;* or, Female Difficulties," *Modern Philology* 73 (1976): 368–81. Staves offers an analysis of the relationship between violence and anxiety in Burney's first novel as it undergirds a structure of female helplessness in the face of the tyranny of decorum. Staves rightly focuses on the pervasiveness of physical assaults in *Evelina* as central to Burney's vision.

3   All quotations are from *Cecilia; or, Memoirs of an Heiress,* with preface and notes by Annie Raine Ellis, 2 vols. (London: George Bell and Sons, 1882). Volume and page numbers are given parenthetically in the text. The 1904 George Bell edition has been reprinted in a Virago Press paperback (New York: Penguin Books, 1986). The welcome new annotated Oxford World's Classics *Cecilia,* ed. Margaret Anne Doody and Peter Sabor (London: Oxford University Press, 1988), appeared after this book went to press.

3   *Evelina:* Protecting the Heroine

1   *The Works of the Marchioness de Lambert,* 2 vols. (London: W. Owen, 1769), 1:68. For commentary on the marquise's ideas, and other views of early women's education, see Octave Gréard, *L'Education des femmes par les femmes* (Paris: Librairie Hachette et Cie., 1889), and Phyllis Stock, *Better than Rubies: A History of Women's Education* (New York: E. P. Putnam's Sons, 1978).

2   *The Works of the Marchioness de Lambert,* 1:233–34. In *Madame de Lambert (1647–1733) ou le féminisme moral,* University Studies, ser. 2, Romance Languages and Literatures, vol. 7 (New York: Peter Lang, 1984), Marie-José Fassiotto cites the French original of "Réflexions nouvelles sur les femmes" from *Oeuvres complètes de Madame la Marquise de Lambert, suivies de ses lettres à plusieurs personnages célèbres* (Paris: Léopold Collin, 1808): "Je demande aux hommes, de la part de tout le sexe; que voulez-vous de nous? Vous souhaitez tous de vous unir à des personnes estimables, d'un esprit aimable et d'un coeur droit; permettez-leur donc l'usage des choses qui perfectionnent la raison. Ne voulez-vous que des grâces qui favorisent les plaisirs? Ne vous plaignez donc pas si les femmes étendent un peu l'usage de leurs charmes" (131). For another discussion, see Emmanuel de Broglie, "Les mardis et les mercredis de la marquise de Lambert, 1710–1733," *Correspondant* 179 (1895): 140–62, 319–45.

3   Walter Allen, *The English Novel: A Short Critical History* (New York: E. P. Dutton, 1954), 95.

4   Robert Palfrey Utter and Gwendolyn Bridges Needham, *Pamela's Daughters* (New York: Macmillan, 1936), 93.

5   Carey McIntosh analyzes the ways language reflects class in *Evelina,* distinguishing between the vulgar, the petty-bourgeois, the genteel, and the noble, in *Common and Courtly Language: The Stylistics of Social Class in 18th-Century English Literature* (Philadelphia: University of Pennsylvania Press, 1986), 114–18.

6   For an excellent analysis of Evelina and the marketplace, see Judith Newton, "Evelina; or, The History of a Young Lady's Entrance into the Marriage Market," *Modern Language Studies* 6 (1976): 48–56.

7   Among the offenses punishable with a stint in the pillory (an instrument that remained in use in England until 1837) were publishing books

without a license or libeling the government ("anti-ministerial writings"). See Bloom's note in the Oxford edition of *Evelina*, 436.

8 Wigs were no longer in fashion for younger men at this period, and Lovel wears a heavily pomaded and curled "frizle-frize top" of his own hair (*Evelina*, 394). In Lovel's defense, Susan Staves suggests that it is time for a revaluation of the fop figure with respect to nonviolence. See Staves, "A Few Kind Words for the Fop," *Studies in English Literature* 22 (1982): 413–28.

9 Patricia Meyer Spacks discusses Evelina's verbal artistry in *Gossip* (New York: Knopf, 1985), 156–64.

10 Staves, "*Evelina;* or, Female Difficulties," *Modern Philology* 73 (1976): 374.

11 In "Of the Pernicious Effects Which Arise from the Unnatural Distinctions Established in Society," chap. 9 in Mary Wollstonecraft, *A Vindication of the Rights of Woman*, ed. Carol H. Poston (New York: Norton, 1975), 141.

12 Spacks, "Ev'ry Woman is at Heart a Rake," *Eighteenth-Century Studies* 8 (1974): 31.

13 Sarah Fielding, *The Adventures of David Simple*, ed. Malcolm Kelsall (London: Oxford University Press, 1969), 101.

14 For a different kind of discussion of this scene, see Earl R. Anderson, "Footnotes More Pedestrian than Sublime: A Historical Background for the Footraces in *Evelina* and *Humphry Clinker*," *Eighteenth-Century Studies* 14 (1980): 56–68.

15 Armstrong, *Desire and Domestic Fiction: A Political History of the Novel* (New York: Oxford University Press, 1987), 112.

16 Johnson, *A Dictionary of the English Language* (New York: Arno Press, 1979). This edition is a facsimile of the 1755 edition printed in London by W. Strahan.

17 Allen, *The English Novel*, 96.

18 Cited by Burney in her *Memoirs of Doctor Burney* (London: Edward Moxon, 1832), 2, 121; also cited by Joyce Hemlow, *The History of Fanny Burney* (Oxford: Clarendon Press, 1958), 96.

19 *The Complete Letters of Lady Mary Wortley Montagu*, ed. Robert Halsband, 3 vols. (Oxford: Clarendon Press, 1965), 1:44. In 1753, Lady Mary wrote her famous warning to her daughter Lady Bute that a woman should "conceal whatever learning she attains, with as much solicitude as she would hide crookedness or lameness" (2:22).

20 *The Whole Duty of a Woman*, Written by a Lady (London: J. Gwillim, 1695), 6; cited by Angeline Goreau in *Reconstructing Aphra: A Social Biography of Aphra Behn* (New York: Dial Press, 1980), 41.

21 Spacks, *Imagining a Self: Autobiography and Novel in Eighteenth-Century England* (Cambridge, Mass.: Harvard University Press, 1976), 57.

22 Barrett, *The Heroine; or, Adventures of Cherubina*, 3d ed., 3 vols. (London: Henry Colburn, 1815). The epigraph appears on the title page of each volume.

23 Barrett, *The Heroine*, 1:31.

24 Ibid., 34.

25   Ibid., 26–28.
26   Ibid., 33–34.
27   Macaulay, letter 22 in *Letters on Education* (London: Dilly, 1790). Reprinted in Wollstonecraft's *Vindication,* 199.

4   *Camilla:* Silencing the Heroine

1   Hemlow, *The History of Fanny Burney* (Oxford: Clarendon Press, 1958), 255.

2   Coral Ann Howells, "'The Proper Education of a Female . . . is Still to Seek': Childhood and Girls' Education in Fanny Burney's *Camilla; or, A Picture of Youth,*" *British Journal for Eighteenth-Century Studies* 7 (1984): 193.

3   *A Father's Legacy to his Daughters, by John Gregory . . . To which is added, Mr. Tyrold's Advice to his Daughter . . . from "Camilla" by Mrs. d'Arblay. Also a Picture of the Female Form, by G. Horne . . .* (Poughmill near Ludlow: G. Nicholson, 1809). G. Horne is George Horne, Bishop of Norwich, and the complete title of his work is *A Picture of the Female Character, as it ought to appear when formed.*

4   Ann Radcliffe, *The Mysteries of Udolpho,* ed. Bonamy Dobreé (Oxford: Oxford University Press, 1980), 5.

5   See notes to the Edward A. Bloom and Lillian D. Bloom edition of *Camilla,* 941.

6   Judith Newton has pointed out in *Women, Power, and Subversion: Social Strategies in British Fiction, 1778–1860* (Athens: University of Georgia Press, 1981; New York and London: Methuen, 1985), 25–26, that *Evelina* may be in part a response to that autobiographical event. The infamous, toadlike Solmes and the unrelenting insistence of the Harlowes in Richardson's *Clarissa* come to mind here as well.

7   See Margaret Anne Doody, "George Eliot and the Eighteenth-Century Novel," *Nineteenth-Century Fiction* 35 (1980): 260–91 and *Frances Burney: The Life in the Works* (New Brunswick, N.J.: Rutgers University Press; Cambridge: Cambridge University Press, 1988), on *Camilla* and stylistic innovation.

8   Edward A. and Lillian D. Bloom identify the reference to the *Peruvian Letters* as a mistaken allusion to either Montesquieu's or Lyttleton's *Persian Letters* and ascribe this error to Mrs. Mittin's ignorance of the difference between Persia and Peru. In fact, Burney certainly means Madame de Graffigny's work, which would be much more appropriate reading material for the sentimental Mrs. Berlinton than the earlier satirical works.

9   Burney has Mr. Tyrold ascribe *Spectator* 17 on unattractiveness to Addison when in fact it was written by Steele, and he slightly misquotes the admonition that "great Tenderness and Sensibility in this Point is one of the greatest Weaknesses of Self-love." The *Spectator* essay begins: "Since our Persons are not of our own Making, when they are such as appear Defective or Uncomely, it is, methinks, an honest and laudable Fortitude to dare to be Ugly." From *The Spectator,* ed. Donald F. Bond, 5 vols. (Oxford: Clarendon Press, 1965), 1:75, 74.

5   *Cecilia:* Money and Anarchy

1   Margaret Anne Doody remarks on this lineage in *Frances Burney: The Life in the Works* (New Brunswick, N.J.: Rutgers University Press; Cambridge: Cambridge University Press, 1988), chap. 5.

2   Bakhtin, *Rabelais and His World,* trans. Helene Iswolsky (Bloomington: Indiana University Press, 1985).

3   In particular, see Leach, "Time and False Noses," in *Rethinking Anthropology,* ed. E. Leach (London: Athlone Press, 1961), 132–36, and Turner, *The Ritual Process: Structure and Anti-Structure* (Ithaca: Cornell University Press, 1977).

4   Stallybrass and White, *The Politics and Poetics of Transgression* (Ithaca: Cornell University Press, 1986), 19.

5   Castle, "Eros and Liberty at the English Masquerade, 1710–1790," *Eighteenth-Century Studies* 17 (1983–84): 155–76; idem, "The Carnivalization of Eighteenth-Century Narrative," *PMLA* 99 (1984): 903–16; idem, *Masquerade and Civilization: The Carnivalesque in Eighteenth-Century Culture and Fiction* (Stanford: Stanford University Press, 1986). This work represents a major contribution to eighteenth-century studies, and my own reading of *Cecilia* is indebted to Castle's analysis.

6   Castle, "Carnivalization of Eighteenth-Century Narrative," 903–16.

7   Carroll Smith-Rosenberg discussed this distribution in "Mis-Remembering Richardson: Representations of the American Middle Class," unpublished paper discussed at the "Language, Culture, Gender, and Power" group at the University of Pennsylvania on 28 May 1986, 35.

8   See Bakhtin, "Discourse in the Novel," the final essay in *The Dialogic Imagination,* ed. Michael Holquist (Austin: University of Texas Press, 1981), 263 and passim.

9   Bakhtin, *Rabelais and His World,* 5–11.

10   See Wayne Booth, "Freedom of Interpretation: Bakhtin and the Challenge of Feminist Criticism," *Critical Inquiry* 9 (1982): 45–76, for a discussion of the ways recent critics have employed Bakhtin's idea that there is no neutral language and that the self is dialogic rather than monologic.

11   For this criticism, see Terry Eagleton, *Walter Benjamin: Toward a Revolutionary Criticism* (London: Verso, 1981), 148; Roger Sales, *English Literature in History, 1780–1830: Pastoral and Politics* (London: Hutchinson, 1983), 169; and Stallybrass and White, *Politics and Poetics of Transgression,* 12–16.

12   Judy Simons comments on the parallels between *Cecilia* and *Pride and Prejudice,* though she concludes that Austen "developed and substantiated the realist vision that Fanny Burney introduced" and argues that Burney's approach is more "tentative" than Austen's. See Simons, *Fanny Burney* (Totowa, N.J.: Barnes & Noble Books, 1987), 65–66.

13   *The Novels of Jane Austen,* 3d ed., ed. R. W. Chapman, 5 vols. (Oxford: Oxford University Press, 1982), 2:245.

6   *The Wanderer:* Money and Entrapment

1   This discussion occurs early in Doody's *Frances Burney: The Life in the Works* (New Brunswick, N.J.: Rutgers University Press; Cambridge: Cambridge University Press, 1988).

2   Martha G. Brown argues that Burney's use of conventional themes and plots makes her novels assimilable into the romance tradition, and Brown contends that reading "feminism" into Burney's fiction falsifies this derivation from romance. See Brown, "Fanny Burney's 'Feminism': Gender or Genre?" in *Fetter'd or Free: British Women Novelists, 1670–1815,* ed. Mary Anne Schofield and Cecilia Macheski (Athens: Ohio University Press, 1986), 29–39. Brown sees an apparent political argument with respect to women only in *The Wanderer.*

3   Mary Wollstonecraft Shelley, *Frankenstein, or The Modern Prometheus,* ed. James Rieger (Indianapolis: Bobbs-Merrill, 1974): 116–17.

4   Judy Simons asserts, "Emotion and common sense coexist in the creation of a female persona in the sour, realistic assessment of *The Wanderer,* as Juliet and Elinor form two sides of the feminist coin," in *Fanny Burney* (Totowa, N.J.: Barnes & Noble Books, 1987), 113.

5   Hemlow, *The History of Fanny Burney* (Oxford: Clarendon Press, 1958), 225.

7   "A very woman" and Her Readers

1   *Critical Review* 46 (September 1778): 202–4.

2   *Gentleman's Magazine* 48 (September 1778): 425.

3   *Monthly Review* 58 (April 1778): 316.

4   *The Dial* (16 May 1893): 317.

5   *The Spectator* 70 (20 May 1893): 673.

6   William Dean Howells, *Heroines of Fiction* (New York: Harper & Brothers Publishers, 1901), 1:22, 23.

7   R. Brimley Johnson, *The Women Novelists* (1919, Essay Index Reprint Series; Freeport, N.Y.: Books for Libraries Press, 1967).

8   Muriel Masefield, *Women Novelists from Fanny Burney to George Eliot* (1934, Essay Index Reprint Series; Freeport, N.Y.: Books for Libraries Press, 1967), 32.

9   Christopher Lloyd, *Fanny Burney* (London: Longmans, Green and Co., 1936), 75.

10   James R. Foster, *History of the Pre-Romantic Novel in England* (New York: MLA Monograph, 1949), 221, 222.

11   Kemp Malone, "*Evelina* Revisited," *Papers on Language and Literature* 1 (1965): 19.

12   Lionel Stevenson, "Varieties of the Novel," *Studies in Burke and His Time* 13 (1972): 2256.

13   Michael O'Neill, review of *Evelina, British Journal for Eighteenth-Century Studies* 6 (1983): 85–86.

14   Karl Danz, "Frances Burneys *Evelina* (1778) und das Aufkommen der Frauenromane," *Anglia* 48 (1924): 358–74.

15   Staves, "*Evelina;* or, Female Difficulties," *Modern Philology* 7 (1976): 368–82; Newton, "Evelina: or, The History of a Young Lady's Entrance into the Marriage Market," *Modern Language Studies* 6 (1976): 48–56.

16   Bloom and Bloom, "Fanny Burney's Novels: The Retreat from Wonder," *Novel* 12 (1979): 220, 221.

17   Poovey, "Fathers and Daughters: The Trauma of Growing Up Female," in *Men and Women,* ed. Janet Todd, *Women & Literature,* n.s., 2 (1981): 39–58.

18   Rogers, "Fanny Burney: The Private Self and the Published Self," *International Journal of Women's Studies* 7 (March–April 1984): 110–17.

19   In addition to the work already cited, see Judy Simons, *Fanny Burney* (Totowa, N.J.: Barnes & Noble Books, 1987), and Jane Spencer, *The Rise of the Woman Novelist: From Aphra Behn to Jane Austen* (Oxford: Basil Blackwell, 1986).

20   An exception to this failure is the important work by Kristina Straub, "Fanny Burney's *Evelina* and the 'Gulphs, Pits, and Precipices' of Eighteenth-Century Female Life," *The Eighteenth Century: Theory and Interpretation* 27 (1986): 230–46; idem, *Divided Fictions: Fanny Burney and Feminine Strategy* (Lexington: University Press of Kentucky, 1987).

21   Parke, "Vision and Revision: A Model for Reading the Eighteenth-Century Novel of Education," *Eighteenth-Century Studies* 16 (1982–83): 167, 168.

22   Staves, "*Evelina;* or, Female Difficulties," 381.

23   Newton, "Evelina," in *Women, Power, and Subversion: Social Strategies in British Fiction, 1778–1860* (Athens: University of Georgia Press, 1981; New York and London: Methuen, 1985), chap. 1, 54.

24   Figes, *Sex & Subterfuge: Women Writers to 1850* (London: Macmillan, 1982), 33.

25   Poovey, *The Proper Lady and the Woman Writer: Ideology as Style in the Works of Mary Wollstonecraft, Mary Shelley, and Jane Austen* (Chicago: University of Chicago Press, 1984), 25.

26   *Gentleman's Magazine* 52 (October 1782): 485.

27   *Monthly Review* 67 (December 1782): 453, 456. The *George Bateman* review that accuses Blower of imitating Burney appears in *Monthly Review* 66 (March 1782): 237.

28   *The Saturday Review of Politics, Literature, Science, and Art* [London] 55 (17 March 1883): 347, 348.

29   The "Great Cham" is, of course, Samuel Johnson. *Spectator* 55 (6 January 1883): 18, 19.

30   Straub, *Divided Fictions;* Doody, *Frances Burney: The Life in the Works* (New Brunswick, N.J.: Rutgers University Press; Cambridge: Cambridge University Press, 1988).

31   Copeland, "Money in the Novels of Fanny Burney," *Studies in the Novel* 8 (1976): 24–37, 29.

32   Cutting, "Defiant Women: the Growth of Feminism in Fanny Burney's Novels," *Studies in English Literature* 17 (1977): 522–24.

33   Bloom and Bloom, "Fanny Burney's Novels," 223, 227, 228.

34   Doody, "A Journal to 'Nobody': the Life of Fanny Burney." Talk given to the American Society for Eighteenth-Century Studies in Williamsburg, Virginia, 13 March 1986.

35   Spacks, "Ev'ry Woman is at Heart a Rake," *Eighteenth-Century Studies* 8 (1974): 41.

36   Spacks, *Imagining a Self: Autobiography and Novel in Eighteenth-Century England* (Cambridge, Mass.: Harvard University Press, 1976), 181.

37   See Claudia Marina Vessilli, *Cecilia Tra I "Courtesy Books" e la Vindication of the Rights of Woman* (Rome: Edizioni Dell'Ateneo & Bizzarri, 1979). [Università degli Studi di Trieste, Facoltà di Lettere e Filosofia, Instituto di Filologia Germanica — 8.]

38   *Critical Review* 18 (September 1796): 40.

39   *The British Critic* 8 (November 1796): 527, 528, 533.

40   *Monthly Review,* ser. 2, 21 (October 1796): 156, 161, 163.

41   Bodleian MS. Don.c. 56, ff. 87–88; cited by Roger Lonsdale, "Dr. Burney and the *Monthly Review,* Part I," *Review of English Studies,* n.s., 14 (1963): 351.

42   Lonsdale, "Dr. Burney," pt. 1, 350.

43   Lonsdale, "Dr. Burney," pt. 1, 350. It may be that at that point Dr. Burney assumed he might as well urge Charles to write the review, if people would think he had written it in any case; it may also be that Charles declined his father's request before Griffiths became involved in the discussion.

The elder Burney had himself never been opposed to self-puffery: he made frequent allusions to himself or to his works in the reviews that he published unsigned, and his anonymously published *Verses on the Arrival in England of the Great Musician Haydn (1791)* was reviewed by its author himself, though Griffiths may not have been aware that Burney had written the work when he assigned him the review (Lonsdale, "Dr. Burney," pt. 1, 352). And Burney's father was not averse to *ad feminam* criticism himself. Of Hester Thrale Piozzi's *British Synonymy (1794),* he wrote in the *Monthly Review:*

> We always expected from this Lady's pen emanations of genius, seasoned with wit, humor, and learned allusions: but we were fearful that she would not submit to the trammels of good taste and sound judgment. She had frequent flashes, but no steadiness in her fire; its fuel, like green wood, crackles, and produces corruscations which alarm, but which afford neither light nor heat of long duration.

He concluded, "We are acquainted with very few females, and not with many males, who are able to write such a book." These passages are cited by Lonsdale, "Dr. Burney and the *Monthly Review,* Part II," *Review of English Studies,* n.s., 15 (1964): 29. (See also Benjamin C. Nangle, "Charles Burney, Critic," in *The Age of Johnson: Essays Presented to Chauncey Brewster Tinker* [New Haven: Yale University Press, 1941]: 99–109.) It should be noted that Hester Thrale Piozzi, an old friend of the Burney family, had been alienated from them for ten years by the time this review appeared.

44   *Analytical Review* 24 (August 1796): 142.

45   *Times Literary Supplement,* 15 December 1972, 1531–32. See Margaret Anne Doody, *Frances Burney: The Life in the Works.* Doody makes a strong argument for restoring Burney's formal given name, Frances, and points out in addition the irony that library patrons cannot even rely on knowing under which name to find Burney's works catalogued.

46   *The Philadelphia Minerva* 2 (19 November 1796): 2.

47   Moreux, review in *Studies in Burke and His Time* 17 (1976): 152–53.

48   Polly Shulman, "The Perils of Evelina, Cecilia, Eugenia, Lavinia, Honoria, Henrietta, & c.," *Voice Literary Supplement* 30 (November 1984): 6.

49   *The Novels of Jane Austen,* 3d ed., ed. R. W. Chapman, 5 vols. (Oxford: Oxford University Press, 1982), 5:49.

50   *The British Critic,* n.s., 1 (April 1814): 374, 385, 386.

51   Croker, *Quarterly Review* 11 (April 1814): 123, 126.

52   Taylor, *Monthly Review* 76 (April 1815): 412.

53   Ibid., 412, 413.

54   Croker, *Quarterly Review* 11 (April 1814): 124.

55   Ibid., 125–26.

56   Ibid., 130.

57   Ibid., 124.

58   Ibid., 129.

59   These citations come from Hunt's "Men and Books" essay in *New Monthly Magazine* (January 1833), n.s. 37, 48–59, reprinted in *Leigh Hunt's Literary Criticism,* ed. Lawrence Huston Houtchens and Carolyn Washburn Houtchens (New York: Columbia University Press, 1956), 416, 417.

60   All quotations from Hazlitt's review are from *Edinburgh Review* 24 (April 1815): 336–37, 338.

61   Joseph A. Grau lists the editions of Burney's works in *Fanny Burney: An Annotated Bibliography* (New York: Garland Publishers, 1981). Grau notes a French translation of *The Wanderer* entitled *La Femme Errante,* by J. B. J. Breton de la Martinière and A. J. Lemierre d'Argy, which appeared in Paris in 1815. Margaret Anne Doody and Peter Sabor are editing *The Wanderer* for the Oxford World's Classics, as they have edited *Cecilia* (1988), with an expected publication date of 1989 or 1990. In 1988, Pandora Press (Unwin Hyman) published the novel with an introduction by Margaret Drabble.

62   S. Bugnot, "*The Wanderer,* de Fanny Burney: Essai de Rehabilitation," *Etudes Anglaises* 15, no. 3 (July–September 1962): 225–32.

63   See Copeland, "Money in the Novels of Fanny Burney," 24–37, and Bloom and Bloom, "Fanny Burney's Novels," 215–35.

64   Cutting, "Defiant Women," 519–30. Cutting also discusses *The Wanderer* in "A Wreath for Fanny Burney's Last Novel — *The Wanderer*'s Contribution to Women's Studies," *Illinois Quarterly* 37 (1975): 45–64, but there she

apologizes for Burney's limitations, rigidity, and moralism in praising *The Wanderer* largely as a neglected contribution to the feminist movement.

65   Doody, *Frances Burney: The Life in the Works.* Cited from typescript.

66   Croker, *Quarterly Review* 11 (April 1814): 123–30.

67   Macaulay, *Edinburgh Review,* ser. 2, 161 (January 1843): 29–36.

68   Bloom and Bloom, introduction to *Camilla* in the World's Classics series (London: Oxford University Press, 1983), xiv.

69   Macaulay, *Critical and Historical Essays,* ed. F. C. Montague (London: Methuen, 1903), 3:306.

70   *Thraliana, The Diary of Hester Lynch Thrale (later Mrs. Piozzi),* 2 vols., ed. Katharine C. Balderston (Oxford: Clarendon Press, 1942) 1:368.

71   Watt, *The Rise of the Novel: Studies in Defoe, Richardson, and Fielding* (Berkeley: University of California Press, 1957).

72   McKeon, *The Origins of the English Novel, 1600–1740* (Baltimore: Johns Hopkins University Press, 1987).

73   For discussions, see Marilyn Butler, *Romantics, Rebels and Reactionaries: English Literature and its Background, 1760–1830* (Oxford: Oxford University Press, 1981), and Terry Lovell, *Consuming Fiction* (London: Verso, 1987), particularly chap. 3, "The Novel as Commodity: 1770–1830."

74   Cited by Derek Roper, *Reviewing before the Edinburgh, 1788–1802* (Newark: University of Delaware Press, 1978), 158–59.

75   Cited by W. F. Galloway, Jr., "The Conservative Attitude Toward Fiction, 1770–1830," *PMLA* 55 (1940): 1041.

76   Ibid.

77   Cited by W. H. Rogers, "The Reaction Against Melodramatic Sentimentality in the English Novel, 1796–1830," *PMLA* 49 (1934): 104.

78   Mitford to Elford, 29 June 1819, cited in "A Minor Classic," *New York Times,* 26 July 1940, 16. The *Times* article was written on the centenary of Burney's death.

79   E. V. Lucas, *The Life of Charles Lamb* (London: Methuen, 1905), 2:32–33. Lucas is quoting Thomas Allsop's record of an 1820 conversation. Cited by H. E. Haworth, "Romantic Female Writers and the Critics," *Texas Studies in Literature and Language* 17 (1976): 725.

80   Cited by Haworth, "Romantic Female Writers," 727.

81   Cited by Roper, *Reviewing before the Edinburgh,* 126.

82   From the *Critical Review;* cited by Roper, *Reviewing before the Edinburgh,* 131. See also Katherine Ellis, "Charlotte Smith's Subversive Gothic," *Feminist Studies* 3 (1976): 51–55, and Katharine M. Rogers, "Inhibitions on Eighteenth-Century Women Novelists: Elizabeth Inchbald and Charlotte Smith," *Eighteenth-Century Studies* 11 (1977): 63–78.

83   Bage, *Man As He Is,* 2 vols. (Dublin: P. Byrne and B. Smith, 1793), 1:i.

84   See Michael Munday, "The Novel and Its Critics in the Early Nineteenth Century," *Studies in Philology* 79 (1982): 205–26.

85   *Sylph* 5 (October 1795): 35–36. Cited by John T. Taylor, *Early Opposi-*

tion to the English Novel: The Popular Reaction from 1760 to 1830 (New York: King's Crown Press, 1943), 53, and by Leslie M. Thompson and John R. Ahrens, "Criticism of English Fiction 1780–1810: The Mysterious Powers of the Pleading Preface," *Yearbook of English Studies* 1 (1971): 125.

86   Johnson, "Life of Dryden," in *Lives of the English Poets,* ed. G. B. Hill, 3 vols. (Oxford: Oxford University Press, 1905), 1:410. Johnson referred to criticism as "a kind of learning then almost new in the English Language" (1:366) in his discussion of Dryden's *Essay on Dramatick Poets.*

87   Kernan, *Printing Technology, Letters and Samuel Johnson* (Princeton: Princeton University Press, 1987), 70.

88   On the history of book reviewing see, in addition to the studies already cited, Edward A. Bloom, "'Labors of the Learned': Neoclassic Book Reviewing Aims and Techniques," *Studies in Philology* 54 (1957): 537–63; Walter Graham, *English Literary Periodicals* (1930; New York: Octagon Books, 1966); Joseph B. Heidler, *The History, from 1700 to 1800, of English Criticism of Prose Fiction* (Urbana: University of Illinois Press, 1928); Jon Klancher, "Reading the Social Text: Power, Signs, and Audience in Early Nineteenth-Century Prose," *Studies in Romanticism* 23 (1984): 183–204; and Robert D. Mayo, *The English Novel in the Magazines: 1750–1815* (Evanston, Ill.: Northwestern University Press, 1962).

89   [Colburn's] *New Monthly Magazine and Humorist* 66 (December 1842): 527, 532.

90   *Quarterly Review* 70 (June 1842): 243–87; *Blackwood's Edinburgh Review* 51 (June 1842): 784–94; *Monthly Review,* ser. 2, 158 (April 1842): 488; *Monthly Review,* ser. 2, 160 (September 1842): 19.

91   Croker, *Quarterly Review* 70 (June 1842): 251.

92   Macaulay, "Madame d'Arblay," in *Critical and Miscellaneous Essays,* rev. ed. (Philadelphia: A. Hart, 1852), 5:14, 66, 67.

93   Thackeray, *Contributions to the "Morning Chronicle,"* ed. Gordon N. Ray (Urbana: University of Illinois Press, 1955), 185.

94   *The Dial* 1 (May 1880): 31.

95   *The Nation* 51 (4 September 1890): 193.

96   *Atlantic Monthly* 91 (June 1903): 826.

97   *The Nation* 94 (28 January 1905): 141.

98   *The Nation* 81 (28 December 1905): 527; *The Bookman* 28 (September 1905): 199, 200.

99   Bailey, *Quarterly Review* 204 (January 1906): 89–90. This long review (twenty-two pages) claimed to offer psychobiographical insight into Burney's artistic temperament, but its reductive view of "woman" as psychological category disqualifies its interpretations.

100   Quennell, *New Statesman* 20 (3 August 1940): 114.

101   Claire Tomalin, *New Statesman* 83 (21 April 1972): 529–30; *Times Literary Supplement,* 15 December 1972, 1531–32; Irma S. Lustig, *Studies in Burke and His Time* 15 (1974): 287–96; *Times Literary Supplement,* 30 January 1976, 103; *The Spectator* 236 (21 February 1976): 20; Peter Glassman, *Hudson Review* 30

(1977): 138–46; Jonathan Keates, *The Spectator* 245 (1 November 1980): 21–22; *Times Literary Supplement,* 4 January 1985, 8. It should be noted that headlines are generally composed by editors, not by the writers whose stories they title.

102   Spacks, *Philological Quarterly* 53 (1974): 663.

103   Brookner, "Stranded in France," *Times Literary Supplement,* 30 January 1976, 103.

104   Bernikow, *Ms.,* April 1977, 42.

105   Drabble, "Travels of a Housewife," *The Spectator* 236 (21 February 1976): 20.

106   See Bloom and Bloom, "Fanny Burney's Novels," 215–35, and Spacks, "Dynamics of Fear," in *Imagining a Self,* 158–92.

107   See Staves, *"Evelina;* or, Female Difficulties," 368–81; Newton, *Women, Power and Subversion,* chap. 1; Straub, "Fanny Burney's *Evelina,*" 230–46; and Parke, "Vision and Revision," 162–74.

108   Several changes interacted to produce the new "profession" of letters in the eighteenth century that gave birth to the literary periodical press: new printing technologies, middle-class literacy, and a growing market economy in which books functioned as did other commodities. For interesting discussions, see the introduction and chap. 1 of Alvin B. Kernan, *The Imaginary Library: An Essay on Literature and Society* (Princeton: Princeton University Press, 1982), and his *Printing Technology, Letters and Samuel Johnson* (Princeton: Princeton University Press, 1987).

109   See D. J. Palmer, *The Rise of English Studies* (New York: Oxford University Press, 1965).

110   Raymond Williams notes that the word "ideology" first appeared in English (from the French of Destutt de Tracy) in 1796, and remarks on the word's pejorative meaning as "false consciousness" as well as on its neutral uses as a system of ideas appropriate to a class and as "the set of ideas which arise from a given set of material interests." See Williams, *Keywords: A Vocabulary of Culture and Society* (New York: Oxford University Press, 1976), 126–30. See also Fredric Jameson, "The Ideology of the Text," *Salmagundi* 31–32 (1975–76): 204–46, and *The Political Unconscious: Narrative as a Socially Symbolic Act* (Ithaca: Cornell University Press, 1981), where Jameson uses the term "ideology" in Althusser's sense as "a representational structure which allows the individual subject to conceive or imagine his or her lived relationship to transpersonal realities such as the social structure or the collective logic of History" (30).

111   Jauss, "Literary History as a Challenge to Literary Theory," *New Literary History* 2 (1970): 7–37. Jauss also discusses what he calls the reader's "horizon of expectations."

112   Cited by Emily Martin, *The Woman in the Body: A Cultural Analysis of Reproduction* (Boston: Beacon Press, 1987), 11.

113   The 1987 revelation that Paul de Man, the leading American proponent of deconstruction, who died in 1983, wrote dozens of columns for collaborationist newspapers in his native Belgium in 1940–42 has prompted

renewed debate about the politics of deconstruction. For a preliminary re-
sponse to these revelations, see Jacques Derrida, "Like the Sound of the Sea
Deep within a Shell: Paul de Man's War," trans. Peggy Kamuf, *Critical In-
quiry* 14 (1988): 590–652. De Man's articles for *Le Soir* and *Het Vlaamsche Land*
have been collected in Paul de Man, *Wartime Journalism, 1940–42,* ed. Werner
Hamacher, Neil Hertz, and Tom Keenan (Lincoln: University of Nebraska
Press, 1988). Commentaries on these writings can be found in *Responses: On
Paul de Man's Wartime Journalism,* ed. Werner Hamacher, Neil Hertz, and
Tom Keenan (Lincoln: University of Nebraska Press, 1988). In addition,
numerous articles have appeared in scholarly journals and in the popular
press.

114   Jim Merod, *The Political Responsibility of the Critic* (Ithaca: Cornell
University Press, 1987), 80.

Selected Bibliography

Ackerknecht, E. H. *Medicine at the Paris Hospital, 1794–1848*. Baltimore: Johns Hopkins University Press, 1967.

Adelstein, Michael E. *Fanny Burney*. New York: Twayne, 1968.

Adburgham, Alison. *Women in Print: Writing Women and Women's Magazines from the Restoration to the Accession of Victoria*. London: Allen and Unwin, 1972.

Allen, Walter. *The English Novel: A Short Critical History*. New York: E. P. Dutton, 1954.

Altman, Janet Gurkin. *Epistolarity: Approaches to a Form*. Columbus: Ohio State University Press, 1982.

Altick, Richard D. *The English Common Reader: A Social History of the Mass Reading Public, 1800–1900*. Chicago: University of Chicago Press, 1957.

Althusser, Louis. *Lenin and Philosophy*. Trans. Ben Brewster. London: New Left Books, 1971.

Anderson, Earl R. "Footnotes More Pedestrian than Sublime: A Historical Background for the Footraces in *Evelina* and *Humphry Clinker*." *Eighteenth-Century Studies* 14 (1980): 56–68.

Armstrong, Nancy. *Desire and Domestic Fiction: A Political History of the Novel*. New York: Oxford University Press, 1987.

Armstrong, Nancy. "The Rise of Feminine Authority in the Novel." *Novel* 15 (1982): 127–45.

Armstrong, Nancy, and Leonard Tennenhouse, eds. *The Ideology of Conduct: Essays in Literature and the History of Sexuality*. New York: Methuen, 1987.

Bage, Robert. *Man as He Is*. 2 vols. Dublin: P. Byrne and B. Smith, 1793.

Bakhtin, Mikhail. *The Dialogic Imagination*. Ed. Michael Holquist. Austin: University of Texas Press, 1981.

Bakhtin, Mikhail. *Rabelais and His World*. Trans. Helene Iswolsky. Bloomington: Indiana University Press, 1985.

Balderston, Katharine C., ed. *Thraliana: The Diary of Mrs. Hester Lynch Thrale (later Mrs. Piozzi)*. 2 vols. Oxford: Clarendon Press, 1942.

Ballard, George. *Memoirs of British Ladies, Who Have Been Celebrated for Their Writings or Skill in the Learned Languages, Arts and Sciences*. 2d ed. London: T. Evans, 1774.

Barbauld, Anna Laetitia, ed. *The Correspondence of Samuel Richardson.* 6 vols. London: Richard Phillips, 1804.

Barker, Francis. "The Tremulous Private Body." In *1642: Literature and Power in the Seventeenth Century.* Ed. Francis Barker et al., 1–10. Colchester: University of Esssex, 1981.

Barrett, Eaton Stannard. *The Heroine, or Adventures of Cherubina.* 3d ed. 3 vols. London: Henry Colburn, 1815.

Bersani, Leo, and Ulysse Dutoit. *The Forms of Violence: Narrative in Assyrian Art and Modern Culture.* New York: Schocken Books, 1985.

Blake, John R. "Women and Medicine in Ante-Bellum America." *Bulletin of the History of Medicine* 39 (1965): 99–123.

Blake, William. *The Complete Poetry and Prose of William Blake.* Rev. ed., ed. David V. Erdman. Berkeley: University of California Press, 1982.

Bloch, Maurice, and Jean H. Bloch. "Women and the Dialectics of Nature in Eighteenth-Century French Thought." In *Nature, Culture and Gender,* ed. Carol P. MacCormack and Marilyn Strathern, 25–41. Cambridge: Cambridge University Press, 1980.

Bloom, Edward A. "'Labors of the Learned': Neoclassic Book Reviewing Aims and Techniques." *Studies in Philology* 54 (1957): 537–63.

Bloom, Edward A., and Lillian D. Bloom. "Fanny Burney's Novels: The Retreat from Wonder." *Novel* 12 (1979): 215–35.

Bloom, Harold, ed. *Fanny Burney's "Evelina".* Modern Critical Interpretations. New York: Chelsea House Publishers, 1988.

Bloom, Lillian D. "*Camilla:* The Author as Editor." *Bulletin of Research in the Humanities* 82 (1979): 367–93.

Blumer, George. "History Taking." *Connecticut State Medical Journal* 13 (1949): 449–53.

Bodek, Evelyn Gordon. "Salonières and Bluestockings: Educated Obsolescence and Germinating Feminism." *Feminist Studies* 3 (1976): 185–99.

Bond, Donald F., ed. *The Spectator.* 6 vols. Oxford: Clarendon Press, 1965.

Boone, Joseph Allen. *Tradition Counter Tradition: Love and the Form of Fiction.* Chicago: University of Chicago Press, 1987.

Booth, Wayne. "Freedom of Interpretation: Bakhtin and the Challenge of Feminist Criticism." *Critical Inquiry* 9 (1982): 45–76.

Brown, Homer Obed. "The Errant Letter and the Whispering Gallery." *Genre* 10 (1977): 573–99.

Brown, John, M.D. *Horae Subsecivae.* 3 vols. London: A. and C. Black, 1897.

Brown, Martha G. "Fanny Burney's 'Feminism': Gender or Genre." In *Fetter'd or Free: British Women Novelists, 1870–1815,* ed. Mary Anne Schofield and Cecilia Macheski. Athens: Ohio University Press, 1986:29–39.

Browne, Alice. *The Eighteenth-Century Feminist Mind.* Detroit: Wayne State University Press, 1987.

Bradbrook, Frank. *Jane Austin and Her Predecessors.* Cambridge: Cambridge University Press, 1966.

Bugnot, S. "*The Wanderer* de Fanny Burney: Essai de réhabilitation." *Etudes Anglaises* 15 (1962): 225–32.

Burney, Frances. *Camilla; or, A Picture of Youth.* Ed. Edward A. and Lillian D. Bloom. London: Oxford University Press, 1972.

Burney, Frances. *Cecilia; or, Memoirs of an Heiress.* Ed. Annie Raine Ellis. London: George Bell and Sons, 1882.

Burney, Frances. *Cecilia; or Memoirs of an Heiress.* Ed. Margaret Anne Doody and Peter Sabor. London: Oxford University Press, 1988.

Burney, Frances. *Diary and Letters of Madame d'Arblay.* 4 vols. Ed. Charlotte Barrett. London: George Bell and Sons, 1891.

Burney, Frances. *The Early Diary of Frances Burney, 1768-1778.* Ed. Annie Raine Ellis, London: George Bell and Sons, 1889.

Burney, Frances. *Evelina; or The History of a Young Lady's Entrance into the World.* Ed. Edward A. Bloom. London: Oxford University Press, 1970.

Burney, Frances. *The Journals and Letters of Fanny Burney (Madame d'Arblay).* 12 vols. Ed. Joyce Hemlow et al. Oxford: Clarendon Press, 1972-84.

Burney, Frances. *Memoirs of Dr. Burney.* 3 vols. London: Edward Moxon, 1832.

Burney, Frances. *The Wanderer; or, Female Difficulties.* 5 vols. London: Longman et al., 1814.

Burney, Frances. *The Wanderer; or, Female Difficulties.* Intro. Margaret Drabble. Winchester, Mass.: Pandora Press, 1988.

Butler, Marilyn. *Romantics, Rebels and Reactionaries: English Literature and its Background, 1760-1830.* Oxford: Oxford University Press, 1981.

Carr, David. "Narrative and the Real World: An Argument for Continuity." *History and Theory* 25 (1986): 117-31.

Carroll, Bernice A., ed. *Liberating Women's History: Theoretical and Critical Essays.* Urbana: University of Illinois Press, 1976.

Cash, Philip, Eric H. Christianson, and J. Worth Estes, eds. *Medicine in Colonial Massachusetts, 1620-1820.* Boston: Publications of the Colonial Society of Massachusetts, 1980.

Castle, Terry. "The Carnivalization of Eighteenth-Century Narrative." *PMLA* 99 (1984): 903-16.

Castle, Terry. "Eros and Liberty at the English Masquerade, 1710-1790." *Eighteenth-Century Studies* 17 (1983-84): 155-76.

Castle, Terry. *Masquerade and Civilization: The Carnivalesque in Eighteenth-Century English Culture and Fiction.* Stanford: Stanford University Press, 1986.

Chapman, R. W., ed. *Jane Austen's Letters to her sister Cassandra and others.* 2d ed. London: Oxford University Press, 1952.

Chapman, R. W., ed. *The Novels of Jane Austen.* 3d edition. 5 vols. Oxford: Oxford University Press, 1982.

Clark, Anna. "The Politics of Seduction in English Popular Culture, 1748-1848." In *The Progress of Romance: The Politics of Popular Fiction.* Ed. Jean Radford, 47-72. History Workshop Series. London: Routledge and Kegan Paul, 1986.

Clay, Christopher. "Marriage, Inheritance, and the Rise of Large Estates in England, 1660-1815." *Economic History Review* 2d ser. 21 (1968): 503-18.

Cohen, A., ed. *The Soncino Chumash: The Five Books of Moses with Haphtaroth.* London: Soncino Press, 1947.

Cohen, Murray. "Eighteenth-Century English Literature and Modern Critical Methodologies." *The Eighteenth Century: Theory and Interpretation* 20 (1979): 5–23.

Collins, A. S. *The Profession of Letters: A Study of the Relation of Author to Patron, Publisher and Public, 1780–1832.* London: George Routledge and Sons, 1928.

Copeland, Edward W. "Money in the Novels of Fanny Burney." *Studies in the Novel* 8 (1976): 24–37.

Copley, Stephen, ed. *Literature and the Social Order in Eighteenth-Century England.* London: Croom Helm, 1984.

Cousins, Norman. *Anatomy of an Illness as Perceived by the Patient: Reflections on Healing and Regeneration.* New York: W. W. Norton, 1979.

Crown, Patricia. "Visual Music: E. F. Burney and a Hogarth Revival." *Bulletin of Research in the Humanities* 83 (1980): 435–72.

Cutting, Rose Marie. "A Wreath for Fanny Burney's Last Novel — *The Wanderer*'s Contribution to Women's Studies." *Illinois Quarterly* 37 (1975): 45–64.

Cutting, Rose Marie. "Defiant Women: The Growth of Feminism in Fanny Burney's Novels." *Studies in English Literature, 1500–1900* 17 (1977): 519–30.

Danz, Karl. "Frances Burneys *Evelina* (1778) und das Aufkommen der Frauenromane." *Anglia* 48 (1924): 358–74.

Davidoff, Leonore, and Catherine Hall. *Family Fortunes: Men and Women of the English Middle Class, 1780–1850.* Chicago: University of Chicago Press, 1987.

Davis, Lennard J. *Factual Fictions: The Origins of the English Novel.* New York: Columbia University Press, 1983.

Davis, Lennard J. *Resisting Novels: Ideology and Fiction.* New York: Methuen, 1987.

DeGowin, Elmer L., and Richard L. DeGowin. *Bedside Diagnostic Examination.* 3d ed. New York: Macmillan, 1976.

de Lauretis, Theresa, ed. *Feminist Studies/Critical Studies.* Bloomington: Indiana University Press, 1986.

de Moulin, Daniel. "Historical Notes on Breast Cancer, with Emphasis on the Netherlands. I. Pathological and Therapeutic concepts in the Seventeenth Century." *The Netherlands Journal of Surgery* 32–34 (1080): 129–34.

de Moulin, Daniel. *A Short History of Breast Cancer.* The Hague: Martinus Nijhoff, 1983.

Devlin, D. D. *The Novels and Journals of Fanny Burney.* New York: St. Martin's Press, 1987.

Dobbin, Marjorie W. "The Novel, Women's Awareness, and Fanny Burney." *English Language Notes* 22 (1985): 42–52.

Dobrée, Bonamy, ed. *The Letters of Philip Dormer Stanhope, 4th Earl of Chesterfield.* 6 vols. London: Eyre and Spottiswoode [The King's Printers Edition], 1932.

Donovan, Josephine. "The Silence is Broken." In *Women and Language in Literature and Society.* Ed. Sally McConnell-Ginet, Ruth Borker, and Nelly Furman, 205–18. New York: Praeger Scientific Press, 1980.

Doody, Margaret Anne. "Deserts, Ruins and Troubled Waters: Female Dreams in Fiction and the Development of the Gothic Novel," *Genre* 10 (1977): 529–72.

Doody, Margaret Anne. *Frances Burney: The Life in the Works*. New Brunswick: Rutgers University Press, and Cambridge: Cambridge University Press, 1988.

Doody, Margaret Anne. "George Eliot and the Eighteenth-Century Novel." *Nineteenth-Century Fiction* 35 (1980): 260–91.

Eagleton, Terry. *Criticism and Ideology: A Study in Marxist Literary Theory*. London: Verso, 1978.

Eagleton, Terry. *The Function of Criticism: From the Spectator to Post-Structuralism*. London: Verso, 1984.

Eagleton, Terry. "Ideology, Fiction, Narrative." *Social Text* 2 (1979): 62–80.

Eagleton, Terry. *Walter Benjamin: Toward a Revolutionary Criticism*. London: Verso, 1981.

Edgeworth, Maria. *Belinda*. Vol. 3 of *Tales and Novels*. 10 vols. Longford ed. London: George Routledge and Sons, 1893.

Ehrenpreis, Irvin, and Robert Halsband. *The Lady of Letters in the Eighteenth-Century*. Los Angeles: Publications of the William Andrews Clark Memorial Library, 1969.

Ellis, Katherine. "Charlotte Smith's Subversive Gothic." *Feminist Studies* 3 (1976): 51–55.

Epstein, William H. "Professing the Eighteenth Century." *ADE Bulletin* 81 (1985): 20–25.

Fassiotto, Marie-José. *Madame de Lambert (1647–1733) ou le féminisme moral*. New York: Peter Lang, 1984.

Fauchery, Pierre. *La Destinée féminine dans le roman européen du dix-huitième siècle, 1713–1808. Essai de gynécomythie romanesque*. Paris: Armand Colin, 1972.

Fielding, Sarah. *The Adventures of David Simple*. Ed. Malcolm Kelsall. London: Oxford University Press, 1969.

Figes, Eva. *Sex & Subterfuge: Women Writers to 1850*. London: Macmillan, 1982.

Fordyce, James. *Sermons to Young Women*. 2 vols. 4th ed. London: A. Millar and T. Cadell, 1767.

Foster, James R. *History of the Pre-Romantic Novel in England*. New York: MLA Monograph, 1949.

Foucault, Michel. *The Birth of the Clinic: An Archaeology of Medical Perception*. Trans. A. M. Sheridan. New York: Vintage Books, 1975.

Galloway, W. F., Jr. "The Conservative Attitude Toward Fiction, 1770–1830." *PMLA* 55 (1940): 1041–59.

Garrison, F. H. "The History of Cancer." *The New York Academy of Medicine* 2, 4 (April 1926): 179–85.

Gelfand, Toby. "Demystification and Surgical Power in the French Enlightenment." *Bulletin of the History of Medicine* 57 (1983): 203–17.

Gilbert, Sandra M., and Susan Gubar, *The Madwoman in the Attic: The Woman Writer and the Nineteenth-Century Literary Imagination*. New Haven: Yale University Press, 1979.

Gillis, Christina Marsden. *The Paradox of Privacy: Epistolary Form in "Clarissa".* Gainesville: University of Florida Press, 1983.

Gillis, Christina Marsden. "Private Room and Public Space: The Paradox of Form in *Clarissa." Studies on Voltaire and the Eighteenth Century* 176 (1979): 153–68.

Gisborne, Thomas. *An Enquiry into the Duties of the Female Sex.* 4th ed. London: T. Cadell, Jr., and W. Davies, 1799.

Glassman, Peter. "Acts of Enclosure." *Hudson Review* 30 (1977): 138–46.

Goldsmith, Elizabeth C., ed. *Writing the Female Voice: Essays in Epistolary Literature.* Boston: Northeastern University Press, 1989.

Goreau, Angeline. *Reconstructing Aphra: A Social Biography of Aphra Behn.* New York: Dial Press, 1980.

Graff, Gerald, and Reginald Gibbons, eds. *Criticism in the University.* Tri-Quarterly Series on Criticism and Culture, no. 1. Evanston, Ill.: Northwestern University Press, 1985.

Graham, Walter. *English Literary Periodicals.* New York: Octagon Books, 1966.

Grau, Joseph A. *Fanny Burney: An Annotated Bibliography.* New York: Garland Publishers, 1981.

Greene, Gayle and Coppélia Kahn, eds. *Making a Difference: Feminist Literary Criticism.* London and New York: Methuen, 1985.

Gregory, John. *A Father's Legacy to his Daughter . . . To which is added, Mr. Tyrold's Advice to his Daughter . . . from "Camilla" by Mrs. d'Arblay. Also a Picture of the Female Form, by G. Horne. . . .* Poughmill near Ludlow: G. Nicholson, 1809.

Gregory, John. *A Father's Legacy to His Daughters.* 4th ed. London: W. Strahan and T. Cadell, 1774.

Gubar, Susan. "'The Blank Page' and the Issues of Female Creativity," *Critical Inquiry* 8 (1981): 243–63.

Gutwirth, Madelyn. *Madame de Staël, Novelist: The Emergence of the Artist as Woman.* Urbana: University of Illinois Press, 1978.

Halsband, Robert, ed. *The Complete Letters of Lady Mary Wortley Montagu.* 3 vols. Oxford: Clarendon Press, 1965.

Harrison, T. R. *Harrison's Principles of Internal Medicine.* 8th ed., ed. George W. Thorn et al. New York: McGraw-Hill Book Company, 1977.

Hartman, Geoffrey. "Words and Wounds." in *Medicine and Literature.* Ed. Enid Rhodes Peschel, 178–88. New York: Neale Watson Academic Publishers, 1980.

Haworth, H. E. "Romantic Female Writers and the Critics." *Texas Studies in Literature and Language* 17 (1976): 725–36.

Hazlitt, William. *Lectures on the English Comic Writers.* Vol. 6 of *The Complete Works of William Hazlitt.* Ed. P. P. Howe. London: J. M. Dent and Sons, 1931.

Heath, Stephen. *The Sexual Fix.* New York: Schocken Books, 1983.

Heidler, Joseph B. *The History, from 1700 to 1800, of English Criticism of Prose Fiction.* Urbana: University of Illinois Press, 1928.

Hellerstein, Erna Olafson, Leslie Parker Hume, and Karen M. Offen, eds.

Victorian Women: A Documentary Account of Women's Lives in Nineteenth-Century England, France, and the United States. Stanford: Stanford University Press, 1981.

Hemlow, Joyce. "Fanny Burney and the Courtesy Books." *PMLA* 65 (1950): 732–61.

Hemlow, Joyce. *The History of Fanny Burney.* Oxford: Clarendon Press, 1958.

Hemlow, Joyce. "Letters and Journals of Fanny Burney: Establishing the Text." In *Editing Eighteenth-Century Texts.* Ed. D. I. B. Smith, 25–43. Toronto: University of Toronto Press, 1968.

Hemlow, Joyce, ed. *A Catalogue of the Burney Family Correspondence, 1749–1878.* With Jeanne M. Burgess and Althea Douglas. New York: New York Public Library, 1971.

Hobsbawm, E. J. *Industry and Empire: From 1750 to the Present Day.* Volume 3 of *The Pelican Economic History of England.* Harmondsworth: Penguin, 1968.

Hoffmann, Paul. *La Femme dans la pensée des lumières.* Paris: Editions Ophrys, 1977.

Horner, Joyce M. *The English Women Novelists and their Connection with the Feminist Movement, 1688–1797.* Northampton, Mass.: Smith College Studies in Modern Languages, vol. II., 1930.

Houtchens, Lawrence Huston, and Carolyn Washburn Houtchens, eds. *Leigh Hunt's Literary Criticism.* New York: Columbia University Press, 1956.

Howells, Coral Ann. "'The Proper Education of a Female . . . is Still to Seek': Childhood and Girls' Education in Fanny Burney's *Camilla; or, A Picture of Youth.*" *British Journal for Eighteenth-Century Studies* 7 (1984): 191–98.

Humiliata, Sister Mary. "Standards of Taste Advocated for Feminine Letter Writing, 1640–1797." *Huntington Library Quarterly* 13 (1950): 261–77.

Jacobus, Mary. *Reading Woman: Essays in Feminist Criticism.* New York: Columbia University Press, 1986.

Jameson, Fredric. "The Ideology of the Text." *Salmagundi* 31–32 (1975–76): 204–46.

Jameson, Fredric. *The Political Unconscious: Narrative as a Socially Symbolic Act.* Ithaca: Cornell University Press, 1981.

Jauss, Hans Robert. "Literary History as a Challenge to Literary Theory." *New Literary History* 2 (1970): 7–37.

Jewison, Norman. "The Disappearance of the Sick Man from Medical Cosmology, 1770–1870." *Sociology* 10 (1976): 225–44.

Johnson, R. Brimley. *The Women Novelists.* 1919; rpt. Freeport, N.Y.: Books for Libraries Press, 1967.

Johnson, Samuel. *A Dictionary of the English Language.* 1755; rpt. New York: Arno Press, 1979.

Johnson, Samuel. *The Lives of the English Poets.* 3 vols. Oxford: Oxford University Press, 1905.

Jordanova, L. J. "Guarding the Body Politic: Volney's Catechism of 1793." In *1789: Reading Writing Revolution.* Ed. Francis Barker et al., 12–21. Proceedings of the Essex Conference on the Sociology of Literature, July 1981. Essex: University of Essex, 1982.

Jordanova, L. J. "Natural Facts: A Historical Perspective on Science and Sexuality." In *Nature, Culture and Gender*. Eds. Carol P. MacCormack and Marilyn Strathern, 42–69. Cambridge: Cambridge University Press, 1980.

Kauffman, Linda S. *Discourses of Desire: Gender, Genre, and Epistolary Fictions*. Ithaca: Cornell University Press, 1986.

Kay, Carol. "On the Verge of Politics: Border Tactics for Eighteenth-Century English Studies." *Boundary 2* 12 (1984): 197–215.

Kelly, Gary. *The English Jacobin Novel, 1780–1805*. Oxford: Clarendon Press, 1976.

Kernan, Alvin B. *The Imaginary Library: An Essay on Literature and Society*. Princeton: Princeton University Press, 1982.

Kernan, Alvin B. *Printing Technology, Letters and Samuel Johnson*. Princeton: Princeton University Press, 1987.

Kestenbaum, Victor, ed. *The Humanity of the Ill: Phenomenological Perspectives*. Knoxville: University of Tennessee Press, 1982.

Keynes, G. "Carcinoma of the Breast: A Brief Historical Survey of the Treatment." *St. Bartholomew's Hospital Journal* 56 (August 1952): 462–66.

Kiely, Robert. *The Romantic Novel in England*. Cambridge: Harvard University Press, 1972.

Klancher, Jon P. *The Making of English Reading Audiences, 1790–1832*. Madison: University of Wisconsin Press, 1987.

Klancher, Jon P. "Reading the Social Text: Power, Signs, and Audience in Early Nineteenth-Century Prose." *Studies in Romanticism* 23 (1984): 183–204.

Kowaleski-Wallace, Beth. "Milton's Daughters: The Education of Eighteenth-Century Women Writers." *Feminist Studies* 12 (1986): 275–93.

Kris, Kathryn. "A 70-Year Follow-up of a Childhood Learning Disability: The Case of Fanny Burney." *Psychoanalytic Study of the Child* 28 (1983): 637–52.

Lambert, Marquise de. *The Works of the Marchioness de Lambert*. 2 vols. London: W. Owen, 1769.

Leach, Edmund. "Time and False Noses." In *Rethinking Anthropology*. London: Athlone Press, 1961: 132–36.

Lerch-Davis, Genie S. "Rebellion Against Public Prose: The Letters of Dorothy Osborne to William Temple (1652–54)." *Texas Studies in Literature and Language* 20 (1978): 386–415.

Lewison, Edward F. "Saint Agatha, the Patron Saint of Diseases of the Breast, in Legend and Art." *Bulletin of the History of Medicine* 24 (1950): 409–20.

Lewison, Edward F. "The Surgical Treatment of Breast Cancer. An Historical and Collective Review." *Surgery* 34 (November 1953): 904–53.

Lloyd, Christopher. *Fanny Burney*. London: Longmans, Green, 1936.

Lonsdale, Roger. "Dr. Burney and the *Monthly Review*, Part I." *Review of English Studies* 14 (1963): 346–58.

Lonsdale, Roger. "Dr. Burney and the *Monthly Review*, Part II." *Review of English Studies* 15 (1964): 27–37.

Lonsdale, Roger. *Dr. Charles Burney: A Literary Biography*. Oxford: Clarendon Press, 1965.

Lorde, Audre. *The Cancer Journals.* Argyle, N.Y.: Spinsters Ink, 1980.

Lovell, Terry. *Consuming Fiction.* London: Verso, 1987.

Lucas, E. V. *The Life of Charles Lamb.* 2 vols. London: Methuen, 1905.

Lustig, Irma S. "The Prudent Heart: Fanny Burney's Journals Restored." *Studies in Burke and His Time* 15 (1974): 287–96.

Macaulay, Thomas Babington. *Critical and Historical Essays.* Ed. F. C. Montague. London: Methuen, 1903.

MacCarthy, Bridget G. *The Female Pen.* New York: William Salloch, 1948.

Macherey, Pierre. *A Theory of Literary Production.* Trans. Geoffrey Wall. Boston: Routledge & Kegan Paul, 1978.

Malone, Kemp. *"Evelina* Revisited." *Papers on Language and Literature* 1 (1965): 3–19.

Martin, Emily. *The Woman in the Body: A Cultural Analysis of Reproduction.* Boston: Beacon Press, 1987.

Masefield, Muriel. *Women Novelists from Fanny Burney to George Eliot.* 1934; rpt. Freeport, N.Y.: Books for Libraries Press, 1967.

Mayo, Robert D. *The English Novel in the Magazines: 1750–1815.* Evanston, Ill.: Northwestern University Press, 1962.

McCarthy, William. *Hester Thrale Piozzi: Portrait of a Literary Woman.* Chapel Hill: University of North Carolina Press, 1985.

McIntosh, Carey. *Common and Courtly Language: The Stylistics of Social Class in 18th-Century English Literature.* Philadelphia: University of Pennsylvania Press, 1986.

McKendrick, Neil, John Brewer, and J. H. Plumb. *The Birth of a Consumer Society: The Commercialization of Eighteenth-Century England.* Bloomington: Indiana University Press, 1982.

McKeon, Michael. *The Origins of the English Novel, 1600–1740.* Baltimore: The Johns Hopkins University Press, 1987.

Meade, Richard Hardaway. *An Introduction to the History of General Surgery.* Philadelphia: Saunders, 1968.

Meese, Elizabeth A. *Crossing the Double-Cross: The Practice of Feminist Criticism.* Chapel Hill: University of North Carolina Press, 1986.

Merod, Jim. *The Political Responsibility of the Critic.* Ithaca: Cornell University Press, 1987.

Miller, J. Hillis. "Narrative and History." *ELH* 41 (1974): 455–73.

Miller, Nancy K. "Emphasis Added: Plots and Plausibilities in Women's Fiction." *PMLA* 96 (1981): 36–47.

Miller, Nancy K. *The Heroine's Text: Readings in the French and English Novel, 1722–1782.* New York: Columbia University Press, 1980.

Milton, John. *Complete Poems and Major Prose.* Ed. Merritt Y. Hughes. Indianapolis: Odyssey Press, 1957.

Mink, Louis O. *Historical Understanding.* Eds. Brian Fay and Eugene O. Golob. Ithaca: Cornell University Press, 1987.

Mink, Louis O. "Narrative Form as a Cognitive Instrument." In *The Writing of History: Literary Form and Historical Understanding.* Ed. Robert H. Canary and Henry Kozicki, 129–49. Madison: University of Wisconsin Press, 1978.

Montague, Edwin, and Louis L. Martz. "Fanny Burney's *Evelina*." In *The Age of Johnson: Essays Presented to Chancey Brewster Tinker*. Ed. F. W. Hilles, 171–81. New Haven: Yale University Press, 1949.

Montaigne, Michel de. *Essais*. 5 vols. Paris: Imprimerie Nationale, 1963.

Moore, Anthony R. "Preanesthetic Mastectomy: A Patient's Experience." *Surgery* 83 (February 1978): 200–205.

Munday, Michael. "The Novel and Its Critics in the Early Nineteenth Century." *Studies in Philology* 79 (1982): 205–26.

Nangle, Benjamin C. "Charles Burney, Critic," In *The Age of Johnson: Essays Presented to Chauncey Brewster Tinker*. Ed. F. W. Hilles, 99–109. New Haven: Yale University Press, 1949.

Newton, Judith Lowder. "Evelina; or, The History of a Young Lady's Entrance into the Marriage Market." *Modern Language Studies* 6 (1976): 48–56.

Newton, Judith Lowder. *Women, Power, and Subversion: Social Strategies in British Fiction, 1778–1860*. Athens, Ga.: University of Georgia Press, 1981; rpt. New York and London: Methuen, 1985.

Nussbaum, Felicity A. *The Brink of All We Hate: English Satires on Women, 1660–1750*. Lexington: University Press of Kentucky, 1984.

Nussbaum, Felicity, and Laura Brown, eds. *The New Eighteenth Century: Theory — Politics — English Literature*. New York: Methuen, 1987.

Olshin, Toby. "'To Whom I Most Belong': The Role of the Family in *Evelina*." *Eighteenth-Century Life* 6 (1980): 29–42.

Palmer, D. J. *The Rise of English Studies*. New York: Oxford University Press, 1965.

Parke, Catherine. "Vision and Revision: A Model for Reading the Eighteenth-Century Novel of Education." *Eighteenth-Century Studies* 16 (1982–83): 162–74.

Pepys, Samuel. *The Diary of Samuel Pepys*. 11 vols. Eds. Robert Latham and William Matthews. Berkeley: University of California Press, 1970–83.

Perry, Ruth. *The Celebrated Mary Astell: An Early English Feminist*. Chicago: University of Chicago Press, 1986.

Perry, Ruth. *Women, Letters, and the Novel*. New York: AMS Press, 1980.

Pollak, Ellen. *The Poetics of Sexual Myth: Gender and Ideology in the Verse of Swift and Pope*. Chicago: University of Chicago Press, 1985.

Poovey, Mary. "Fathers and Daughters: The Trauma of Growing Up Female." In *Men and Women* (ed. Janet Todd). *Women & Literature* n.s. 2 (1981): 39–58.

Poovey, Mary. "Ideology and *The Mysteries of Udolpho*." *Criticism* 21 (1979): 307–30.

Poovey, Mary. *The Proper Lady and the Woman Writer: Ideology as Style in the Works of Mary Wollstonecraft, Mary Shelley, and Jane Austen*. Chicago: University of Chicago Press, 1984.

Porter, Roy. "The Patient's View: Doing Medical History from Below." *Theory and Society* 14 (1985): 175–98.

Porter, Roy, ed. *Patients and Practitioners: Lay Perceptions of Medicine in Preindustrial Society.* Cambridge: Cambridge University Press, 1985.

Power, Sir D'Arcy. "The History of the Amputation of the Breast to 1904." *Liverpool Medico-Chirurgical Journal* 42 (1934): 29–56.

Rather, L. J. *The Genesis of Cancer: A Study in the History of Ideas.* Baltimore: The Johns Hopkins University Press, 1978.

Redford, Bruce. *The Converse of the Pen: Acts of Intimacy in the Eighteenth-Century Familiar Letter.* Chicago: University of Chicago Press, 1986.

Reiser, Stanley Joel. *Medicine and the Reign of Technology.* Cambridge: Cambridge University Press, 1978.

Riese, W. "The Structure of the Clinical History." *Bulletin of the History of Medicine* 16 (1944): 437–49.

Rivers, Isabel, ed. *Books and Their Readers in Eighteenth-Century England.* Leicester: Leicester University Press, and New York: St. Martin's Press, 1982.

Rogers, Katharine. *Feminism in Eighteenth-Century England.* Urbana: University of Illinois Press, 1985.

Rogers, Katharine. "Inhibitions on Eighteenth-Century Women Novelists: Elizabeth Inchbald and Charlotte Smith." *Eighteenth-Century Studies* 11 (1977): 63–78.

Rogers, Katharine. "Fanny Burney: The Private Self and the Published Self." *International Journal of Women's Studies* 7 (1984): 110–17.

Rogers, W. H. "The Reaction Against Melodramatic Sentimentality in the English Novel, 1796–1830." *PMLA* 49 (1934): 98–122.

Roper, Derek. *Reviewing before the Edinburgh, 1788–1802.* Newark: University of Delaware Press, 1978.

Rosbottom, Ronald C. "Motifs in Epistolary Fiction: Analysis of a Narrative Sub-genre," *L'Esprit Créateur* 17 (1977): 279–301.

Rousseau, G. S. "Literature and Medicine: The State of the Field." *Isis* 72 (1981): 406–24.

Rousseau, Jean-Jacques. *Les Confessions.* Ed. Jacques Voisine. Paris: Garnier Frères, 1980.

Sales, Roger. *English Literature in History, 1780–1830: Pastoral and Politics.* London: Hutchinson, 1983.

Scarry, Elaine. *The Body in Pain: The Making and Unmaking of the World.* New York: Oxford University Press, 1985.

Schafer, Roy. "Narration in the Psychoanalytic Dialogue." *Critical Inquiry* 7 (1980): 29–53.

Schecter, David Charles, and Henry Swan. "Of Saints, Surgical Instruments, and Breast Amputation." *Surgery* 52 (October 1962): 693–98.

Scheuermann, Mona. *Social Protest in the Eighteenth-Century Novel.* Columbus: Ohio State University Press, 1985.

Seamon, Roger G. "Narrative Practice and the Theoretical Distinction between History and Fiction." *Genre* 16 (1983): 197–218.

Sedgwick, Eve Kosofsky. *The Coherence of Gothic Conventions.* London: Methuen, 1986.

Shelley, Mary. *Frankenstein, or the Modern Prometheus.* Ed. James Rieger. In-
    dianapolis: Bobbs-Merrill, 1974.
Shevelow, Kathryn Ann. "'Fair-Sexing It': Richard Steele's *Tatler* and the
    Evolution of a Feminized Prose in English Periodical Literature." Ph.D.
    Dissertation. University of California, San Diego, 1981.
Sigerist, Henry E. "The Social History of Medicine." *The Western Journal of
    Surgery, Obstetrics, and Gynecology* 48 (1940): 715-22.
Simons, Judy. *Fanny Burney.* Totowa, N.J.: Barnes & Noble Books, 1987.
Spacks, Patricia Meyer. "Ev'ry Woman is at Heart a Rake." *Eighteenth-Century
    Studies* 8 (1974): 27-46.
Spacks, Patricia Meyer. *Gossip.* New York: Alfred A. Knopf, 1985.
Spacks, Patricia Meyer. *Imagining a Self: Autobiography and Novel in Eighteenth-
    Century England.* Cambridge: Harvard University Press, 1976.
Spencer, Jane. *The Rise of the Woman Novelist: From Aphra Behn to Jane Austen.*
    Oxford: Basil Blackwell, 1986.
Stallybrass, Peter, and Allon White. *The Politics and Poetics of Transgression.*
    Ithaca: Cornell University Press, 1986.
Starobinski, Jean. "The Body's Moment." *Yale French Studies* 64 (1983): 273-
    305.
Staves, Susan. "*Evelina;* or, Female Difficulties." *Modern Philology* 73 (1976):
    368-81.
Staves, Susan. "A Few Kind Words for the Fop." *Studies in English Literature*
    22 (1982): 413-28.
Stevenson, Lionel. "Varieties of the Novel." *Studies in Burke and His Time* 13
    (1972): 2251-59.
Stewart, Keith. "Towards Defining an Aesthetic for the Familiar Letter in
    Eighteenth-Century England." *Prose Studies* 5 (1982): 179-92.
Steward, Wolf, et al. "Instruction in Medical History Taking." *Journal of Medi-
    cal Education* 27 (1952): 244-52.
Stock, Phyllis. *Better than Rubies: A History of Women's Education.* New York:
    E. P. Putnam's Sons, 1978.
Stone, Lawrence. *The Family, Sex and Marriage in England, 1500-1800.* New
    York: Harper & Row, 1977.
Stratton, Jon. *The Virgin Text: Fiction, Sexuality, and Ideology.* Oklahoma Proj-
    ect for Discourse and Theory. Norman: University of Oklahoma Press,
    1987.
Straub, Kristina. *Divided Fictions: Fanny Burney and Feminine Strategy.* Lexing-
    ton: University Press of Kentucky, 1987.
Straub, Kristina. "Fanny Burney's *Evelina* and the 'Gulphs, Pits, and Preci-
    pices' of Eighteenth-Century Female Life." *The Eighteenth Century: The-
    ory and Interpretation* 27 (1986): 230-46.
Suleiman, Susan Rubin, ed. *The Female Body in Western Culture: Contemporary
    Perspectives.* Cambridge: Harvard University Press, 1986.
Swift, Jonathan. *Gulliver's Travels.* Rev. ed., ed. Robert A. Greenberg. New
    York: W. W. Norton, 1970.

Taylor, John T. *Early Opposition to the English Novel: The Popular Reaction from 1760 to 1830.* New York: King's Crown Press, 1943.

Thackeray, William Makepeace. *Contributions to the "Morning Chronicle".* Ed. Gordon N. Ray. Urbana: University of Illinois Press, 1955.

Thompson, E. P. "Eighteenth-Century English Society: Class Struggle without Class?" *Social History* 3 (1978): 133–65.

Thompson, E. P. *The Making of the English Working Class.* New York: Vintage Books, 1966.

Thompson, Leslie M., and John R. Ahrens. "Criticism of English Fiction 1780–1810: The Mysterious Powers of the Pleading Preface." *Yearbook of English Studies* 1 (1971): 125–34.

Todd, Janet. *Women's Friendship in Literature.* New York: Columbia University Press, 1980.

Tompkins, J. M. S. *The Popular Novel in England, 1770–1800.* 1932; rpt. Lincoln: University of Nebraska Press, 1961.

Trumbach, Randolph. *The Rise of the Egalitarian Family: Aristocratic Kinship and Domestic Relations in Eighteenth-Century England.* New York: Academic Press, 1978.

Turner, Victor. *The Ritual Process: Structure and Anti-Structure.* Ithaca: Cornell University Press, 1977.

Utter, Robert Palfrey, and Gwendolyn Bridges Needham. *Pamela's Daughters.* New York: Macmillan, 1936.

Vessilli, Claudia Marina. *Cecilia Tra I "Courtesy Books" e la Vindication of the Rights of Woman.* Rome: Edizioni Dell'Ateneo & Bizzarri, 1979.

Wangensteen, Owen H., and Sarah D. Wangensteen. *The Rise of Surgery: From Empiric Craft to Scientific Discipline.* Minneapolis: University of Minnesota Press, 1978.

Warren, Samuel. *Affecting Scenes: Being Passages from the Diary of a Physician.* 2 vols. New York: J. and J. Harper, 1837.

Watt, Ian. *The Rise of the Novel: Studies in Defoe, Richardson, and Fielding.* Berkeley: University of California Press, 1957.

White, Hayden. *The Content of the Form: Narrative Discourse and Historical Representation.* Baltimore: The Johns Hopkins University Press, 1987.

White, Hayden. "The Question of Narrative in Contemporary Historical Theory." *History and Theory* 23 (1984): 1–33.

White, Hayden. "The Value of Narrativity in the Representation of Reality." *Critical Inquiry* 7 (1980): 5–27.

Williams, Raymond. *Keywords: A Vocabulary of Culture and Society.* New York: Oxford University Press, 1976.

Wollstonecraft, Mary. *A Vindication of the Rights of Woman.* Ed. Carol H. Poston. New York: W. W. Norton, 1975.

Woolf, Virginia. *A Room of One's Own.* New York: Harcourt, Brace and Jovanovich, 1929.

Wright, C. E. "The Barrett Collection of Burney Papers." *The British Museum Quarterly* 18 (June 1953): 41–43.

Index